American Trails Series
XIV

"Beyond This Place There Be Dragons"
can be found lettered by imaginative cartographers on ancient maps as a substitute for the more prosaic "Terra Incognita."

So, too, was much of the Far West, especially the "Great Basin" desert region, an unknown land, even by the mid-1800s. Mountain men, fur trappers and adventurers had penetrated it. But for the most part they did not or could not record their travels. Word of trails, grass and water were imparted verbally and were only vaguely descriptive.

It was a bare, bleak, sun-scorched, forbidding land. A *jornada del muerto* or journey of death for many. And rarely more dramatized than by the gold-rush-bound emigrants known as the Death Valley '49ers, the first-known party to cross the desolation of south-central Nevada and into the dragon's lair—Tomesha, the land of ground afire.

beyond this place there be dragons

The Routes of the Tragic Trek
of the Death Valley 1849ers
through Nevada, Death Valley,
and on to Southern California

by

GEORGE KOENIG

THE ARTHUR H. CLARK COMPANY
Glendale, California   1984

to the late
LIEUTENANT JOHN BECK
officer and gentleman
friend and fellow traveler of the '49er trail

Contents

Contents

Maps

Illustrations

Introduction

I have not attempted to see differently from others
but to look further. —ALEX DE TOCQUEVILLE

The Death Valley 1849ers were the stuff of which legends are born. Knowing little more than that the Pacific Ocean was to the west, they indomitably forged their way across the wastelands of southern Nevada into the "valley of death".

Stubbornly, heroically, they persevered through a land where water was more precious than gold, where lack of forage meant life or death for oxen and those dependent upon them.

Their judgment was oft faulty. Their spirit was not. As Sarah Royce, of another group of emigrants, wrote:

> Turn back! What a chill the words sent through one. Turn back on a journey like that, in which every mile had been gained by most earnest labor, growing more and more intense until, of late, it had seemed that the certainy of advance with every step was all that made the next step possible . . .

Yet in a notable exception, two did turn back in classic heroism to save, if they could, those they had been forced to leave behind in Death Valley, trudging some 250 miles each way. Truly they exemplified that greater love hath no man than he be willing to lay down his life for his friends.

More years ago than I care to recall, I decided to retrace the escape route of that historic party of '49ers who had strayed into Death Valley on their way to the goldfields of California.

I wasn't sure why I wanted to undertake such a task. After all, the route had already been plotted, mapped and written about by acknowledged authorities. Yet these had invariably evolved through the simple and suspect expediency of picking up other writings until conjecture assumed an aura of fact.

And who was to say aye or nay? Assuredly it would be impossible to fix exact routes and campsites in a land where, within relatively few miles of similar scenery and options, there could be any number of spots for pin-pointed searchings. Nor, with sparse exception, does physical evidence remain. Remnants of wood and iron, if not ravaged by time and weather, or scavenged over a hundred years, would be hopelessly lost, scattered and/or intermixed with the leavings of later day miners.

Even the occasional '49er rock inscriptions, of which five have been found,* can be suspected of having been done by unknown persons at an unknown time. And for unknown purposes since, for the most part, they are where few if any would ever be apt to see them.

Yet the challenge remained. Perhaps for at least a pictorial review of the Death Valley route. After all even the "I was there" account of William Manly tended to bog the average reader with a blurring and blending of going up this mountain, down that canyon, repetition that makes it difficult to visualize and appreciate. To those who have little opportunity or reason to huff and puff their way into the bleak and barren back-country of Death Valley there would well be curiosity as to just what the mountains and canyons look like.

It would be nice to actually see, pictorially, Manly's view of, "It did not seem very far to the snowy peak to the north of us." It would also help to pin down his trail since such views from the many canyons are unique. What did the dramatic rock falls they encountered look like? Where? What of "the grandest sight we ever beheld" that could so inspire even bone- and spirit-weary Manly to such poetic heights?

I returned from that original trek without one photo.

Nothing seemed to fit. Despite all presumptions, I could not find, and thus photograph, any "snowy peak" view from the accepted routing. Somewhat surprisingly, twists and turns and sheer cliffs cut off such views from all canyons—save one. So, too, was the impressive sight from atop the Panamint Mountains to apply to but a singular site.

Just how well did Manly recall, descriptively, their epic trek? Was he indeed a hero—or hoax, without a supporting witness?

He proved to have done remarkably well. The "lost journal of

---

*Jayhawker Canyon, Emigrant Wash, Marble Canyon, Nye Canyon, Beaver Dam Wash.

Louis Nusbaumer", also a member of the famous Long Camp, was found to substantiate him.

The accuracy of Manly's book, *Death Valley in '49,* published in 1894, 44 years later, was not a matter of memory alone, but of sharpening by several rewritings. His first manuscript, written in 1852 from trail notes, was destroyed by fire. A "lost" account was reportedly dictated to a Bancroft representative. The San Jose *Pioneer* of April 21 and 28, 1877, published a short dictated account. A detailed serialized version "From Vermont to California" appeared periodically in the *Santa Clara Monthly* from 1887 to 1890. And other writings appeared from time to time in the *Pacific Tree & Vine* (San Jose, Calif.), *Inyo Independent* (Bishop, Calif.) and *The Pioneer* (San Jose). In addition, Manly carried on considerable correspondence and conversations with his fellow '49ers. Thus it is far less a matter of fitting Manly to theory than of adapting to Manly himself. He was in truth the '49er's guide as he is ours.

But Manly is not unflawed. There are gaps in accounting for days and dates. These cannot be sloughed off for they often determine trails taken. Too easily, too often a three day "leg" has been fitted into one for association with familiar present day sites. At times even the '49ers tend to identify places near their trail with those later in the news of the day. Such as L. Dow Stephens associating their route with Mountain Meadows, which became notorious for its infamous massacre. And when Searles became publicized for its borax it was easy enough to identify it as one of the alkaline lakes on their route. It would certainly be understandable in describing their way through an unknown, unmapped region, to those who had never been there and could best picture it in relating to current place names.

There were other accounts, notably that of Asa Haynes, Sheldon Young and Louis Nusbaumer, and a great many later recollections, including those of John Colton and the Brier family. For the most part they are as fragmented as the '49ers themselves as they approached Death Valley. Trails parted as individuals and small groups looked out for themselves with varying judgments over the best route to try. Did they go this or thataway? They may have instinctively followed Indian or game trails, although strangely they failed to give credit to either. Some took what seemed easier grade choices. Or were influenced by a glimpse of greenery in the distance. Even a mirage was instrumental. Bearings were often based on the setting sun as "west", although unknown to them the sun sets to the southwest in early winter months of the year.

Frustrating as the gaps, confusion and conflicts may be, sympathetically the '49ers are more to be praised for what they did remember than faulted for what they did not.

Yet, varied as their ways were, they did rejoin from time to time. Notably at "Providence Springs" where previously separated parties witnessed the same events. Meager and controversial as the clues may be, they must link together to form a chain without inexplainable, casually accepted missing links. If one '49er says he was at a certain place on a certain date and met others, a correlation of accounts must also place the others at the same place at the same time.

Retracing the trails is much like the old puzzle drawings of connecting numbered dots to form a picture. At times it can be done, with surprising frequency, from rather specific clues and confirmations. "Connecting lines" must be more generalized from directions and mileages. Yet even these can be given the weight of circumstantial evidence by on-the-scene leg work viewing terrain probabilities and impossibilities, the logical and the unlikely.

The sands of the desert and time have long since obliterated the '49er trail. Yet men and women will persist in pursuing it as long as the shadowy hills beckon and fingering canyons lure them on. There is the fascination of a whodunit in knowing just where the Bennetts-Arcans sweated out four weeks for the return of two men sent ahead for help and who, if they had any sense of self-preservation, would never return; and in determining where the Jayhawkers fled across "a mountain of silver" still sought after more than a century as the legendary "Lost Gunsight Lode", and a nearby cache of gold coins buried as too heavy to carry further. Too, few places are more shrouded in mystery than aptly-named "Providence Springs." Was it indeed where some have all too easily placed it without fitting all of the pieces?

This book is not a duplication of other books on the story of the

Death Valley '49ers. Nor is there an intention to be different for the sake of being so. At times it is controversially iconoclastic, leaving chips to fall where they may. Too long has fancy become fact simply by passive acceptance and repetition, invariably quoting and compounding earlier errors.

It is, instead, a concentration on the retracing of the trail itself—where they went, why and when. And the importance of the latter has been long overlooked since it governed the distances between camps, the obstacles influencing the pace of travel and the important correlations with the accounts of various contingents. It is easy enough to quote out of context, but all of the links must be forged to form an unbroken chain.

While much has been written on the Death Valley to Los Angeles part of their trail, that between "Mt. Misery" and Death Valley has been quite untouched. Understandably so for it lies across a lonely desolate land, much of it now "out of bounds" by the military and Atomic Energy Commission since the early 1940's. The little that has been written on this portion is unfortunately flawed, accepted as authoritative simply because few have the opportunity to dispute it.

Following up on my initial efforts I was caught up in a broader scope. Having learned to doubt the accepted Panamint crossings, how could I be sure that the '49ers entered Death Valley via Furnace Creek Wash? This then led into what is now the Atomic Energy Commission area of Nevada. Confirmation of those findings inevitably led to just how the '49ers got there. "Just around one more bend," I told myself, "just over one more hill." But the hills continued endlessly and the bends without number. Finally I called a halt at what was really the start of the Death Valley story—"Mt. Misery," straddling the Nevada-Utah border.

Acknowledgments

Just as "no man is an island unto himself," I am indebted to many for their helpfulness and friendship over the years. To those not included I ask for forgiveness and understanding of my faults of memory and files.

Lt. John Beck
L. Burr Belden
A. A. Brierly
Nye Butler
Dr. Thomas Clements
Helen Coyle
Guard Darrah
E. I. Edwards
Charles Ferge
Harry Gower
LeRoy Hafen
Guy Hamblin
Charles Kelly
Curt Kincer
Sewell Lofinck
Don Meadows
Dale Morgan
Lee Mortensen

David Myrick
Haydee Noya
Allan Ottley
Lauritz Petersen
Ellen Primeaux
Mary Ream
Mary Rice
Lloyd Rooke
Matt Ryan
Lewis Sharp
Dan Sheahan
Priscilla Traunstein
Carl Wheat
Walt Wheelock
Slim & Sylvia Winslow
Hank Whittenmyer
Art Woodward
Harold Weight

The Cast

The introduction by name of some 300 to 500 men, women and children in the wagon train that left Salt Lake City to chance the relatively unknown southern route in 1849 is a Herculean task. And except for infinitely detailed histories, needless for all practical purposes.

Those who remained with or rejoined the main trail, including a number of "horse and mule packers" are noted only in passing.* A list, as complete as possible, of the "shortcutters" who comprised the Death Valley '49ers is included as Appendix A.

A few of the key participants, however, do warrant a special introduction to help identify them, their entrances and participation:

WILLIAM LEWIS MANLY—Author of the classic account of the trek in which he played a major role.

SHELDON YOUNG AND ASA HAYNES—Two of the '49ers who kept diaries of their journey.

THE BRIERS—A family of five traveling, at times, with the Jayhawkers.

THE WADES—A family of six who invariably lagged behind, likely allowing small water seeps, exhausted by the others, to refill.

THE BENNETTS-ARCANS—A party of about 14, including Manly, the Bennetts a family of 5, the Arcans a family of 3.

JOHN COLTON, L. D. STEPHENS, ALONZO CLAY, ED DOTY, CHARLES MECUM, BILL ROOD, "DEACON" RICHARDS, and TOM SHANNON—Prominent role Jayhawkers.

LOUIS NUSBAUMER—A German, with a small group of six, who meticulously kept a journal.

JIM MARTIN—Who traveled, on and off, with the Briers.

JOHN ROGERS—Manly's companion on their historic and heroic rescue trek from and back to Death Valley.

---

*Except for the Savage-Pinney Party of 11 who were to re-enter the '49er saga near Death Valley.

The Parties, Their Routes
and the Treks

Salt Lake City - 1849

The overture to the Death Valley '49ers saga started in mid-1849 in the fledgling Mormon settlement of Salt Lake City.

Founded two years before (July 24, 1847), it had barely been proclaimed the State of Deseret (July 2-3, 1849) when its population of about 5,000 was inundated with California bound gold seekers.

The cry of "Gold! In California!" had spread like wildfire. Within three weeks during the Spring of 1849, as the first spring grasses could provide forage for the trek, nearly 18,000 crossed the Missouri River heading westward. One observer counted 1,100 wagons on the prairies beyond Independence, Missouri.[1]

As the only sizeable settlement enroute to the rainbow's end, many gravitated into Salt Lake City. Here they recuperated and milled about uncertainly. Word had drifted back of the ill-fated Donner Party in which 42 out of 90 perished, some by cannabalism, crossing the Sierra Nevada in the winter of 1846-7. Still, another report sought to soften the dire prospects with, "Emigrants who reach the Sierra by the first of October are safe. Those who come later and encounter snow should retreat or turn southward along the eastern base of the California Mountains."

Should they chance it? With the Mormons themselves hard pressed for survival there were scarcely sufficient supplies, and little or no employment, for the gathering wagons to layover until Spring.

Rumors abounded of a little known southward route. Death Valley '49er W. L. Manly writes, "No wagons were reported as ever getting through that way, but a trail had been traveled through that barren desert country for perhaps a hundred years and the same could be easily broadened into a wagon road."[2]

---

[1] Also, according to Bancroft, over 775 ships reached California harbors, crammed with the fortune-bound.

[2] This was a northerly extension of the Old Spanish Trail from Santa Fe which made a great loop around the chasmic Colorado River country to near Green River, Utah, before circling south and on to the Southern California settlements. From present day Parowan north to Salt Lake City it became known as "The Mormon Trail".

Debates waged pro and con. Finally they found a Captain Jefferson Hunt who offered to guide them to Los Angeles for $10 a wagon. Few of the '49ers were to agree on Hunt's capabilities. Many became vehemently critical. None seemed to be aware or to record that Hunt had been over the trail the year before.

In 1846-7 a party of 18 or 19 Mormons, including Hunt and two sons, had been sent to the San Bernardino area for seed, cuttings and cattle. Their availability had been known to members of the famed Mormon Battalion who had been in that area during the war with Mexico. While there is some confusion on dates, it is generally accepted that this supply party left Salt Lake City on November 16, 1846, reaching Chino on or about Christmas Eve. The return, February 15 to May 15, 1847, encumbered with cattle, was slow and difficult. Out of 200, 97 cows survived and one bull out of 30. Although using a map provided by mountain man "Duff" Weber, who had been over the trail earlier with Kit Carson, they found it "hard to follow and we lost the trail often."

Nor was a '49er wagon to be the first vehicle over the route. After their discharge, a contingent of the Battalion left Southern California in April of 1848, reaching Salt Lake City, via Chino, in June. They brought one wagon through safely, with possibly another abandoned enroute. Notably, too, one of the members, a Mr. Davis, brought his wife who thus became the first known woman over the trail.[3]

Yet it was, as Hunt knew from experience, a rough route with sometimes uncertain water, sparse forage and hostile Indians.

Hesitatingly the wagons began to rendezvous near Provo, south of Salt Lake City. There was by now a touch of Fall in the air. Arguments raged over the alternatives. Even families were divided, although sometimes motivated by an instinctive desire not to risk the loss of all over one route. Caught between the devil and the deep, some gambled they could still make it westward via the Humboldt River trail. Others were reluctant to hazard family, possessions and themselves, so late in the year.

---

[3] Hunt left with those returning to Salt Lake City via the northern route. In another of history's interesting footnotes, Henry Bigler of this contingent, was one of the Mormons who stopped off to earn a few days employment at Sutter's mill and witnessed the gold discovery at Coloma on January 24, 1848. He was also fated to be a member of the Hunt '49er wagon train.

Indecision started to fade as a group of 114 to 130 men, guided by a James Waters, started south in September. The Record Book of Chino Rancho notes their arrival as October 27-29, 1849, having "made fast time . . . enjoyed good health . . . but lost about 30 animals from scarcity of water and grass."

They were followed by the Gruwell-Derr Party with 23 to 49 wagons, 300 men plus women and children.[4] Unwilling or unable to pay Hunt his $10 per wagon fee, they employed a Mexican guide. That their problems were many is indicated by Hunt catching up with their main body at the Mojave River.

The tide had turned. And in early October Hunt's wagon train began to move south. A mixture of easterners, midwesterners, overseas emigrants and Mormons; families and single men; some with wagons and some with pack animals. Just how many wagons there were varies according to accounts—from 84 to 125. The exact number is difficult to ascertain as late-comers joined, others dropped out and wagons broke down or were abandoned. Approximated, too, were some 300 to 500 men, women and children, plus some 500 oxen, horses and mules.

Had they made the right decision? Sarah Royce[5] was among those who elected to stay with the Humboldt trail and Hastings Cut-off. Leaving Salt Lake City August 30 they crossed the Sierra Nevada summit October 19, 51 days later. She was to write that snow had started and only 10 days after they crossed the summit the mountains were blocked with snow by the stormiest winter California had known for years. Had those who were to form Hunt's train left earlier, in August, they too might have made it. As is, although they little knew it, they had made the best of a difficult decision.

Of the way south, including the various "horse and mule packers" and those who kept to the main trail, is a story unto itself. A new and different tale was in the news of a shortcut map!

Some attributed the map to an Elijah "Barney" Ward, said to have been over the trail three times. Others credit, or blamed, a "Williams

---

[4] In two sections; one the Pearson-Dallas Party, co-led by Charles Dallas, wagonmaster of the wagon train with which Manly had started west.

[5] *A Frontier Lady: Recollections of the Gold Rush and Early California,* New Haven, Yale University Press, 1932.

of Salt Lake," possibly the "Old Bill" Williams who guided Fremont's
4th Expedition. Many fingered a "Captain O. K. Smith" from New
York, contradictorily described as a Mormon and a "gentile."[6] Some
said it was one of Fremont's maps "which showed them if they went
straight out from the trail it would only be 300 miles to the mines."

Just whose map it was will undoubtedly never be known. But
obviously there was a map of sorts. Such maps were probably compilations from various reports of mountain men, early explorers, etc.,
sometimes relayed verbally or literally "mapped on buckskin." However crude and faulty, they offered the promise of a shorter, faster trip,
easier on people, stock and supplies. It could also help to miss the rainy
season that they heard set in from Los Angeles north to the gold fields
at this time of year. To some it could mean getting to the diggin's
"before the gold was gone."

However cursed their shortcut map was to be, it was probably as
reliable as any of that day. Vague, generalized, and for those afoot or
with pack animals, and not with wagons in mind. And there is a consistency that a shortcut did exist.

Fremont's 1845 route cut through Nevada striking southwest from
Ruby Valley, skirting the infamous Alkali Desert, swinging southwesterly to Walker Lake, approximating the 39th parallel. A route
"traversed by mountains white with snow (October) while below
the valleys had none. Instead of a barren country, the mountains were
covered with grasses of the best quality."

Hastings had recommended his cut-off as being "300 miles shorter
than the more northern route and perfectly safe for wagon trains."
Howard Egan was to make a Salt Lake City-Sacramento round trip
in ten days by mule in 1855, approximating the 40th parallel. A route
later followed in the main by the Pony Express. Captain Simpson in
1859 blazed a somewhat similar route. A number of other shortcuts
were heard of, but no one was sure just where. Just somewhere between Salt Lake City and the southern rim of the Great Basin.

---

[6]Irresistibly it is footnoted that an Orsen Kirk Smith was traced to Lincklaen, Chenango
County, New York. Just when he left for California is unknown; only that he arrived in Stock-
ton in 1849, became Sheriff of Tulare County in 1852, fought in the Tule Indian War of 1856,
was an Assemblyman from Fresno 1860, Census Marshal for San Luis Obispo 1870, and reported "murdered" February 17, 1871.

So it was that the Death Valley '49ers fell victim to their time. The die had been cast. And on November 4, 1849, the wagon train came to a parting of the ways near present day Cedar City, Utah. All except seven wagons turned westward. Hunt, announcing that he had bargained to take them to Los Angeles over his route, bid farewell to the dissidents with, "Even if one wagon decides to go the original route I shall feel bound by my promise to go with that lone wagon. But if all decide to go (on the shortcut) I will go with you, even if the road leads to hell."

Mt. Misery overlooking Beaver Dam Wash, "a sheer precipice of a thousand feet or more"

Bigler's inscription at Mt. Misery's base
"I cut the three first letters of my name"

A clipping from the *Deseret News*,
Great Salt Lake City, Sept. 7, 1850

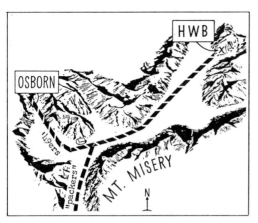

CALIFORNIA EMI-GRANTS.
TAKE NOTICE!!

ELIJAH WARD, (generally known by his mountain name, Barney Ward,) intends leaving Utah Valley, on or about the first of October next, for the SOUTHERN MINES in California. Mr. Ward is thoroughly acquainted with the SOUTHERN ROUTE, and will pilot Emigrants through to said mines for ten dollars per wagon; and ten dollars for every company of five persons with packs, or pack animals. As fast as Emigrants come in, and can get ready for the journey, they will pass on through Great Salt Lake City, and Utah Valley, and encamp on Hobble Creek, about ten miles south of the Utah Settlement, where they will find GOOD FEED AND WATER TO RECRUIT THEIR TEAMS. Any further information wanted, can be obtained by calling at my dwelling in Utah Settlement.
ELIJAH WARD, Pilot.

N. B. No one will be permitted to travel in the train, until his fare is paid to the Pilot.

The contemplated route to the Southern Mines, is no worse than the usual route from the States hither, so far as rocks and mountains are concerned; although the deserts are more extensive.

We expect to leave the old road, near the foot of the mountain, and near Mahave (or Mahawbee) Creek. I will pilot the company either to Williams' Ranche, or to the Gold Mines in that region, just as a majority of the company shall decide, for their convenience.   E. W.

G. S. L. City, Sept. 2, 1850. 13 No. 3 in.

"Mount Misery"

Death Valley, which they were to know, and became so historically identified, was not to be the great obstacle in itself. It was the climax of a month and a half struggle across sun-scorched wastelands, lost amid seemingly endless bare, bleak mountains, great sandy valleys and alkalined dry lake beds. Death Valley was to be, in short, the proverbial straw to break the camel's back.

Thus it was at "Mt. Misery," straddling the Utah-Nevada border that the Death Valley '49er story actually begins. Up to now they had just been another party of overland emigrants. Here they etched their way into the pages of history.

Central Nevada ahead of them is for the most part, as it was then, a lonely, desolate land. Tenuously prospected during the mining booms of Freiburg, Tem Piute and the Gold Flat camps, even those skeletal remains have gradually all but been obliterated by the swirling sands of time. Little wonder a great expanse of it was carved out by the Atomic Energy Commission where its awesome tests could be carried out undisturbed.

But in early November of 1849, in a relatively verdant elevation, all went well. Indeed, the "shortcut to hell" was not taken as madly as might seem. Purportedly Jedediah Smith had used it on his 1826-27 trek. It also approximated the old Clover Creek-Meadow Valley route used by miners and Mormons filtering into the Beaver Dam area as early as 1857. In the 1860's the Mormons, in establishing such settlements as Joseco, Barclay and Panaca, followed Clover Creek Valley in preference to a more direct route to the north (via Modena) because it provided "the best water and grass." By the 1870's it was a popular cut-off to Pahranagat and Pahrump Valley. And its feasibility was underlined by Union Pacific Railroad for its route between Salt Lake City and Las Vegas. It was a natural gateway that was not at all incompatible with the '49ers shortcut map.

But the route is for the knowing, not those innocent of when and where to turn left or right. And three days later the '49ers were stopped by "a sheer precipice of a thousand feet or more."

From a distance their route had seemed deceptively easy going. Knolls, saddles and ravines blended into the illusion of a mesa extending hazily westward. Even the 6,000-foot heights were lost in the expanse of similar surroundings, giving little hint of the encircling canyons ahead. And now they were stranded on a high narrowing promontory above the deep, sandy gorges of Beaver Dam Wash.

According to Manly, "Immediately in front of us was a canyon, impassable for wagons and down into this the trail descended. Men could go, horses and mules perhaps, but wagons could no longer follow the trail, so we proposed to search (for) a pass. Wood and bunch grass were plenty but water was a long way down the trail and had to be packed up to camp."

Those with agility and ability laboriously hauled the water up by bucket. According to Brier Jr., "a Frenchman did so for others for a dollar a bucket." Mecum was also to recall "the deep canyon where the little Frenchman hauled up so much water"—later noting that the Frenchman perished with Robinson as they neared Los Angeles.

Repeated references to "the trail" which they could no longer follow strongly indicates it was not the one they were blazing. Rather, it was one of the old Indian trails that cut across Beaver Dam Wash at this point and the locale of a number of cave sites.

The more venturesome descended into the small meadowland below, where there was ". . . plenty of water and grass," scouting for a way out. Whatever the choices and chances they were neither obvious nor easy.

Unencumbered by wagons, the "horse and mule packers"—including the O.K. Smith, Flake-Rich, Stover and Savage-Pinney parties —precariously switch-backed their way down into the canyon and on through the narrow and rugged defile to the south. Among the advance parties to descend the trail which double-teamed wagons were to eventually follow was Henry W. Bigler. His journal entry of "Sat. Nov. 3rd" records, "Laid by until nearly noon for our animals to rest and eat grass. I cut the 3 first letters of my name on a rock and the date." Fortunately that inscription still remains to identify just where the '49ers descended and continued on.

They had reached Mt. Misery "at the end of three days travel" (November 4, 5, 6).

Two days were spent in scouting with discouraging results. On the third morning (Nov. 9) many of the wagons, including that of Mr. Rynierson[1] deciding that discretion was the better part of valor, turned back to the main trail to rejoin Hunt.

But there were still scouts out, for Haynes wrote that he was one of a small party who spent three days searching for an escape route in what he named "Buckskin Canyon." Before they made it back to camp with the news that a "pass" had been found, still more wagons turned back, including that of Alexander Erkson who tells that "On my way back from Mt. Misery I climbed up on a big rock and inscribed the date—Nov. 10, 1849."

The wagons had now been reduced to "about 27."

Apparently the rest of the day was spent in readiness, for both Young and Haynes log being in camp this date, and both log travel on the 11th; Young with "25 miles westerly" and Haynes with "one day to a pleasant valley."

It was a slow and difficult descent and the wagons began to stretch out. Bennett fell even further behind when only a short distance on the way he broke an axle, returning to get a replacement from the wagon of an unknown Kentuckian who died and was buried atop Mt. Misery.[2]

In one of his occasionally confusing recollections, Manly says "When all was ready we followed the others who had gone ahead. The route led at first directly to the north and a pass was said to be in that direction. . . . After the wagons straightened out nicely a meeting was called to organize so as to travel systematically." A little later he notes, "I sometimes remained out all night (scouting) and soon became satisfied that going north was not taking us in the direction we ought to go."

The inference of heading north when they reached the bottom is

---

[1] Manly says Rynierson left on the 7th. But 3 days on the turn-off (4, 5, 6), and two days of scouting and the death of the Kentuckian on the third, with Rynierson pulling out soon after the incident, would make it the 9th.

[2] Strangely while it would seem this first fatality on the cutoff would be more commented upon, except for Manly only one other did so—Jacob Stover, who was to follow the Smith-Flake-Rich trail to the south.

a jump-in-time error of memory. The enclosing cliffs at the northern end are sheer. And there is no way they could have continued days north to allow for him being out several nights scouting. Not at this point. Also Haynes and Young log *westerly* courses from November 11 through 17.

The answer is more readily apparent when actually viewing the terrain. From their encampment atop Mt. Misery the trail did start north, but the distance was short before it swerved to the bottom. Further north was rough and gutted. And any thoughts of wagons following the rim southward would have stopped at precipitous Pine Park canyon-wash. They had been given a Hobson's choice.

Nor did continuance on the other side seem much better. Initial scouting reports said, ". . . the trail on the west side could be ascended on foot by both men and women, but it would take years to make it fit for wheels." But it was, as it is still, the only practicable route up the westward rim.

Channeled by the surrounding cliffs, they proceeded somewhat westerly through the bottom land meadows towards a large cul-de-sac. The rise to the top was steep but a far cry from the barriers that Mt. Misery had presented. Here a steep slope was later used by prospectors and cattlemen, and hacked out as a rough road by the Bauer family who ranched in the meadows below; a road used by Charles Kelly, in a Model A Ford, who first found the Bigler inscription.

A cliff wall, near the base of this road, is covered with time-dimmed names, mostly of later pioneers in the area, including Osborn, Hamblin and Pulsipher. Almost lost among them is an indecipherably weathered short name or initials and the date "49"! Questioned as it might be, it helps to point the way onward, upward and westward.[3]

---

[3] *Desert Magazine*, Feb. 1939. The Bigler and Osborn inscriptions are also detailed in the Los Angeles Westerners *Brand Book* #10, 1963, article "Betwixt the Devil and the Deep".

Westward Ho! Again!

TO SAND SPRING VALLEY

Two of the '49ers now play key roles in retracing the continuance of the trail. Sheldon Young and Asa Haynes.

Unfortunately all traces of the original Sheldon Young "log" have been lost. It does survive as a typed copy in the "Jayhawker Collection" at the Huntington Library. This copy bears the typed imprint of "The Jayhawkers of '49 Headquarters, Kansas City, Mo." Alas all traces of that organization have also disappeared. And while some of the '49ers heard that Young had 100 or 200 copies of his account privately printed, none have ever surfaced.

How accurate is the typed copy? *Quien sabe?* Even the most conscientious typist could be faced with judgmental decisions whether an "8" was an "S", etc. Still one does not throw out the baby with the bath water. Apparently John Colton, the indefatigable "secretary" of the '49ers, had the original for a time. Given to comments and corrections on such things he editorially filled in a gap-covering paragraph between Young's entries of Oct. 23 and Nov. 10, but left the remainder unquestioned and unchanged. Thus we can accept Young's basic validity for most, if not all, at least as long as it does not clash with the accounts of others and shared events.

There are confirming reports that Young had been a sailor, which lends a certain authoritativeness to his "logging," particularly his directional bearings. Yet out of his element and in a strange new land this too can be tempered by terrain and the variances of headings during a day.

Of Asa Haynes' journal there is doubt, not of the factualness of what he had written, but in the uncertainty of piecing it together. It is to the well-won credit of John Beck, whose patient, painstaking research unraveled the maze of not one but four accounts: (1) the original diary, (2) a Haynes dictated copy of the original from Death

Valley to Walker Pass, (3) a slightly overlapping copy of the section from Mt. Misery to Panamint Valley, and (4) a set of recalled diary notes. Indicative of Beck's authoritative analysis was establishing that the copied portion and notes were written by Haynes' daughter, Nancy J. Wiley, at her father's dictation and approval. Also that the mileage figure "8" had frequently been traced over into 4's in a well-intentioned but faulty interpretation of Haynes' scrawlings.

The supplemental portions were obvious attempts by Haynes at elaboration and clarification of his earlier on the spot entries. That they often resulted in occasional variances and duplications lessens little their acceptance. But to weed them out, separate and correlate them chronologically, including dovetailing with Young's comparable entries, was a task few researchers have had the fortitude to face. That it was done so well by Beck, enables us to now follow along a clearly blazed trail that has borne up under even this author's "Doubting Thomas" misgivings that would not rest until the route had personally been followed for any faults and failings of theory.

Chroniclers among the short-cutters are rare. They were either not given to writing or could not. That Haynes and Young did so is invaluable.

Young's entries are dated, logging directions and miles but with a paucity of names and descriptions. Haynes' entries are sparse and undated. Alone each might be suspect. Together they corroborate each other too closely to be coincidental. And both support and supplement the recollections of others.

As if to make amends for Mt. Misery, the chaparral hills beyond began to flatten out into more easily traveled terrain interspersed with small grassy valleys. Periodically groups would forge ahead scouting and clearing trail. Brier Jr. recalled that after the descent from Mt. Misery they camped that night "among the quaking bogs at the edge of a dark drain of the Mountain Meadows" and "the day following we advanced by a long and easy grade to a summit . . . the air was sharp . . . the men circled about the greasewood fires and sang the old songs some of which were parodied in a manner to turn regrets into laughter. I well remember the chorus of 'Carry Me Back,' and that of 'Oh, Susanna,' accompanied by the strains of Nat Ward's fiddle."

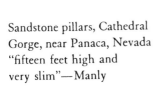

A page of the Asa Haynes journal

Cover title of Sheldon Young's log reproduced from page 258 of Dr. Margaret Long's *The Shadow of the Arrow*

Sandstone pillars, Cathedral Gorge, near Panaca, Nevada "fifteen feet high and very slim"—Manly

One might question his recollection of the ease of grade going up, but not their relief in the now pleasant traveling. One also shared by Manly writing, "Thus far the country had been well watered and furnished with plenty of grass . . . the men . . . making a regular picnic of it. There were no hardships and one man had a fiddle which he tuned up evenings and gave plenty of fine music. Joy and happiness seemed the rule and all of the train were certainly having a good time of it."

Because of the dependency upon two witnesses supporting each other both are now quoted in side by side comparison. For simplicity both have been stripped to bare bones essentials:

	Young	*Haynes*
Nov. 10	Lay in camp	(Third of "3 days scouting")
Nov. 11	Westerly . . . 25 miles . . . grass and water	1 day to pleasant valley
Nov. 12	Lay in camp	Traveled NW 1 day
Nov. 13	Westerly . . . camped at a warm spring . . . 12 miles . . . good roads, plenty of wood and grass . . . rained	Traveled 12 miles west to a spring and cornfield

In leaving Mt. Misery on the 11th, Young could not have been referring to the grass and water beneath Mt. Misery as 25 miles distant. Rather that they did not lose any time in continuing on to where they also found water and grass.

Also to be kept in mind is that any day-to-day differences are accounted for by parties forging ahead of the others, helping to clear and guide the way.

Following terrain of least resistance they gravitated into the area just south of Panaca, Nevada, angling towards a prominent saddle and the most visibly obvious pass in the Highland Range, camping at what is now known as "Bennett Spring."[1]

---

[1] Although the pass elevation is 5600 feet it is but 900 feet above the valley floor. The spring (actually two) is traditionally named for Asabel Bennett who, in 1858, guided a Mormon expedition seeking a possible refuge from Johnson's U.S. Army troops. The account by James Martineau, topographer and historian for that expedition, appeared in *The Improvement Era*, July 1928 although originally penned in 1910. Martineau says Bennett told them the story of the '49 trek while they traveled "over the same route for 120 miles", pointing out their old trail

In confirmation of the locale, Manly describes their passing "pillars of sandstone, fifteen feet high and very slim and strange," an apt description of the distinctive formations of Cathedral Gorge State Park and unique in that region.

But, as Manly reports, "gradually there came a change as the wagon wheels rolled westward. The valleys seemed to have no streams in them and the mountain ranges grew more and more broken; in the lower ground a dry lake could be found and water and grass grew scarce."

	Young	*Haynes*
Nov. 14	Bore north of west . . . 10 miles . . . hard roads . . . dry camp . . . neither grass nor water . . . rained and snowed in the afternoon	W 12 miles to snow camp . . . no water
Nov. 15	6 miles north of west . . . water but not much grass . . . dry sandy desert . . . went 8 miles and camped on the opposite side of the valley . . . no wood or water . . . Northwest course	W 15 miles to dry camp across the valley

That Young's directions are northwesterly and Haynes' westerly can be attributed to the latter's briefer generalized entries. As an ex-sailor, familiar with compass bearing sightings, credence is given to Young. At least the things on which they are in agreement leaves little questioning that they were traveling relatively close together.

From saddle-summit of the Highland Range the '49ers worked their way down the slopes in a generally northwest course, calling a halt near the foot. The following day they headed toward the large playa in Dry Lake Valley (aka Bristol Valley and before that as Desert Valley), one of the many dry lake beds they were to encounter. Nor

---

and campsites along that portion. Martineau also says that Bennett attributed their short-cut map to Fremont and incompatibly describes Bennett as "an educated man". Whether it was a fault of Bennett's recollection or in the relayed telling, Bennett made no mention of the Manly-Rogers rescue in Death Valley and said that only one woman was left at the end.

were these to be avoided as without prospects of water despite their
sunbaked alkalined surfaces. At times water can be found along the
edges, especially after recent rains. Invariably it was not the most
potable but often better than none. Pausing briefly they curved around
the lake bed and continued across the flats toward the Pahroc Range.

	Young	*Haynes*
Nov. 16	No grass or water. Dismal looking country . . . 8 miles and camped at a spring. Not much grass. Bore north of West.	W 8 miles to water
Nov. 17	Rough road for 4 miles . . . came into a narrow valley. No running water. Rain-water in puddles. Grass scarce, wood none. Went 10 miles Northwest.	NW 15 miles

Channeled by terrain offering little alternate choices, both record
almost identical mileages, water and northwesterly course.

The route into Dry Lake Valley via Bennett Spring later became
a portion of one of the well traveled Pioche-Hiko routes in the silvered
'70s. In turning northerly up the valley the '49ers were heading towards the two main mining-day routes from Pioche to the White
River and Railroad valleys. The first to be sighted would be that via
Stampede Gap, Coyote Spring and over the lower north end of the
Pahroc[2] Range. Attracted to this first opportune crossing they veered
toward it, missing Coyote Spring a few miles further north. The
other route, still further north, from Pioche to Bristol Well, Silver
King Pass and rounding the end of the Pahrocs would be an uncertain haze and hillock-hidden choice even if seen in scouting. Although
both wind up in the old Sierra Valley or White River sink, it is the
former that fits the course of events that followed.

Crossing the Pahroc Range pass they camped, on the 16th, near
Black Rock Spring atop a barren highland. The next day they angled
down the gully-gashed western side into the narrow northern limits

---

[2] Found spelled both Pahrock and Pahroc.

of Pahroc Valley where it forms the beginning of the White River Valley (aka Sierra Valley).

Although the White River is mapped through here it is rarely if ever more than a dry wash. But in the slender flat valley shallow basins are common where rain waters puddle before slowly seeping away. One thing is sure, hemmed in by ranges on both sides there was little other than a northwesterly course to follow.

But now, after a week on the trail, dissention arose. "I went to the leaders," Manly says, "and told them we were going back toward Salt Lake again, not making any headway toward California."

Manly implies that this pronouncement was right after they left Mt. Misery. But as noted earlier, he also said that in scouting ahead he had remained out all night at times, although that was in an area where there was neither time, distance or corroboration of others to do so.

Subsequently he also writes that his solo scouting satisfied him that "going north was not taking us in the direction we ought to go." And that a series of meetings followed. It was about the third night the Jayhawkers were overtaken that Manly visited their camp, protesting the course being taken. That he ". . . went over to their camp again the next night," repeating his protestations, and on the following morning the Bennetts-Arcans broke away to the west.

Obviously a number of days had passed before that rebellion. A couple of happy days and nights of song, three days of growing discontentment and a meeting, another meeting the next night and the breakaway the next day, all add up to a week from Mt. Misery.

But the Jayhawkers continued on.

	Young	*Haynes*
Nov. 18	Good roads . . . 15 miles . . . grass and water scarce . . . followed a narrow valley bearing NW	N of W 20 miles
Nov. 19	5 miles . . . plenty of grass and water . . . the best grass since we left the Platte	6 miles W to good water & grass.

Distracting as it may be, it may be well to set at rest previous theorizations that the '49er route was via Hiko-Crystal Springs and the well known grasslands of the Pahranagat Valley. Unfortunately that theory gained acceptance by repetitive appearance in print rather than delving into other possibilities. Yet understandably so, for it still is a vast, empty and relatively inaccessible "back country" area.

Familiarity with Pahranagat Valley is usually due to Highway #93 south from Ely, jogging near Hiko to continue on to Las Vegas; and west-east #375 from Tonopah continuing as part of #93 to Caliente and Panaca.

From Beaver Dam's "Mt. Misery" to Hiko is almost due west in contrast to the '49ers dissention over going north. It is also only about 75 miles vs. Young's logging of 103 miles and Haynes a close 113 to "the best grass since the Platte."

Then there is the matter of days. Accepting that the '49ers left November 11, and with nothing to refute the Haynes-Young subsequent turn south on November 19-20, there are 9 to 10 days to be accounted for. Yet in taking two days to make some 35 miles from Beaver Dam to Panaca, it leaves 7-8 to make 45 miles more to Hiko—over flat terrain where they would have easily averaged 15 to 20 miles a day.

Also, as noted the Bennetts-Arcans now broke off to turn west— a direction they would already have been heading enroute to Hiko. Too, with the Jayhawkers continuing north then turning south to intersect the west bound Bennetts-Arcans, requires a triangulation of routes. It could not be as they reached the Pahrocs, for by then the Pahranagat greenery could have been sighted, convincing proof to all that they were on the right road and eliminating any bickering about hewing to a north course that might take them back to Salt Lake City.

Nor, in view of their subsequent swing south would the Pahranagat meadows have been the turning point for the Jayhawkers. Blocking ranges would eliminate any resumptive westward move until so far south they would have wound up on the Old Spanish Trail and not in Death Valley.

Keeping in mind that the '49ers traveled northerly for several days they would be well up in Dry Lake Valley. Here no westward wagon crossing is practicable until many miles farther north in the visibly lowering end of the range.

Here the Pahrocs and the narrowing valley along its eastern slopes end in the surprising meadowlands of the Hot Creek area.[3] While its verdancy has been enhanced by enlarging the springs for cattle ranching, it has been known for as long as can be remembered for its expanse of grass and water.

Intriguingly, in a letter from Tom Shannon to fellow forty-niner Clay, dated January 21, 1895, he writes:

> . . . I made two discoveries on the desert and do not know if anyone shared them. The first was a well of warm water that ebbed and flowed. When I first came upon it, it seemed to be a well about 8 feet in diameter, perfectly round and smooth. It was 8 or 9 feet to the water. While I was contemplating how I could get some water, both to drink and to wash, it became agitated and slowly rose to within three feet of where I stood so that I put my hand into it and felt its temperature. It was right for a warm bath. This flow was accompanied by a roaring and gurgling sound and the earth trembled slightly under my feet. As I found the (water) undrinkable I determined to take a plunge, but when about ready the water began sinking with a gurgling sound. I stood and saw it recede to where it was at first. In ten minutes it came up again and I plunged in to take a quick bath but it went down before I could get out so I had to wait the next flood tide and it came, but I thought it was an eternity getting there . . .

Shannon does not date nor does he state just where this unique spring might have been. He simply notes it being "on the desert," indicatively precluding it being along the Platte or along the trail south from Salt Lake City. The process of elimination leaves the location somewhere between Mt. Misery and Death Valley.

But where? There are any number of geyser-spring areas in Nevada, although primarily in the north-central section. The closest to the '49er trail seemed to be about 50 miles north of Pioche. Could they have wandered that far afield?

And what of the Pahranagat? With all of its water sources no

---

[3] There are a number of places mapped as "Hot Creek", "Warm Springs" or "Hot Springs" in Nevada. This particular location is between the northern end of the Pahroc-Seaman ranges and Sunnyside where a network of intermittent streams, fed by springs in the flanking mountains, converge into the White River Valley near the present Adams McGill Reservoir.

such springs are known at present or in the past. Yet Shannon had seen a most unusual spring. Wherever it was it could provide a key to a pivotal point.

It is an age-old story that springs can come and go with the years. Time and searchings went on. "Old timers" who might have known had moved on. If information on such a spring did by chance turn up and, incompatible to the trail retracing, it would have to be chalked off as one of those unfathomable contradictions. Indeed as the quest went on the writer even hoped the answer would not be found lest it muddy the waters beyond all explanation.

But many months and field trips later The Answer came. From Lewis Sharp, of the old ranch and post office of Sharp, Nevada, at the foot of the Grant Range on the western edge of the White River Valley meadows.[4]

> There was a spring south of the old Hot Creek Ranch on the west side of the buttes that would answer your description. It was about 8 feet across. A man went in below the spring and ran a tunnel to top it. He got a large flow of warm water and ran it down into the valley and made a small ranch known as the Moon River Ranch.

Was this Shannon's spring? No others even remotely eligible have ever come to light. And the Moon River Ranch certainly fits with the '49ers trail—two miles or so from the Jayhawker camp amid "the best grass since the Platte." That no others report that particular spring can be attributed to Shannon wandering about or scouting during the layover and happening upon the strange spring.

Important a supplement as it is to the White River Valley routing it is just that—a supplement. In no way has route plotting been governed by the finding of the spring. Rather, it happens to be one of those happy coincidences that delight the researcher who is sometimes fearful of the findings but savors the rewards all the more.

After the Bennetts-Arcans broke away the morning of the 18th,

---

[4] Mr. Sharp's father once co-owned the old Freiburg Mine. Today the family ranch is at Nyala in Railroad Valley, "just over the hill" from abandoned Sharp, since reborn as Adaven.

Apparently there were two "Freiburgs". One, some mines in the Worthington Range near Tem Piute, dating back to 1865 and reorganized as the *Freyburg* District by George Ernest in 1869, although two years later the State Mineralogist re-spelled it as Freiburg. There was also a Freiburg in the Golden Gate Range near Oneota and purportedly a stage and wagon stop during the later mining booms.

Westward through Coal Valley to the pass into Garden Valley
Jayhawkers abandon their northward course to rejoin the Bennetts-Arcans

Hot Creek meadows with Shannon's unique spring
and "the best grass since we left the Platte"

the Jayhawkers continued northerly, reaching the meadowland on the 19th. Here man and beast recuperated with plenty of water and the best grass since the Platte.

But there were disquieting doubts. To the north the distance stretched hazily and endlessly between long, high ranges with no visible pass westward. Southerly, where the dissidents had gone, they could see the sun setting through an invitingly wide pass. Could the Bennetts-Arcans have been right after all? The sun set in the west, didn't it?[5] And Fremont had said that the way to California was to the west.[6] Swallowing their pride, the Jayhawkers turned south.

That the Jayhawkers did not reverse their direction without mutterings and misgivings is revealed in John Groscup's letter of January 18, 1865 to the Jayhawker Reunion:

> . . . and I shall never forget that at the head of the valley where we camped before we turned south . . . council was held which way we should go, to the north or to the south. . . . It was very rough south and plenty of snow peaks there and open and barren north . . . thought we should go that way but there was one man in the company who you all know. He could lay off all the mountains and call them by name whether they hit or not. He made the start and we all followed, and so down into the Great American Desert we went . . .

He could have been referring to Manly who was always out scouting, and disagreeing over the route he "frequently told them so." And couldn't resist rubbing it in a little that the Jayhawkers "at last concluded to accept my advice." But Manly was not at the meadows camp. Possibly the reference was to Rev. Brier who was frequently given to, and dimly viewed for, his vocal pontifications. Assuredly it was a time of edgy tempers and critical views of their fellow travelers.

---

[5] Repetitiously, although the reminder seems warranted, the sun sets to the southwest at this time of the year.

[6] A little over four years later, Fremont on his lesser known Fifth Expedition, traveled a similar course to the '49ers—from Cedar City, Utah, to Pioche and into the White River Valley; across Garden Valley and the Worthingtons into Penoyer Valley; on to Lida and Saline Valley into the Darwin area before crossing the Sierra Nevada at Walker Pass.

Considering the relative proximity of the two routes across Nevada, one muses that Fate could have placed the Pathfinder in the steps of the '49ers who had placed so much faith in his routings. Unfortunately, in the rather meager account of the Fifth there is no mention of seeing any trail signs, camps or discards of the '49ers.

Manly says that it was on the second night, i.e. the 19th, that "the Jayhawkers hove in sight in the rear." But according to Young and Haynes the Jayhawkers turned south on the 20th. With fairly long upgrade travel they were likely seen near dusk although arriving late that night.

And Manly does provide some clues that his party took three days for the cut-off. He tells of camping where the oxen fondly foraged on white sage. That they reached an Indian cornfield and piles of seed supplies. And that "one day I climbed a high mountain" before the Jayhawkers rejoining. All of which is a lot of activity for just two days and more easily acceptable as three.

That Manly does scramble things a bit at this point, including a belated reference to pillars of sandstone, actually passed a few days earlier at Cathedral Gorge and not indigenous here, is regrettable but understandable as part of a general background fill-in to his more important Death Valley story.

So it was that on the 18th the Bennetts-Arcans had turned off through one of the few good passes westward. That they did so prematurely was undoubtedly due to the elevations that blocked their view of the meadowlands the Jayhawkers found on the 19th.

Working their way down the western slope of the Seaman Range, crossing the soft sands and clay playa of Coal Valley, the Bennetts-Arcans camped near the site of Oneota[7] on the 20th. That night the reunited '49ers camped together and the next morning the Jayhawkers again took the lead.

	Young	*Haynes*
Nov. 20	This day left Ward's Muddy[8] and bore Southwest . . . struck another valley. Went 16 miles. Good roads. Dry camp. Not much grass.	20 miles . . . S . . . no water or grass

---

[7] Not the Oneota near the California border about 30 miles southwest of Columbus Salt Marsh. Coal Valley's Oneota was, in the early 1900's, developed as an irrigation project that didn't succeed. Remnants of a large cement reservoir still remain, gradually being covered by sand.

[8] Perhaps just a coincidence, but the White River Wash is actually the upper end of the Muddy River Channel. Young's naming of it as an anticipated location is intriguing. Again, the map which many blamed for leading them astray may have indeed been a good if crude guide.

	Young	*Haynes*
Nov. 21	2 miles . . . water . . . good roads . . . some rain . . . mountains covered with snow . . . snow in evening . . . went 16 miles . . . water and grass. West.	(5?) (15?) miles . . . found water and grass . . . snow
Nov. 22	Snow . . . two inches at 9 o'clock . . . 4 miles and camped . . . mostly squalls all day	SE 4 miles . . . layed by

Haynes' mileage for the 21st is indecipherable. The faded entry can be read as "5"—suspiciously low for the easy going grade—or "15", which totals 36 for Young, 39 for Haynes for the three days. The small difference could be due to differing estimates and/or slightly varying routes across the open terrain.

Just as they did not note splitting from the Bennetts-Arcans, neither report the rejoining. We know only from Manly that they all camped together, and that the Jayhawkers again took the lead the next day.

The '49ers were now in what is popularly known as high desert country. Snow is a familiar winter sight in the 8,000 to 10,000 foot ranges. Even the flat sandy valleys between are over 5,000, enclosing varying sized dry lake beds, their sticky clay surfaces mucky in the rains, cracked and billowing with dust when sun scorched. Although cleaving passes are few, erosion has created wide gaps connecting the series of high valleys, providing relatively easy if meandering travel.

Forging westward, at least at first, the setting sun beckoned enticingly through a broad gateway between the isolated buttes leading into Garden Valley, descriptively known as Hercules Gap.

The logic of heading for it was not theirs alone. In early Nevada mining days it was a roadway between Tem Piute, Freiburg and Sharp with Pioche and the Bristol mines to the east, and the junction with the old Cherry Creek-Hiko road to the Mt. Irish and Pahranagat mines.[9]

---

[9] In a 1964 field trip it was still marked by a mileage sign of "63 to Pioche, 13 to Sharp, 35 to Hiko".

Sand Springs South to Death Valley

"We had no instruments except a small pocket compass and could never tell where we were . . . we were lost . . . nearly dead from want of food and water . . ."—Colton

"The clear days and nights furnished us with the means of telling the points of the compass as the sun rose and set . . ."—Manly

"We did not know where we were, but I know we were much further off than we realized . . ."—Stephens

From Sand Springs Dry Lake the desolate expanse of Penoyer Valley stretched out before them, its sandy tentacles disappearing into distant rows of bare, bleak, black ridges.[10] Although the range immediately west was ending temptingly low there were no signs of water or grass as far as the eye could see.

Perhaps as never before they had arrived at The Moment of Truth. The decisive point when no longer channeled by terrain the choice was theirs from a great arc sweeping across the wastelands that seemed to extend into eternity.

From a high butte Manly saw a "snowy range ahead . . . the last range to cross before we entered the long-sought California." But he also reflected that "I believed that we were much farther from a fertile region than most of our party had any idea of."

The animals worn out, the emigrants exhausted, spirits dulled with despair, the wagon train began to disintegrate. Individually and collectively they began to scatter in search of water and even the poorest of grazing. The best route ahead was any man's choice.

Gone was the bonding philosophy that they were dependent upon one another "as one family." That if an ox should fail the others would share the burden, or if a man should weaken through need he should be helped lest he delay the rest. Unity, as their strength and salvation, gave way to sheer survival.

-----

[10]Cartographically the western portion along the Quinn Canyon Range is known as Sand Springs Valley, the eastern portion as Penoyer. That they are physically inseparable led to moves to redesignate the entire valley as Sand Springs Valley.

By now they had covered about 300 miles from Mt. Misery and each mile was becoming longer than the one before.[11] More than ever they began to string out, each segment struggling at its own pace, sometimes within sight of the others if only for swirls of dust in the distance, or simply following the tracks of those already lost to view. Those best fitted undoubtedly drove desperately ahead; the stragglers, just as desperate, staggering into camps guided by their fires.

It was near Sand Spring that the accounts of Manly, the Briers, Young and Nusbaumer unanimously report, although varying in details, the capturing of Indians in an endeavor to obtain information about water and their location.

Manly says that after finding a rain water basin in the rocks they captured *an* Indian who, in the morning, showed them (1) "a small ravine four miles away which had water in it, enough for our use," and (2) a water hole in a steep rocky cliff, at which point the Indian bounded away "after the fashion of a mountain sheep."

Brier Jr. recalls "a German" capturing two scantily clad savages at a slow pulsing spring. And "comprehending at length that water was the pressing want, they pointed toward a mountain, where base lines marked the confines of the desert, some ten miles to the south of west" where they found a spring "clear and cold and covered by a great flat rock."[12]

Teutonic Nusbaumer, who may well have been the German referred to, writes with striking similarity:

> A couple of our men caught two Indians who told us it was impossible to get through (westerly) as there was no water and the mountains were too steep to cross. They advised us to go further south. They also showed us a spring at a time when our animals were just ready to give out for want of water. Unfortunately the men let the Indians go free when they could have assisted us as guides.

---

[11] Two-hundred and eighty-nine according to Young's logging Nov. 11-Dec. 10, a little more per Haynes. All mileages should allow for estimations and side searchings for water, grass and terrain choices. One example is Mecum's ". . . traveled all day and then had to retrace our steps to get a drink," leaving uncertain just how often a day's travel was now forward or backtracked.

[12] The Brier story of finding a small spring at a "fissure" and of captured Indians pointing to a mountain about 10 miles southwest where they found another spring or "tank" covered by a flat rock, has been interpreted as reaching springs in the Belted Range to the west after leaving Papoose Dry Lake. But sequentially they then tell of the Papoose partings, indicating the Indians and springs incident occurred earlier.

Young, in his entry of November 26, notes, although not tying in his similar incident with any water discovery:

> This day lay in camp. Caught two Pi Ute Indians. Found that we were too far north, let one of them go again and kept the other for a guide. Caught another in the morning.

Whether all four incidents were one and the same is uncertain. Assuredly they occurred about the same time and locale, although they may have been coincidentally separate incidents. And one can but muse upon the Indian's advice. There are springs in the surrounding ranges for those who know where. And while some thought the Indians, coveting their wagons and cattle, were misdirecting them, it does not fit with them showing the '49ers springs "at a time when our animals were ready to give out for want of water." Too, in advising they were too far north, with its implicit counter move south, the '49ers were being directed into an area with a number of springs. At least to the desert wise and sharp of eye. In all probability the Indians were acting in good faith and of a possible knowledge of a trail to California far to the south.[13]

Despite these rays of hope, prospects were bleak with despair and doubt.

According to John Rogers' short account in the *Merced Star,* April 26, 1894:

> ... (we) traveled on till about the 1st of December. The company being dissatisfied, sixteen wagons were piled up and burned. Next morning the owners of the wagons packed their traps on their cattle and drove off. The rest of the party hitched up and continued on their journey in that way for about ten days when another split up occurred. They all left except three wagons. The latter party comprised Aharts (Ehrhardts) from Iowa, Bennett from Wisconsin and a man from Chicago named Arcane, the latter two having families. Manly and I stopped with them.

Although Rogers' account is far less than flawless there is little reason to doubt the essential factualness of his recollection. A split at Sand Springs late in November would be "about the first of

---

[13] Archeological excavations in the area have turned up both Pueblo and Paiute pottery, indicating Indian trade routes between Nevada and California.

December"—i.e. nearing that month. A second split "about ten days later" would be in early December at Papoose Dry Lake, a dating supported by Manly's account.

That 16 wagons were destroyed is doubtful. Accepting 27 wagons starting on the shortcut this would leave only 11 to continue on towards Death Valley, of which 7 are recalled by Manly as comprising the Bennett-Arcan contingent. Rogers' tally of three wagons left also conflicts with the Bennetts and Arcans having two wagons each, and fails to note that of the Wades, Nusbaumer, and one, the owners of which Manly could not recall. Possibly the 16 should be 6. Any accounting is complicated by wagons frequently being cut down into "carts." While they may have been recorded as wagons burned or abandoned, they could be recounted again later having amoebically divided and multiplied into 2-wheeled cart-wagons.

An example of this is Young, who makes no mention of their wagons until Death Valley where he logs, "Dec. 27 . . . our only alternative was to leave our wagons and carts." This could also apply to Martin's group. Haynes, at the McLean Spring camp in Death Valley, says, "we left our wagons" but he may have been referring collectively to the various Jayhawkers in camp. Colton, in a letter to *The Pioneer* (Nov. 20, 1895) also reports that while at McLean ". . . we had previously cut our wagons down to small carts."

Chances are that no one contingent left all of their wagons at Sand Springs. Rather it was a general lightening of the burden in facing the trek through the great sandy expanse they could see to the south.[14]

Manly, in a July 1894 letter to Colton writes:

> I saw a man named Barton who 3 years ago went hunting the Gunsight Lead and he says he found the camp where Jim Martin left his wagons. . . . The stones where you left your camp kettle still remain as you left them. Here he found a silver dollar, black but good, a hard wood picket pin and some small wagon irons. He says there were places where the wagon and ox tracks were plain to be seen . . .

---

[14] Old wagon remains were found on the southwest slope of the Worthingtons, approximating Haynes' crossing. Along with other evidence of wagon remnants and discarded equipment from Sand Springs to White Blotch, it lends credence to this being the "emigrant route" known to those who have lived long in that land.

In a letter to Clay, Nov. 25, 1894, he writes an almost identical description except adding that Barton found the old campsite "100 miles east of Death Valley . . . he (Barton) says the squaws rolled the wagon tires 75 miles to Pioche and got a big price for them." And reiterates that "this was the camp where Jim Martin left his wagons."

Since Manly's classic account later also notes that "Martin's mess unyoked their oxen from the wagons" near the Amargosa, a relatively few miles east of Death Valley, it is apparent that Martin's mess, like others, abandoned equipment at more than one locale.

While milages were often hazily recalled, certain confirmation of the above camp can be taken from the fact it is about 100 miles from Death Valley to Sand Springs, and from there about 75 miles east to Pioche. And in Thompson & West's *History of Nevada,* 1881, there is a coincidental description of Indian farming at early day Crystal Springs, close to Hiko and Pioche:

> To irrigate the land under tillage they had constructed several ditches, which were creditable to these primitive engineers. . . . To dig (these ditches) they had procured iron from abandoned emigrant wagons, which they had patiently cut and shaped and fastened with strong twine upon wooden handles, to be used for picks and spades.

Fatalistically, Nature also dipped into her bag of tricks as if to prove the susceptibility of men to will o' the wisp pursuits of the illusory and elusive. In the March 1903 *Out West* magazine, Brier Jr. writes:

> We journed fifty miles with the Timpanute (sic) and descended into the first real desert I had ever seen and saw here, for the first time, the mirage. We had been without water for twenty four hours when suddenly there broke into view to the south a splendid sheet of water which all of us believed was Owen's Lake. As we hurried towards it the vision faded and near midnight we halted on the rim of a basin of mud with a shallow pool of brine.

The incident, gilded with more flowery descriptions, also appeared in *The Grizzly Bear,* June 1911.

While he was only 7 or 8 years old at the time, and later some were to discount the recollections of "the Brier cub," it was an impressionable experience—and one undoubtedly recalled many times in family conversations and in the extensive collaborative writings with his father.

Turn south they did—into what was to be, a century later, the Atomic Energy Test Site area. By the time they realized the mirage was an illusion they were too committed to turn back to what offered no better promise.

Oddly enough it was probably the Indians and their springs that spared and separated them. Limited gestured communication left indecision as to just where and how far some of the springs were. And a notable divergence occurs between Young and Haynes.

	Young	*Haynes*
Nov. 26	Lay in camp . . .caught 2 Indians . . . found we were too far north . . . let 1 go . . . caught another in the evening	SE 8 miles . . . water
Nov. 27	Lay in camp	20 miles S . . . no water
Nov. 28	16 miles . . . good roads . . . dry camp. South	S 10 miles . . . water . . . no grass
Nov. 29	6 miles West to spring . . . water and grass . . . damed dubious country	E by S . . . 10 miles
Nov. 30	Lay in camp . . . shoeing oxen	SW 6 miles
Dec. 1	Left in evening . . . 6 miles . . . dry camp . . . grass	20 miles SW . . . water . . . no grass

In the six days Young logs three in camp, 16 miles south, 6 west and 6 with no direction given. In comparison Haynes was on the move each day, with 18 of his 74 miles in an easterly direction.

Endeavoring to follow the Indian directions "toward a mountain where base lines marked the confines of the desert," Young's party worked their way to distinctive White Blotch Butte near the end of Sand Springs Valley where it parts the openings southward like a boulder dividing a stream. In the meantime, Haynes' group leaving the Worthingtons via a more southern pass and finding some springs in the continuing elevations just ahead of them, gravitated into Desert Valley, also known as Tickaboo or Tickapoo Valley.[15]

---

[15]Concensus is for "boo", with "poo" as a slurred usage.

South from Sand Springs Dry Lake and Valley toward White Blotch Butte.
Across this expanse a mirage lured the '49ers south into the AEC area.
As Young forked to the right, the Jayhawkers canted southeast to the left.

Approaching White Blotch Butte from Sand Springs
"This day we came across a shrub called the
Spanish Bayonet"—Sheldon Young, Dec. 2, 1849

The location of their campsites in this area can only be hinted at by the finding of ox shoes and miscellaneous wagon parts at Sand Springs and near White Blotch Butte, in addition to the wagon remains found on the slopes of the Worthingtons.[16] However questioned, it is some corroboration of this section for Rogers' reported wagons abandonment, Manly's report on Martin's camp found by Barton, and Young's reshoeing of oxen November 30.

Just as Young and Haynes were now to part ways, so did the latter and larger group splinter again and again. The "Mississippians", "Georgians" and other Jayhawker contingents become indefinably intermingled as some fell behind, rejoined and formed new alliances.

SHELDON YOUNG

With Young and Haynes parting, dramatically evidenced by their Nov. 26-Dec. 1 entries, there is no longer need for the detailing that corroborated their similarities. And lest inclusion of more complete entries clutter and outweigh the increasing individualization of the other parties, they have been cut to bare-bone dates, mileages (without the repetitious use of "miles") and directions (i.e. SW instead of Southwest, etc.)

Both groups are now on somewhat parallel courses, separated by a low range extending southward.

Leaving White Blotch Spring, named after that Butte, where they had recuperated for two days, Young's group of about a dozen "independents" wended their way (17 S) Dec. 2 down the arm of the valley skirting the high Belted Range.

On Dec. 3 (16 SW) they camped with "plenty of water." They may have found a pool in the open flat at the edge of a dry lake bed, although this would apt to be meager and brackish. Or they may have found one of the Belted Range springs; and rather than laboring up the slopes with wagons, brought the water back down.

---

[16]There are reports of wagon remains found in 40 Mile Canyon further west, and by S. M. Wheeler, Nevada State Archeologist, near Ammonia Tanks and Captain Jack Spring in the Belted Range, as well as at some of the Indian caves and campsites in the area. The first has never been confirmed. And the only photographic evidence of Wheeler's wagon findings is that of a later light wagon. There is no doubt that the Indians collected findings for possible use, wood for fires, pieces of iron, etc., somewhat obscuring their original abandonment sites.

Here a string of springs extends from Johnnies Water, Cottontail, Wiregrass, Tub, Oak,[17] Whiterock and Captain Jack springs to Tippipah Spring. Scattered between, tucked in small spur canyons and rocky ravines are innumerable intermittent springs and "water holes" whose proclivity depends upon the wetness or dryness of the season. In addition, a supplemental source of water can be found at the "tanks" or shaded rock basins of standing water or damp sand—often stagnant, frequently requiring a little digging, but invariably welcomed by those in dire need—such as "Triple Tanks" south of Papoose Dry Lake and a string of tanks in northern areas of 40 Mile Canyon.

In addition, the Naquintas, just north of Groom Dry Lake, contain at least a half dozen, including Tickaboo, Naquinta, Emigrant and Disappointment springs.[18]

Water, of varying sorts, there was. Finding it another matter. Especially in blind searches. Again one wonders how many Indian and game trails were followed without comment or credit.

After "watering up" they continued Dec. 4 (16 SW), Dec. 5 (14 S). On the 6th (5 S) Young reports snow as they approached the rising heights of the Shoshone Range. He again reports snow on the 9th, three days of travel later. It is not clear from Young's entry of the 6th whether the snow fell on them or was simply seen in the mountains. It could be either or both since they were keeping close to the slopes. Similarly he was in the highlands to the south on the 9th.[19]

---

[17] Later the isolated ranch of cowboy-western novelist B.M. Bower (*Chip of the Flying U*, etc.), wife of Bud Cowan, author of *The Range Rider*. Dan Sheehan of the historic Groom Mine, a day's horseback ride across the valley, courted and married their daughter.

[18] The last two are held by "old timers" of the area to be springs of the '49ers. However distance, direction and timing preclude this. The '49er story may have inspired the namings but it is most unlikely they saw them.

[19] Haynes does not report snow on the 6th. Probably because they were in the low flatlands. The Jayhawkers did not have snow until their sixth day after leaving Papoose. They too had been in the flats. But those who were to veer from Haynes' course southward had, like the Briers, kept to the higher slopes near 40 Mile Canyon. The Bennetts-Arcans reported snow on the 7th in Nye Canyon, probably getting the December 6th snow storm as it moved eastward into the 4-5000-foot ridges enclosing their camp. By the 9th they had moved out and down into the lower elevation of the "Indian Farm".

Although as fragile as the flakes that fell, it can be presumed the snows were experienced by those at higher elevations, missed by those in the low flatlands. However deductive it does help to position the various groups.

After 10 miles WSW on the 10th, they "crossed a desert ... found wood, grass and water in time to save some cattle" on the 11th (12 SW). And on the 12th went "3 miles downstream ... better grass ... camped" and remained at this camp for the next six days.

The "desert" was that of the Jackass Flat extension of the Amargosa, and apparently they reached the fairly good water and grass area embracing Rogers and Longstreet springs, just east of the Fairbanks Ranch. Undoubtedly beckoned on by the greater verdancy of the latter they then continued three miles to where there was a sufficiency to justify a long camp. Here they recuperated, reshod oxen and explored, including the naming of Carter and Mecum among the scouts.[20]

They moved out on the 19th (8 S) over a "soft" sandy road, heading for Furnace Creek Wash. But not necessarily the present highway entrance. In the projecting spur of the Funeral Range just east of Pyramid Peak there is a cut-off pass. In retrospect one might prefer the longer but flat rounding of this spur but many did not. Buel and Todd, for example, map their 1864-5 route through this pass. So does Lt. Wheeler in his 1871-75 mappings. And the H. Washington-surveyed General Land Office maps of 1855-56 show an "old road" (old even at that date, and possibly that of the '49ers) from the Ash Meadows area and approximately four miles north of Death Valley Junction. From here it roughly parallels the present highway but varying one to two miles north of it, skirting the base of the range more than the wash road now used.[21]

[20] Indicative of the shiftings, Mecum is consistently identified as a Jayhawker, even to being listed in the #2 wagon with Clay, Richards and Edgerton. Later, at McLean, he is again with the Jayhawkers. Likely, Mecum was one of the Haynes contingent met by Young at the Fairbanks Ranch.

[21] Although Washington's survey has been criticized, Death Valley-wise Inyo County Surveyor A. A. Brierly defends this portion at least with "Don't let anyone contend this survey was a complete fraud. He ran the San Bernardino Meridian and I never heard of any question as to its accuracy."

Whether its controversial plotting of townships in Death Valley were done later at a desk to pad their activities is debatable. That the survey team was definitely in the area is evidenced by mappings too accurate for hearsay. Interestingly, Travertine Springs was once known as Hadley Springs, after one of the members of that survey.

As mapped, "the old road" continues just north of Furnace Creek, over an old trail, and ends near the present Beatty Junction road, probably when and where the surveyors called a halt.

Groom Dry Lake, looking south
from the historic Groom Mine

The same view a century later.
The '49ers were to enter what
later became the AEC test site.

Papoose Dry Lake, the
"last camp of the families"

However moot the point, Young's mileages and directions place him within the general confines of Furnace Creek Wash.

In leaving the Amargosa desert that they reached on the 11th and recuperated along the edge of it for a week, his entry of the 20th is worth noting in full.

> Dec. 20. This day left Relief Valley, bore a West course over a barren desert, discovered an old pack trail supposed to be Ward's. Went twelve miles and camped without food or water.

Having reached "wood, grass and water just in time to save our cattle," his naming of "Relief Valley" is well put. Intriguing is his thought that the trail might be Ward's. Seemingly he was clinging to the basic authenticity of the "shortcut" map. That this was a pack trail, and whose one can only wonder, and wonder whether it was a well worn Indian trail or of game on the way to water in the highlands, or perhaps at Travertine Springs. While he does not say they followed this trail one would do so instinctively. Given a choice of following a trail to someplace or something valued enough to establish it vs. cutting across virginal ground in unknown terrain the former would be a preference for most.

As they wound their way on the 20th and 21st (W 6?) they periodically glimpsed the Panamints as "a range of snow mountains ahead."

The next two days were spent at Travertine Springs. On the 24th they attempted a three mile aborted effort to cross Death Valley, turned back and went 4 miles NW.

Young's mileages now take on a new significance.

On Dec. 25 they went 8 miles NW, finding springs of fresh water on the east side of the valley—probably the Cow Creek-Nevares Spring area. The water, found by scouting, was probably hauled back to the wagons rather than laboring up the slopes. That night they went another 7 miles, a total of 15 for the day.

On the 26th they went another "8 NW" to the "head of the salt valley . . . small stream of salt water . . . no grass" and *continued 4 miles up the valley,* camping with both grass and water.

His mileages take them beyond McLean, where they probably found too many Jayhawkers encamped for the meager saltish water

and sparse grass, on toward the mesquite greenery of the Midway
Well area beyond the lower salt flats.

Here, on the 27th, they "concluded our only alternative was to
leave our *wagons and carts.*"

ASA HAYNES

Meanwhile, back near Sand Springs, November 26, Haynes and
the others had elected to take the route through Desert Valley on the
east side of the Timpahutes. Here Nusbaumer's small party of six—
"Hadapp, Calverwell from Washington City, Fisch from Indiana,
Isham from Michigan and a colored man named Smith from Missouri," plus Nusbaumer, joined the Bennetts-Arcans, having decided
"Captain Town's party traveled too slowly so we left them and joined
a company of six wagons which we met near one of the dry lakes."

Ranks broken, they continued south and southeast (8 SE on the
26th, 10 E by S on the 29th). On the 30th, with changed minds over
the route selected, they veered six miles SW, over or near Summit
Pass in what is known as "the jumbled hills." On December 1, still
SW, they reached Papoose Dry Lake late in the day after a long 20
mile haul.[22] And just in time to hear Manly, who had been out scouting, report on very dismal prospects ahead.

Haynes here "found water . . . no grass." Water, however uncertain
the quality, is frequently found along the edges of such lake beds.[23]
Mrs. Brier was to describe it as glazed mud covered with shallow
alkaline water. But there are also occasional seeps, such as at "Wet
Weather Spring" about 3 miles to the west, to which they may have

---

[22] In so doing they avoided Groom Dry Lake which they could undoubtedly see in the distance. Papoose Dry Lake, about 15 miles south of it, could also be visible along with signs,
including campfires, of the faster moving Bennetts-Arcans and Nusbaumer who had reached
it the day before.

[23] J. Ross Browne, reporting on similar locales, says "Upon these salt fields (i.e. playas) there
are no signs of animal or vegetable life, though it is a singular circumstance that coming up
through the saline incrustations near the edge of the largest of them (can be found) fine springs
of pure cold water." The pools edging Papoose are neither fine, pure or cold, but can be palat-
able for the desperate.

gone for water. However poor and meager, apparently there was enough, especially after the others left, for the Bennetts-Arcans to layover until the 6th. Grass, however, was another matter, requiring foraging for sparse patches on the sandy slopes. Perhaps deciding this time-taking effort was outweighed by the possibilities of better pickings ahead, Haynes and the Jayhawkers began to pull out westward with little delay. Feeling that the way south left much to be desired, the Jayhawkers were back to California being to the west.

INTERMISSION

It is well to take time out at this point to establish which of the many dry lakes was to be the last camp at which, save for Young, they were together, and which provides a foundation for the routes and events to follow.

It also clarifies confusing references to "where we left the famil*ies*", of which there were four—the Bennetts, Arcans, Wades and Briers. In the parting the Briers were without the company of another family. And the others were never to be with the Jayhawkers again. The Bennetts, Arcans, and trailing Wades were to reach Travertine Springs near Furnace Creek after the Jayhawkers had left. There they turned south, far from any Jayhawker camps. Thus any subsequent reference by the Jayhawkers to family or families, such as in Panamint Valley or at Providence Springs, could only be singular—the Briers.

In locating the "Last Camp" with the families there are five possibilities, however remote some may be. Each has as its crux Manly's view of a "level plain" to which the Jayhawkers headed "due west."

Progressively, north to south, the more prominent and possible routes westward from a dry lake bed are Sand Springs Dry Lake, Groom Dry Lake, Papoose Dry Lake, a playa in Frenchman Flat and Yucca or Tippipah Dry Lake. Sand Springs Dry Lake is ruled out as being too far north and out of the sequence of events. Although it has been theorized that the Jayhawker escape route might have been, be it at prohibitive odds, west from Sand Springs via Gold Flat to Sacrobatus Flat between Beatty and Goldfield, the emigrant accounts unanimously agree that they found themselves too far north at this point. And with the same unanimity report turning south, however misled by the mirage.

From Groom Dry Lake, which fits neither Young nor Haynes, what little is visible of the dogleg into Yucca Flat would be offset by the high wall of the Belted Range to the west.

Frenchman Flat, from the standpoint of a dry lake bed with an open level plain westward into Jackass Flat, blending into the Amargosa, could fit topographically but not chronologically. So, too, with Yucca (aka Tippipah) Dry Lake.

Papoose is a large elongated dry lake south of Groom. To the east the low jumbled hills curve to hem in the Papoose playa. To the west, across a low range, Yucca Flat can be seen from any nearby elevation. To the south a rather rugged mountainous area seemingly bars the way except for the singular opening of Nye Canyon through which, in the far distance, snowclad 11,918-foot Mt. Charleston can be seen.

It is Papoose Dry Lake that provides as no other the approach routes, a practical westward course through the passes in the narrow ridges to a level plain, and for Manly's observation of a great snow-peak to the south.

Here, all of the families were together—for the last time. And from here the various routings fit like the pieces in a jigsaw.

BACK TO HAYNES

From Papoose Dry Lake the various Jayhawkers left intermittently, heading west. Haynes and his companions were among the first, leaving the morning after their late night arrival. Logging 15 SW (Dec. 2) indicates they opted for a dimly discerned route angling southwesterly. While there is another pass more directly west, now a bladed AEC road, the former evidently seemed best to them at the time. A judgment call? An Indian trail? Or was "SW" the main or last direction of the day? *Quien sabe?*

Again there is a reminder that Haynes' entries are not dated. Some datings can be fixed by events that he noted and/or locales and circumstances established by the reports of others. Intervening days are more deductive, supported by on-site observations of terrain and logical routes.

That so little is known of the next portion of the '49er trail is not **surprising.** Except for Haynes' brief entries, there is no chronicler among the fragmented Jayhawkers to detail their way. Young had taken a different route. The Bennetts-Arcans, with the two best diarists—Manly and Nusbaumer—had been left behind to follow another route. The Briers, Colton and others were to depend upon hazy recollections.

Too, all were in dire straights. Days and miles blurred with only survival in mind. Yet the meager information, pieced together, provides a reasonable picture of the ways and days to follow.

To continue with Haynes and his fellow travelers—after crossing the ridges there is no mention of water or grass for three days as they trekked along the waterless eastern side of Yucca Flat. On the fourth (Dec. 5), after traveling 18 miles they reached "water and grass." But they did not tarry for they went 8 miles "S" (?) the next day before laying by for 8 days.

Obviously something unusual had taken place. Or it was the place itself.

Strangely, while they must have found sufficient to sustain an 8 day camp, he does not mention water. Even more puzzling is the directional "S". Haynes entries are not infallible and those pondering his sometimes faded and illegible pencilings were subject to interpretive errors.

From the events, directions and distances preceding and following, he is positioned between latter day Wahmonie[24] and 40 Mile Canyon. It is an empty, thirsty land with few reliable springs. The most noticeable and eligible would be Cane Springs. But if Haynes was here for 8 days (Dec. 6-14) he surely would have mentioned the Bennetts-Arcans who were here, at what they called the "Indian farm," (Dec. 9-19). And neither Manly nor Nusbaumer even hint of sharing that camp with any Jayhawkers.

Did Haynes, like Young, proceed through Jackass Flat to the springs just east of Fairbanks Ranch? Not likely. Not with logging W 14, W 20, W 6 from their 8 day camp to a 5 day camp at the latter on the 16th.[25] Yet that 5 day camp cannot be ignored. It is only explainable if the Dec. 6 entry should be N, not S. Here they would have neared Topopah Spring, tucked within the slopes to the north,

[24] Wahmonie, about 4 miles northwest of Cane Springs, lived a short but merry 3 months in 1928, during Nevada's last Great Bonanza days.

located by scouting. A well-worn Indian/game trail to it was later used by early miners.

It is anyone's guess whether Haynes counted his mileage for the next three days as from Topopah Spring itself, or from its approach where they probably camped with the wagons. Either way it better fits his distance to where he records a 5 day camp (Dec. 16-21) with water and grass, later developed as the Fairbanks Ranch.

Young is positioned here December 12 thru 18, and Haynes 16th thru 21st. There is no doubt they were both attracted by the same site. Indeed, Haynes may also have been motivated by the sight of Young's group already there and shared that recuperative opportunity the 16th, 17th and 18th. This would also account for Young's reference to Mecum scouting although he was a Jayhawker and not one of Young's "independents."

But now, as Young headed southerly, Haynes heads W 6 (22nd), NW 8 (23rd), W 8 (24th) and W 18 (25th) where he notes "here we left our wagons" (at McLean Spring).

Haynes' course cannot be reconciled with Furnace Creek Wash. By sight or scouting they decided to go west and northwest, past the site of Leeland, to Indian Pass. According to his Dec. 25th entry they still had wagons (or carts) and one may well speculate on the practicality of Indian Pass. Yet from his *west* directions of the 24th and 25th it is less likely that they went as far as the more easily traversible Daylight Pass, which would have then required a southwest course to McLean Spring.

We know only that Haynes was on a distinctively different route, that he is not mentioned by others as being in the Furnace Creek area, and that he was at McLean with the Jayhawkers and Briers and linked with them thereafter.

Despite the care and conviction of placing Haynes at Fairbanks Ranch the awareness of weaknesses in his journal allows a possibility, however remote, of the 8 day camp being at Indian Springs, about 35 miles "south" of Lathrop Wells.[26] With the usual variables dictated by terrain and estimations, it is conceivable to still chart him into

---

[25] Arriving earlier enough on the 6th, after only 8 miles, he seems to have counted it as one of the 8 days. At the 5-day camp they may have started late, had slow going or problems, and tallies the next 5 days as "layed by".

Death Valley via Indian Pass. And the present 71 miles by road from Papoose to Indian Springs is not far off from his logged 56 miles from Papoose to the 8 day camp, especially with crosscountry short-cuttings.

But while his entries may be questioned they cannot be ignored. In leaving Papoose, heading west with the Jayhawkers, he logs SW, W, SW, W of S, all of which would then require an extremely unlikely consistent south and southeast bearing to Indian Springs. The way west was too open, too inviting for Haynes and the others.

THE JAYHAWKERS

Leaving Young and Haynes "on stage" at McLean Spring for the next Act in the Death Valley drama, let us pick up the other players, the Jayhawkers.

Detailed information is meager indeed. Sparse, hazy recollections are all that bridge this section of the trail from Papoose Dry Lake.

Some or all may have, like Haynes, started over the "pass" southwesterly. Or the one more directly west. Either way they would have soon been blocked by the Belted Range ahead. Here there would be only one pass opportunity, however unlikely, via Tippipah Spring into 40 Mile Canyon—a locale detailed under Briers and Martin.

They are reported to have gone five days without water and encountering snow on their 6th day. As noted previously, the Jayhawkers undoubtedly left Papoose at various times. Those who left December 4 would have experienced the same snow as Young on the 9th, six days later.

Like, or with, Haynes they followed the same general route southwesterly down Yucca Flat until just before Cane Spring. Strung out with irregular knots of small groups they fanned across the wastelands. Since there is no mention of Cane Spring, one not easily overlooked or forgotten, the Jayhawkers probably cut westerly before sighting it, continuing through upper Jackass Flat and encountered snow in the elevations near the south entrance to 40 Mile Canyon.

---

[26] Once known as Rose or Rose's Well, a name picked up from the abandoned Las Vegas & Tonopah Railroad station of Rosewell about 12 miles farther north toward Beatty. In the newest renaming Lathrop Well has become Amargosa Valley which may add to confusion with an old LV&T station of Amargosa, also the former name for Death Valley Junction!

There is even less information on the Jayhawkers' approach to the Amargosa. Did they also reach the well watered camps of Young and Haynes? Perhaps with the latter? Possibly at least some of them. Or perhaps stopped at one of the occasional small oases of greenery and water along the Amargosa River bed—such as Franklin Well— where the 1861 Boundary Party found "tall bunch grass, mesquite, rabbits and Indian brush rancherias." All that is known is that some of them gravitated into Furnace Creek Wash.

The Briers tell of "Capt. Town's party" following them here, although they might have veered off before reaching it. At their memorable Christmas Day camp the Briers name "two young men, St. John and Patrick" as well as Fred Carr and Masterson. And in a vague reference, Brier Jr. infers "the Towns, Wards, Mastersons, Briers and others, bonded by congenial ties and concurrent judgment" were at Travertine Springs.

Manly is to later note that the Jayhawkers were at the McLean camp when the Martin party and Briers pulled in, adding weight to the possibility that these two parties had rejoined after their earlier parting.

Yet Manly also tells of finding the Jayhawker trail[27] at a bitter tasting stream of the Amargosa, but *heard* that the Jayhawkers did not follow it southward but "turned west again, bearing to the north towards a low pass they could see in the mountains." And that "this new direction gave them an *up hill* route for 30 or 40 miles, rough and barren."[28] Although Manly was to offset this somewhat by finding the body of an ox on his route into Furnace Creek Wash, it does add to the speculation that some of the Jayhawkers had fanned out over different entries.

When Manly overtook the Briers at Travertine Springs he reports it as a camp of *one man* with his wife and family. He was told others were somewhere ahead. Still others, named by the Briers at this camp, may have been with the reconnoitering party into the valley, reported

---

[27] On the 24th, per Nusbaumer. Manly says it was a trail undertaken by the Jayhawkers ten days before, i.e. the 14th. Young's crossing was the 19th and 20th, Haynes the 22nd. Manly may have been guessing about 10 days. Or advance parties may well have crossed earlier.

[28] An "up hill route" description may be contrasted by the 1861 Boundary Party's description of the wash itself: ". . . a broad low pass through these mountains leading with scarce any rise from the plain into a dry arroyo named Furnace Creek."

by Brier Jr. who found "Jayhawk wagon tracks and we decided to follow them northward."

Whatever the dearth of information, a sizeable number of Jayhawkers were at Travertine before and with the Briers. Some arrived via Furnace Creek Wash. Some, starting out on a higher course, may have drifted into Echo Canyon, a route to be well worn by miners between Lee's Camp, Schwaub and Furnace Creek. Others, like Haynes, missed Travertine in their farther north crossings via Indian or Daylight Pass.

But in varying sized segments the Jayhawkers began to gather, about the 20th of December for the advance parties, at McLean Spring along Salt Creek, as if some fateful maelstrom had drawn them beyond their control for a final rendezvous in the valley of the shadows of death.

THE BRIERS AND OTHERS

Admittedly taking up the main '49er parties as units may be distracting in the separations. But in view of them being on different routes it is hopefully easier than bouncing back and forth daily. So it is that we now take up the Briers. Theirs is, on the surface, a seemingly simple story of a single family. But it gained in complexity as they moved south from Papoose Dry Lake.

Not ones to lead or go it alone, the Briers went with or followed the Jayhawkers on their intended westward course. When that proved impractical if not impossible, all turned southward along Yucca Flat.

According to Manly, the Doty and Martin messes traveled for five days from the lake camp without finding water. That the Briers were with them is evidenced by witnessing the Martin "mess" breaking away later on.

Because of the bearing on the Brier route, and in turn on a number of others, it may be well to set at rest the conjecture that the Briers reached and followed 40 Mile Canyon.

That canyon is a long north-south defile in the Belted Range. There are few if any enticing passes on the east, except for that at Tippipah Spring. At its south end it empties into Jackass Flat. Just above Tippipah Spring it swings around Timber Mountain and Pah-

Tippipah Springs and the entrance into 40-Mile Canyon

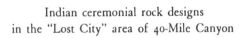

Indian ceremonial rock designs
in the "Lost City" area of 40-Mile Canyon

ute Mesa towards Beatty. Also near Timber Mountain a trail cuts across via Cat Canyon and Beatty Wash. The latter two routes are virtually impassable except afoot, by horse or very light wagons and those with difficulty.

Southward it is deep, volcanically gutted, littered with boulders falling from steep enclosing cliffs, with twists and turns blocking views of how far one might progress. While an early mining days road was once mapped through 40 Mile Canyon from Wahmonie to Tippipah it was an uncertain route. Subject to washouts and rockfalls, traversing it was oft an Herculean task, one the '49ers were in poor condition to handle. Nor would they be in a position to gamble that they would not be helplessly stranded. Even if it had been seen in scouting, 40 Mile Canyon could have been weighed and found wanting over the somewhat parallel open route through Yucca Flat.

Following this the Jayhawkers went five days without finding water. Then according to Manly:

> Martin's mess unyoked their oxen from the wagons, put some small packs on their own backs and loaded some on the backs of their oxen and turned south toward the nearest snowy mountain they could see, the same one toward which the Bennett party had steered from the lake camp. The Doty party kept on straight for another day. Toward morning, as they stood around the fire, a stray cloud appeared and shortly after began to unload a cargo of snow.

The Briers report that a foot of snow fell as they reached a *branch* of 40 Mile Canyon. And that Martin's mess left *after* the snowfall when ". . . the company loaded (packs) on the cattle and burned everything with the wagons. It was a fatal step as we were about 500 miles from Los Angeles with only our feet to take us there."

Before or after? Perhaps both, with some of the faster moving Jayhawkers and Martin party breaking away, leaving others still encamped another day or so.

Would Martin have stayed with the Briers and kept wagons/carts with the providential snow? Or the Briers abandon theirs with other helpful hands available? We know only that Martin's mess started for the same snowy mountain the Bennetts-Arcans had headed for earlier. And that the wagons/carts were abandoned near 40 Mile Canyon in Jackass Flat.

From here the Briers wound up in Furnace Creek Wash. The 9th to the 25th, when they reached Travertine Springs, is, as with most of the Jayhawkers, a blank. To fill in the two weeks is only a faintly heard word that the Briers lay in camp for a week. Undoubtedly they, and the others, progressed in camp to camp stages.

What little is known of this part is more than made up by Mrs. Brier's touchingly recalled memories of following the men who had gone ahead to explore and find water, leaving her behind with three small boys (about 9, 8 and 4 years old) to help bring up the cattle:

> Poor little Kirk gave out and I carried him on my back, barely seeing where I was going, until he would say, "Mother, I can walk now." Poor little fellow. He would stumble on a little way over the salty marsh and sink down, crying, "I can't go on any farther." Then I would carry him again, and soothe him as best I could.
>
> Many times I felt that I should faint and as my strength departed I would sink on my knees. The boys would ask for water but there was not a drop. . . . Night came and we lost all track of those ahead. I would get down on my knees and look in the starlight for the ox tracks and then we would stumble on . . .
>
> About midnight we came around a big rock and there was my husband at a small fire. "Is this camp?" I asked. "No, it's six miles farther," he said.
>
> I was ready to drop and Kirk was almost unconscious, moaning for a drink. Mr. Brier took him on his back and hastened to camp to save his little life. It was 3 o'clock Christmas morning when we reached the springs . . . a Christmas none could ever forget.[29]

That the Briers followed the Jayhawkers instead of Martin is indicated by Mrs. Brier recalling that in their approach to Furnace Creek Wash "we were the second last, Town's party being the last."

As touched upon earlier, there were more at the Travertine camp than can be tightly pinned down.

Manly recalls that only the Briers were in camp.[30] And that when he arrived he found Rev. Brier delivering a lecture to his *boys* on education. But Brier Jr., in *Out West* magazine, 1903, says, "The *men*

---

[29] For those who may chance upon it, a somewhat duplicative account appeared in the *Carson City News,* June 8, 1913, in which she relates, "Poor little Kirk, my eldest, aged 9 years, gave out and I carried him . . . until he would say, 'Mother, I can walk now'," etc. Since Kirk was the youngest, about 4, and Chris the eldest, about 9, the assumption is a reportorial error.

wanted something to remind them of other days and my father gave
them a lecture on education. It was grave, humorous and reminiscent." Mrs. Brier corroborates this with:

> Our company was from the southern states, called the Mississippi
> Boys (and) they called Mr. B. "Parson" . . . One came to him and
> said, "Parson, we would like you to give us a lecture this evening." He
> complied and gave them one on education. All cheered him and our
> Christmas ended . . .

Mrs. Brier also records that "two young men, St. John and Patrick
made up our 'mess' as we called it." And that after the arrival at 3
o'clock on Christmas morning, she was for "lying down immediately,
but good, kind Mr. Masterson insisted upon eating a little and gave
us each a piece of bread."

She is also to tell that "The *men* killed an ox and we had a Christmas dinner of fresh meat, black coffee and a very little bread. I had
one small biscuit. . . ." And:

> Music or singing? My, no. We were too far gone for that. Nobody
> spoke very much, but I know we were all thinking of home back East
> recalling the cheer and good things there. Men would sit looking into
> the fire or stand gazing away silently over the mountains and it was
> easy to read their thoughts. Poor fellows! Having no other woman
> there I felt lonesome at times, but I was glad, too, that no other
> was there to suffer.
>
>   Fred Carr said to me that night, "Don't you think you and the chil-
> dren had better remain here and let us send back for you?" "No," I
> said, "I have never been a hindrance. I have never kept the company
> waiting, neither have my children, and every step I take will be to-
> ward California.

The next morning "the company moved on over the sand to—
nobody knew where"—making a unique discovery also shared by
others. That of an aged Indian. According to Mrs. Brier:

> One of the men ahead called out suddenly, "Wolf! Wolf!" and raised
> his rifle to shoot. "My God, it's a man!" his companions cried. As the

---

[30] One can only muse upon why, with all of the Brier family fondness for telling of their
experiences, there is no mention of Manly at Travertine Springs. Surely it would have been a
notable reunion with someone of another party that they had not seen or heard of since the
Papoose parting three weeks before. But then. Manly's recollective halo also becomes a bit tar-
nished at this time.

Death Valley from Dante's View

McLean Spring, where the Jayhawkers abandoned their wagons and "carts"

company came up we found the thing to be an aged Indian lying on his back and buried in the sand, save his head. He was blind, shriveled and bald and looked like a mummy. He must have been 150 years old. The men dug him out and gave him food and water . . .

According to the "*we* found," the Briers had caught up with those who had moved ahead. According to Brier Jr. it was the reconnoitering party who "came upon an old Indian, buried in the sand and only his head visible" although he also tells of the Indian being released from confinement and "we watched him catch beetles for food and visit the near branch [of the spring] for drink though his eyes may have been dead for a quarter of a century."

Did the reconnoitering party do their exploring the day of the 25th, find the Indian, and return to camp that night for the Christmas ox dinner and educational sermon, thus missing Manly in the interim? Or did the Indian incident occur on the 26th after the company moved out with the Briers in the rear? A small difference perhaps, except to wonder about the Brier's sad plight prior to Travertine and staying but one day to recuperate.

Exact datings are difficult indeed to fix.

Haynes had reached McLean on Christmas, probably late in the day, and says they "layed by four days."

Stephens was also there the 25th, although there is no indication of how much sooner, if at all, he had arrived:

> On Christmas day, 1849, we were all busy making pack saddles and cooking the scanty supply of flour into little biscuits or crackers as they were perfectly hard. We were divided into eight men to two men mess(es) and each had his share allotted. . . . We had a half dozen of the little crackers, about three or four spoonfuls of rice and about as much dried apples . . . which must last until we reach settlements.

Stephens also says, "The Rev. Brier family came up to us (at McLean)" adding, "There were others who came to our camp, one a company of Georgians, about 15 of them. . . . Captain Townshend seemed to be the head man of the Georgia Company." Mindful that the Georgians (which had included Town or Townshend, Masterson, Fred Carr and a John Martin from Texas) and the Mississippians (including Jim Martin from Mississippi, Coker or Croker, as well as the attached Briers) had become indistinguishably intermixed, one must settle for a loosely knotted string of '49ers reaching McLean, some before, some after Christmas day.

Alas, except for the patient, we are not yet through with the Briers on their way into Death Valley.

MARTIN AND COKER

In leaving the Briers near 40-Mile Canyon, Martin's party headed toward the mountain whose snows beckoned the Bennetts-Arcans. Seemingly, in going south, he would have almost inescapably soon reached Cane Springs about Dec. 9 or 10. But the Bennetts-Arcans were already there and neither Manly nor Nusbaumer make any mention of new arrivals and surely they would have.

One can only surmise that on a necessary southeast heading from the 40-Mile Canyon area toward Charleston Peak area, they missed Cane Spring, skirted Skull Mountain into Frenchman Flat. Here they could have opted for the signs of water and greenery where the AEC was to locate their Camp Mercury, or drifted to Indian Springs. Both offer relatively easy, if sandy, going westward.

Some clues lie in another small and equally vague contingent— that of Ed Coker.

Manly, in a letter to Clay (Nov. 23, 1890) says, "Coker was in Jim Martin's party that gave Briers their oxen." And in that part of his book where "Mr. Coker related his experiences to the author somewhat as follows...." Coker says:

> ...we started with our knapsacks and we left the families, for it was plain the women and children must go very slowly (and) a colored man joined us who had been with a party that included Culverwell ...Fisch...and another man whose name I never knew...

That the camp was at Papoose and not 40-Mile Canyon is supported by a combination of things. One, the noting of famil*ies,* and not the singular Brier family. Two, the joining of Smith, who had been with Nusbaumer and Culverwell to Papoose but not mentioned after that.[31]

---

[31] Smith was not one of the two or three blacks with the Mississippians from the start. Smith was an obvious new addition.

From the above potpourri it appears that Coker continued with Martin's mess after parting from the Briers near 40-Mile Canyon, rejoining them from Death Valley to Providence Springs.[32]

THE SAVAGE-PINNEY PARTY

Still another, the most shadowy group of all, and the most intriguing, may have been at the 40-Mile Canyon camp, or met along the Jackass Flat.

Brier Jr., in a letter to the *Inyo Independent* (July 4, 1884) writes, "After we had decided to leave our wagons a company of 11 men, led by Savage and Pinney, taking whatever they could carry on their backs, pushed ahead . . . near the Amargosa, Savage and Pinney, differing with the rest as to the route, remained in camp while their nine companions pushed over into Death Valley."

Brier Jr.'s recollections have been discounted by some '49ers as being a child at the time. But the many times retold story of their trek was undoubtedly a constant subject of family conversations and correspondence. And in their extensive writings the Brier father and son were close collaborators.

Few contingents have been more surrounded by mystery.

According to the accounts of Jacob Stover and William Lorton, among those who packed it by horse, mule and afoot, south from Mt. Misery to rejoin Hunt's trail near Las Vegas, was the Savage-Pinney party who broke away at Coyote or Dead Horse Spring in the Meadow Valley Wash area.

---

[32] Basically the "Mississippians", of which Coker was a member, was a small party of six, including Jim Martin and Jim Woods from Mississippi, a negro Joe, a negro Tom, "Little West" and Ed Coker. But in his own listing Coker also includes Nat Ward, John Martin from Texas, "Old Francis" a French Canadian, Fred Carr "and some others". Who and how many "the others" were is unknown. That Coker lists Jim Martin as from Missouri is a small point since he is consistently "from Mississippi" by others.

Ward, John Martin, Masterson and Carr have also been identified as members of the Georgians. In turn, the Turner brothers, listed as Georgians are also described as "Mississippi boys."

The discrepancies, typical of trying to categorize the parties, is explainable in the intermixing that had taken place. That it is dwelt upon here is only in guesstimating the number of people at the 40 Mile Canyon camp. Acceptably there were the 5 Briers, about a dozen in Coker's grouping of mixed Mississippians and Georgians, including Carr and Masterson, plus possibly "St. John and Patrick." A total of about 19 or 20.

Stover later notes, "I met Pinney and Savage in Nevada City. They gave me a history of those travels after leaving us:"

> We went over the mountains and traveled through a rough country, nothing to shoot, not a living thing to be seen till our horse meat was all gone and we came one night into a camp on a big desert. The boys said we would have to draw cuts in the morning who should be killed to eat. As we did not want to be killed to be eaten or eat anybody when we thought they were asleep we got up and traveled till day; then we took our butcher knives and dug holes in the sand and covered up all but our heads till night when we would come out and travel all night again. By this time we did not fear them and were recruited. The sand was what saved us. We think we kept westward more than we did before we left those seven men,[33] they bore northwest too much to suit us. We had almost given out when we thought we saw water and smoke. That cheered us up and gave us encouragement till we made the lake. It was Owen's Lake.

That the threat of cannabalism occurred not in southeastern Nevada but in the Death Valley area is supported by '49ers other than the Briers.

L. Dow Stephens, of the Jayhawkers, also touches upon this party of 11 after telling of the Briers rejoining at the McLean camp in Death Valley:

> Another party of 11 men passed us who thought they could make it by packing on their backs enough to last them . . . out of the 11 there was but two to finish the trip, the others having died in a pile.

Mecum was also to write, in a letter of January 1872:

> From where we burned our wagons and packed our cattle to Silver Mountain, one other hombre and myself will both remember a long time. Of those boys that left us at Silver Mountain we are disposed to draw the veil, their sufferings were too sickening to dwell upon. I saw Savage afterwards at the mines and his eyes would fill with tears at the mention of that sad time. The next thing I remember of importance was the morning we left our old friend Fish on top of the mountain and Isham in the afternoon . . .

---

[33] There were 9, not 7 others. They have been identified as Chas. McDermot of Kentucky, Mr. Savage of Illinois, Jno. Adams, G. Wiley Webster, T. Ware, Mattison Baker from Utica (New York), Mr. Samore, Mr. Allen, Mr. Moore and Mr. Pinney — 11 in all.

According to Mecum, "Silver Mountain" was between the Death Valley camp where they burned their wagons and the locale of the deaths of Fisch and Isham. Sequentially this would be where they picked up the silver that gave rise to the "Lost Gunsight" legend and where they also buried a cache of gold coins to lighten their packs.

Clarifying the locale, Mecum was again to write, in a letter to Colton February 17, 1903:

> I received a letter from a hyene (sic) in Nevada who claimed to have followed our trail and dug for the gold buried where we burnt our wagons. He is fooled. It was buried at Silver Mountain and not where we burned our wagons.[34]

Early historian Ellenbecker, who was in close contact with many of the Jayhawkers, adds:

> John B. Colton said this gold was left in a canon in the Tuki (sic) mountains just where the Georgians found the Gunsight Silver Lode. This was on the north slope of Telescope Peak.

Be it hearsay, Manly also contributes to the Savage-Pinney story with an interesting conclusion:

> . . . four of the train perished besides the trail (an unknown Kentuckian at Mt. Misery, Culverwell, Fisch and Isham) and it will be remembered that one party of eleven started out on foot before the wagons were abandoned by the rest of the party . . . long afterwards nine skeletons were found at the remains of a camp and the other two were afterwards seen in the gold fields. When spoken to about this party they burst into tears and could not talk of it. So it is known that at least thirteen men perished in the country which has well been named Death Valley.[35]

However shrouded in darkness and rumor, it appears that the Savage-Pinney eleven broke away from the Stover-Lorton et al. packers in southeastern Nevada. Starting from Coyote or Dead Horse Spring, close to the 37° parallel and on a westward course, it would be remarkable if they had not gravitated to the path of the '49ers.

---

[34] He is referring to a Gurley Jones, a mining man with the Pactolus/Mammon Mining Company, who corresponded with Colton in an endeavor to locate both the gold and silver lode in 1903. Jones' map was, for a time, erroneously believed to be one of Manly's maps.

[35] Colton, in Chalfant's *Death Valley, the Facts* says that a child of the Briers is buried in Death Valley, but this is completely unsupported.

Assuredly they did not go south after splitting from the Flake-Rich packers, or southwest following Stover, both of which intersected Hunt's route along the Old Spanish Trail. Nor did they return easterly to that trail with the remnants of "O K" Smith's group. Thus there is little reason to doubt that the eleven kept west on a fateful course across the AEC area into Jackass Flat.

The course, the time, the place, would find them meeting the Briers and later those at McLean.

The hearsay reports of what happened to the nine is conjecture and wildly so. Reports, notably by Stephens and the Briers, that nine skeletons were found by Governor Blasdel on his 1866 expedition have proved unfounded. And tales of nine bodies being found, huddled together near the Slate Range west of Death Valley stretches the imagination even more to depict them perishing en masse. At best it adds a colorful, dramatic touch to a story for awed listeners and readers, intentionally or innocently, to which even the '49ers were not adverse.

Except for Savage and Pinney reaching Owens Lake, and eventually the gold diggings near Nevada City, nothing is known of their route out of Death Valley. And the other nine disappear into history.

For those who may have become lost in the welter of parties, places and dates, the accompanying comparison summary may be a helpful reminder of the '49ers approach into the dragon's lair.

THE BENNETTS - ARCANS, MANLY AND NUSBAUMER

In picking up the trail of the last major group of '49ers it is refreshing and fortunate to have not just one but two remarkable diarists—William Lewis Manly and Louis Nusbaumer.

Whatever Manly's flaws, his is the classic account. According to Manly, his first manuscript was written in 1852 from trail-kept notes, and expanded in his later articles and his 1894 book.

Nusbaumer's methodically recorded journal, written in German, was the only one brought out of Death Valley by the historic "Long Camp" party.[36]

Where Manly is given to generalities, Nusbaumer helps to fill in

---

[36] The long "lost" Nusbaumer journal was published as *Valley of Salt, Memories of Wine* by the Bancroft Library in 1967.

1849	JAYHAWKERS	HAYNES	YOUNG	BRIERS	B/A - MANLY	NUSBAUMER
Dec.2	Begin to leave Papoose Dry Lake	W from Papoose prob. with Jayhawkers	lv.White Blotch Butte and Spring	leave Papoose with Jayhawkers	Remain in Papoose Dry Lake camp	Remains in Papoose Dry Lake camp
3	South along Yucca Flat	At Yucca Flat	Skirting Belted Range to Yucca Flat			
6	5th day without finding water. Approach Jackass Flat	Topopah Spring Lays by 8 days	Yucca Pass – snow	Martin's mess leaves Also Coker?	Leave Papoose	Leaves Papoose Dry Lake camp
7	Continue 1 more day – snow	"	Rounds pass toward Wahmonie	Snow – abandon wagons	Camp near head of canyon (2nd night) – snow	Enroute up Nye Canyon – camp at "Triple Tanks"
8	Route and camps unknown	"	At Jackass Flat	(Rumor of staying in camp a week)	M/R scout ahead to Indian farm – return p.m.	Snow on ground–scouts return from Indian farm
9		"	40-Mile Canyon area – snow		Manly out scouting	Arrive Indian farm – camp 9 days
10		"			Summit view – smoke to south	" "
11		"	At springs east of Fairbanks Ranch		Manly returns to camp on 3rd day	Expects scouts to return that night
12		"	Fairbanks Ranch (6 days)			(in camp)
13	Advance parties into Death Valley. Most via Furnace Creek Wash	"	"			" "
14		Continues through Jackass Flat	"			" "
15			"		(Indian farm)	" "
16		Fairbanks Ranch (5 day camp)	"		"	" "
17-18		"	"		"	" "
19		"	Crosses Amargosa		Leave Indian farm	Leave Indian farm

1849	JAYHAWKERS	HAYNES	YOUNG	BRIERS	B/A - MANLY	NUSBAUMER
Dec.20		Still at Fairbanks Ranch	Furnace Creek Wash			
21	Advance parties begin to reach McLean Spring	" "	Sees snowy mountains ahead			
22		West 6 miles				
23		NW 8 miles	Camp		"Cave Spring" (Devil's Hole)	"Cave Spring" (Devil's Hole)
24		W 8 miles (Indian Pass)	Try to cross Death Valley – 4 NW		Manly follows Jay-hawkers trail Furnace Creek Wash	Lose ox near Death Valley Junction
25		W 18 – "here we left our wagons" (McLean Spring)	7-8 miles find springs east slopes	Travertine Spring arrive 3 a.m.	Manly meets Briers at dusk – Travertine Spring	"lose another ox" abandon wagon
26		camp	Pass McLean Spring go 4 miles – grass and water		Guides B/As into camp	Continues afoot following company
27		camp	Conclude to leave wagons		Manly visits Jayhawker camp	Furnace Creek Wash

with specifics. Even more than Young and Haynes, the two support and supplement each other. While they did not travel together across most of Nevada, they were to fatefully join near Papoose Dry Lake.

It was at a time when Nusbaumer's small party of six felt that the Jayhawkers were traveling too slowly and joined the Bennetts-Arcans wagons. And a time when Manly descriptively dwells upon the views and prospects of his scoutings.

"Our road," Manly says, "had been winding around buttes which looked like Indian baskets turned upside down." And on one of his solo scoutings near Papoose, while the wagons continued on toward it:

> . . . it seemed as if pretty near all creation was in sight. North and south was a level plain, fully one hundred miles wide it seemed . . . on the western edge it was bounded by a low, black and rocky range extending north and south for a long distance, with no pass through it which I could see, and beyond this range was still another apparently parallel to it.
>
> In a due west course from me was the high peak we had been looking at for a month, and the lowest place, which we had named Martin's Pass and had been trying so long to reach, was on the north side. This high peak, covered with snow, glistened in the morning sun, and as the air was clear from clouds or fog with no dust or haze to obscure the view it seemed very near.

The great plain was the expanse of Yucca Flat and Sand Springs Valley. That due west was the high peak they had been looking at for a month is a slip of memory or pen in that they were looking *for* it, not *at* it. Such a month-long view is an impossibility even in the renowned clarity of the desert. Of the westerly snowcaps visible from rises around Papoose Dry Lake, Telescope Peak glistening in the early sun would be the most notable.

Much the same with the "pass" they had been trying so long to reach. Since passes tend to blend into distant mountains, Manly may have been speaking of an objective sought rather than an object seen. Why it was called Martin's Pass is conjectural. Perhaps the two Martins with the Jayhawkers were instrumental in its naming as one they had heard about. Yet they spurned it to go southward.

Peering through a small spyglass, Manly saw the wagons slowly working their way toward "what seemed like a dry lake." Obviously it was not one of earlier familiarity and consequently not far to the north. Apparently Manly's viewpoint was southeasterly of Papoose Dry Lake, which Haynes was approaching from the northeast on November 30 and December 1.

In rejoining the wagons Manly gives two versions. In one he says he began to make his way down the steep, eroded slopes, stopping overnight at a little pool of water ("having been without a drop of it for two days") and the *next morning* he rejoined the wagons which had now reached the lake bed. This would be Dec. 1, and until late that night, as scattered parties dropped by, Manly gave a discouraging report of what lay ahead:

> In the morning (Dec. 2) the Jayhawkers and others of the train that were not considered strictly of our party, yoked up and started due west across the level plain which I predicted as having no water.

In a partially duplicating section he says:

> The author came into camp about *nine o'clock in the evening . . .* "Well", said Captain Doty of the Jayhawkers, "I don't like to hear such discouraging talk from Manly, but I think we will have to steer straight ahead. . . ." When morning came Captain Doty and his party yoked up and set out straight across the desert, leaving seven wagons of the Bennett party still in camp.

Except for indicating the flaws of memory it matters little. Just as in one version he says it was Bennett with whom he talked and who commented on the discouraging report, which sent Sarah Bennett to bed in tears; and in the other speaks only of Doty and his reaction.

Neither Manly nor Nusbaumer tell of why they remained for four more days after the Jayhawkers began to leave. Perhaps to recuperate and get ready for the journey ahead. With two families, including four children, it was not as easy a task as it was for the Jayhawkers. And with the departure of the others enough water could be eked out—"the edge of the lake contained about a quarter inch of water . . . dug some holes here which filled up and (we) were using this water in the camp."

That the Bennetts-Arcans elected to go south was motivated by Manly's report of another large snowpeak to the south—11,918-foot

Mt. Charleston—visible through a canyon extending in that direction.

Admitting that "being due south it was quite off our course," they felt this was offset by better prospects of water.

The canyon possibilities south from Papoose are singularly limited to Nye Canyon—later used by miners, ranchers and known as the old "Engineers Road" after an early railroad survey team. While more of an arroyo, or Arabian wadi, its grade up from Papoose is not steep, but slow, rough going with soft sands and rock scatterings.

Manly says that "Mr. Culverwell and Mr. Fish (sic) stayed with us making another wagon in our train." Note *stayed,* not joined, as they had already joined when they left the Jayhawkers as traveling too slowly.

Nusbaumer records the departure as:

> . . . the sixth of December and traveled until the evening of the 8th without a drop of water and no food for our cattle . . . snow and cold had hardened the ground to such an extent we were compelled to wait until it thawed before we could move on. We were sitting dejectedly around a fire . . . when (we) heard to our greatest joy that one of the scouts had found an Indian family about six miles from our camp, with good water and plenty food. He also had learned from the Indians that Captain Walker had passed south of the farm.

Manly adds that:

> . . . we turned up a canyon leading toward the (snowy) mountain and had a pretty heavy up-grade and a rough bed for a road. Part way we came to a high cliff and in its face were niches or cavities as large as a barrel or larger and in some of them we found balls of a glistening substance . . . we found it sweet but sickish and those who were so hungry as to break up one of the balls and divide it among the others, making a good meal of it, were a little troubled with nausea afterwards . . . the second night we camped near the head of the canyon . . .

That second night snow fell several inches deep. And on the following day Manly and Rogers scouted ahead, finding an Indian camp or farm with its food and water, returning to camp with the good news that evening.

Shortly after Nye Canyon crests for a descent into Frenchman Flat a relative rarity occurs. Eroded tufa and sandstone cliffs pocked

The entrance to Nye Canyon from Papoose Dry Lake toward the Mt. Charleston area
"We turned up a canyon toward a snowy mountain."—Manly

South from Sand Springs
"Our way had been winding among buttes
which seemed like Indian baskets
turned upside down."—Manly

In Nye Canyon
"cliff with niches or cavities
as large as a barrel or larger
...in some we found balls of a
glistening substance."—Manly

From Triple Tanks water basins into Nye Canyon

The "1849" inscription at Triple Tanks

with cavities! Of all sizes, many large enough for shelter and storage.[37]

Just beyond the cavitied cliffs the "wash" temporarily flattens into a bowl-like area. Leading from it is a small ravine, ending in perhaps a hundred yards, at a water-catching rock basin known as "Triple Tanks."

To the casual passer-by there is little to distinguish this cleft from others along the way. But at the entrance, on a concaved side-wall, there are some ancient petroglyphs and two inscriptions, sheltered from weathering by the overhang. One helpfully directs those in need to "TRIPLE TANKS 1/4 MILE." The other, although speaking volumes, simply says "1849."[38]

Excuse can be found for their not knowing that petroglyphs are commonly a sign of nearby water. But it would seem curiosity should have led them to explore the short, well worn trail to the water basin at the end. That they apparently did not is indicated by Nusbaumer's saying they continued until the evening of the 8th without a drop of water. But then one also wonders why snowmelt wasn't used. Likely it was, but deemed too meager to mention in comparison to a pool or stream of water.

Six or eight miles to the Indian farm was not far, but the way was not easy, especially for the emaciated animals hauling heavy loads. Along the way Bennett reluctantly abandoned the tools he had hauled all the way from Wisconsin, along with "almost everything else except bedding and provisions."

In his book Manly says they had to leave some oxen and *a* wagon behind. In his "Vermont to California" version he says some of the wagons. Either way they took water back for the animals and retrieved the wagon(s).

---

[37] While the possibilities of such cavities in other sections may exist, none so notable have been found in extensive searching. From the Pahranagat to the Amargosa this is the only such area seen or known to others.

[38] Although it has been reported as "Nov. 26, 1849" there is not the slightest evidence of month or day. Neither could the report of a "W L MANLY" inscription nearby be confirmed by a fine-comb searching. However, an "1848" was discovered! Along with the "F O BYOR 1847" rock found at Cane Springs these add fuel to the smoldering fires of tales of other and earlier "lost wagon trains."

The inscription "Triple Tanks ¼ Mile" is attributed to an early railroad survey team, and not the early ranchers and cattlemen who were found unfamiliar with it.

The Indian farm, a veritable oasis as it must have seemed, is best described by Manly initially:

> Here was a flat place in a table land and on it a low brush hut. . . . We approached carefully and cautiously, making a circuit around so as to get between the hut and the hill. . . . When within thirty yards a man poked his head out of a doorway and drew it back again quick as a flash . . . a child or two in the hut squalled terribly, fearing, I suppose, they would all be murdered. . . .
>
> The poor fellow was shivering with cold. With signs of friendship we fired off one of the guns, which waked him up a little and he pointed to the gun and said "Walker", probably meaning the same good Chief Walker who had so fortunately stopped us in our journey down the Green River. . . . By the aid of a warm spring nearby they had raised some corn here and the dry stalks were standing around.

While Manly took "Walker" to be the Indian Chief Walkara of his earlier experiences, Nusbaumer associated it with mountaineer Joe Walker. Undoubtedly Nusbaumer was right. Walker had followed Fremont's 1843-44 expedition returning via the Old Spanish Trail just to the south and may have short-cutted near this point hastening to rejoin Fremont.

In any event there are few such springs in the area. Fewer still fitting description, direction and distance than Cane Springs, nestled at the eastern end of Skull Mountain, and the major water supply for Wahmonie, four miles northwest, during its short boom.

Here, Nusbaumer records, they camped for nine days. During this time Manly made another, and perhaps most fateful, of his observation scoutings. Heading for a high elevation:

> I reached the summit . . . and had the grandest view I ever saw. I could see north and south almost without limit. . . . On the west the snow peak [39] shut the view in that direction. To the south the mountains seemed to descend for more than twenty miles and near the base, perhaps ten miles away, were several smokes, apparently from campfires and as I could see no animals or camp wagons anywhere, I presumed them to be Indians.

---

[39] Manly frequently refers to peak and mountain in the singular, just as one should correctly refer to the Sierra Nevada, not Nevadas; but his references usually mean peaks and mountains in the plural.

A few miles to the north and east (stood) sharp peaks . . . of many colors, some of them so red that the mountains looked red hot. . . . It was the most wonderful picture of grand desolation one could ever see. Toward the north I could see the desert the Jayhawkers and their comrades had undertaken to cross. . . .

Poor Manly! In the depths of his despair that "I must keep my worst apprehensions to myself lest they (the others) lose heart and hope and faith," his spirit could still soar to "the grandest view I ever saw."

From the Specter Range the Amargosa Desert dims distantly to the south into Pahrump Valley and to the north far beyond the Jayhawkers' crossing.

The snow peak to the west was obviously not the same one they had pursued to the south. His attention was now focused on Telescope Peak in the Panamint Range.

Northeasterly were the uniquely colorful Calico Hills, caught afire by the sun. The Old Spanish Trail was to the south, but alas they headed west.

Manly calculated it was about ten miles to the base of mountains to the south, which descended for what seemed another twenty. Although distance is deceptive in the clarity of the desert, it is only about 60 miles from Cane Springs to the Old Spanish Trail and would be even less—about 40—a few days later. Two or three days travel southward and they would have reached the main trail, which Hunt was taking, and been spared their ordeal in Death Valley.

Manly returned to camp after three days of scouting, and "I found the boys who went part way with me and whom I had outwalked . . . when all was told it appeared that the route westerly was the only route that could be taken."

But, deviate they might, blunder they did at times, committed they were that each step would be to California to the west.

This was probably the 12th, since they reached the Indian farm on the 9th, which is supported by Nusbaumer:

The information we received in regard to the road ahead of us is not very encouraging. Two of our people have just returned and report that there is no food or water to be had for two or three days in advance. . . . Our entire hope now rests on the report of two others who will be back tonight, the eleventh, or tomorrow.

On the 19th, Nusbaumer records, they left "where we had been camping for 9 days and started for a spring which was said to be about 7 miles from here."

Just where, or if, there was a spring 7 miles away is problematical. While none are known within that radius, small springs do ebb and flow with the tides of time in that country. Possibly it was just a camp rumor or the promise of a distant glimpse of greenness that never panned out.

There has been some conjecture that a wagon or wagons were abandoned here. Probably on the basis of Manly's:

> . . . an ox had been killed . . . with the understanding that when it became necessary to kill another it should be divided in the same manner. Some one of the wagons would have to be left for lack of animals to draw it.

However, this was simply an eventuality to be faced only and if an additional loss of oxen warranted it.

Where Manly is merely descriptive of their route, Nusbaumer details:

Dec. 20   We traveled fifteen miles.
Dec. 21   Twenty one miles in a southwestern direction.
Dec. 22   We found grass and water.
Dec. 23   We traveled thirteen miles. Still in a southwestern direction and entered a beautiful valley considerably lower than we had been before. Here the atmosphere was very warm and there were flies, butterflies, beetles, etc.

That they left Cane Springs via Jackass Flat is unlikely. While the Jayhawkers, etc., had by now moved on across the Amargosa and would not be sighted or met, there is no mention of even following wagon tracks. And the Bennett party could not have missed the verdancy of Fairbanks Ranch, and which was probably hidden from Manly's scouting view by intervening ridges.

Cane Springs is at the eastern end of Skull Mountain. Just beyond that end there is an open route into Rock Valley which also leads into the Amargosa via Ash Meadows.

The "Indian Farm" at Cane Springs, southeast of Wahmonie

Devil's Hole, the cave
springs picturesquely
described by Nusbaumer

Jackass Flat, with the south entrance to 40 Mile Canyon to right.
Here the '49er trails converged in approaching the Amargosa Desert.

Here another remarkable and telling bit of evidence occurred, as Manly notes:

> One night we had a fair camp as we were close to the base of the snow butte and found a hole of clear, or what seemed to be living water. There were a few minnows in it, not much more than an inch long. This was among a big pile of rocks and around these the oxen found some grass.

Nusbaumer, in a continuance of his entry for Dec. 23 also writes:

> At the entrance of the valley, on the right hand side, we found a cave containing a spring with magnificent warm water in which Had (Hadapp) and I took a refreshing bath, the water being about ninety degrees. The cave is of a fairy like aspect. It seems we are on the road to a Happy Christmas!

Temporarily turning time ahead 17 years to May 10, 1866, Governor Blasdel's expedition, having left Furnace Creek Wash for Ash Meadows, reported:

> May 10—Six miles across meadow and sand flats, with small white ash timber and grapevines brought us to a range of low coralline hills with a fine spring . . . in a cave thirty feet long and ten wide.

While there are a number of springs mapped in the relatively well watered Ash Meadows, and probably a number more known to the Indians, none so fit that duplication-defying spot in that isolated island of Death Valley National Monument known as "Devil's Hole."

At the foot of low volcanic cliffs straddling the pass into which one is funneled, lies a freakish fault fissure on the right hand side approaching the Amargosa.

Its main opening appears as a cavernous spring of clear, warm water. Although about a hundred yards in length most of it is underground, ending in a backwall with little surface sign. Spelunkers have followed the underground stream, with occasional fatalities, in quest of its rare blind minnow specimens.

Prosaically described by Blasdel as 10 x 30 feet, the cave opening must have indeed seemed to be of "a fairy like aspect" to Nusbaumer. While minnows are reported in other sinks of the area, they have all been noted in the open flats. Certainly their occurrence at Devil's

Hole, the physical features of cliffs, rocks, pass and summit area, distances and direction, and the singular choice of route towards Furnace Creek Wash, all combine to leave little doubt of this site marking the Bennett-Arcan-Nusbaumer route.

Of Dec. 24, Manly writes:

> Our trail was now descending to the bottom of what seemed to be the narrowest part of the plain, the same one the Jayhawkers had started across farther north ten days before.

They were indeed crossing what seems the narrowest part of the Amargosa which the Jayhawkers had crossed farther north. His approximation of "ten days before" is not inappropriate, probably having been ascertained from later information secured in correspondence with the Jayhawkers.[40]

But now Nusbaumer's little group fell behind, and on Christmas Day,

> ... to lighten the load so one yoke can pull it ... I had to leave behind five good linen shirts, boots, handkerchief, one coat, friend Adolph's hat, stockings and buffalo hide, etc., and only took three shirts, my black cashmere coat, one pair of stockings, one pair of boots, one pair of shoes, one buffalo hide and my cloak, and so did the rest. Friend Hadapp, who also had to sacrifice his best things, is sick. If we succeed in reaching the company ahead of us we intend to load one ox with food and to wander on if our strength, which is very much broken down by poor nourishment, permits.

Later that day he adds:

> ... we broke up camp and moved on with heavy hearts. We had scarcely covered six miles when the one ox collapsed and could not rise, which made it necessary to kill him. We went to work at once and inside of an hour had him skinned and cut up. We erected a smoke house and dried the meat the whole of the following night. On the morning of the 26th we loaded the three remaining oxen with the meat and our clothes and carpets (i.e. blankets) and began to follow the company ahead of us. We had to travel on for two days and nights without food or water for the cattle until we succeeded in

---

[40] Again ironically, as the Bennett party began to cross the Amargosa on Dec. 24, those who had stayed with Hunt had celebrantly arrived at Chino Rancho Dec. 22nd. But for the short-cutters, their travail was only to begin the climatic act that was to end nearly 2½ months later.

catching up with the other company at the foot of a steep mountain where we found that the Indians had shot three of their oxen one night.

So it was that for want of an ox a wagon was lost, and those in the Bennetts-Arcans train reduced from seven to six.

While there have been stories of the remains of wagons, caused by Indian attacks, found near the Furnace Creek Wash entrance, none are substantiated. Yet clouded in the haze of time and the tales of Indians to whom calendrical years were of casual concern, it may have happened—but to another party at another time. Legends of lost wagon trains, with many or all perishing, have persisted too long, too strongly, to be easily dismissed. But among the 1849ers, Nusbaumer's wagon was the only one abandoned in this area.

This was indeed a time when memories welled up out of the past, as painfully recalled as those of the present. Along with Mrs. Brier's famous Christmas Day account, there is Nusbaumer's:

> Dec. 19.   Fifteen years ago, about this same time of the year, in my father's house, with its Christmas preparations, no sorrow, nothing but joy. Last year in Newark (N.J.) with my beloved wife . . . should I ever return to her I will never leave her again, not even for a day . . .
>
> Dec. 24.   One of our oxen is about to die but we will not despair on the eve of the day when our Savior was born. We came about fifteen miles today through abominable alkali swamps and were compelled to camp without water and grass.
>
> Dec. 25.   This is a day of sorrow for us as the ox, before mentioned is not able to go farther and it is necessary to throw out a great deal of our goods. . . . Courage has not failed us yet and we hope with God's help to reach our destination. There is quite a difference between Christmas days in God's different states—in some of them you receive presents, in others you must throw things away. I hope my dear wife is having a happier Christmas day than I am. May God keep her in good health. Should chance deliver this journal into her hands, she will glean from these pages that she was never far from my thoughts and that my heart shall beat for her to the last.

As usual, the indefatigable Manly had gone ahead and on Christmas Day found the Briers in camp at Travertine Springs, close to the present day landmark of Furnace Creek Inn.

On December 26 Manly went back seven or eight miles and escort-
ed his straggling party into camp at Travertine Springs. On the following day he reconnoitered the valley and visited the camp of the
Jayhawkers.

Ostensibly he was alone—

> I shouldered my gun and followed down the canyon. . . . When I got
> near the lower end . . . I saw a very strange looking track . . . I follow-
> ed it to . . . where a small well-like hole had been dug and in this
> excavation was a kind of Indian mummy curled up like a dog. He
> was not dead for I could see him move as he breathed . . . by his looks
> he must be two or three hundred years old. . . . He was evidently crip-
> pled. . . . I took a good long look at the wild creature. . . . I now left
> him and went farther out into the lowest part of the valley.

Obviously it was the same old Indian that the Jayhawkers had
found, and to whom they gave food and water, although Manly
seems only to have looked in curiosity.

Not as reconcilable is Rogers' account. Faulty as it may be it dis-
putes Manly's memory of the incident:

> . . . *Manly and myself* started down the creek exploring . . . we found
> an old Indian who was blind. He was crawling around on the
> ground. He had a little willow basket full of muddy water and had
> a sharp stick which he was using to dig up roots. Manly said he had a
> notion to shoot him. Says I, "The deuce you would. I would as leave
> shoot my father." I took his willow basket and went to the creek and
> rinsed it out and gave him some clear water. I gave him some meat
> and he raised his head and grunted as if he didn't know who was
> there. We started down into the valley . . .

The conflicting versions are interesting indeed![41] Although Rogers
may have turned back before the Jayhawker camp they had at least
started out together.

Be it as it may, Manly camped overnight with the Jayhawkers at
McLean Spring, and learned of their decision to leave the wagons
and continue afoot.

---

[41] Supporting the Jayhawkers and Rogers versions of giving the Indian food and water, Dane
Coolidge in *Death Valley Prospectors* tells an interesting sequel. That the old blind Indian was
the grandfather of Shoshone Chief "Hungry Bill." And that night the old man's daughter crept
by and asked how they had treated him. "They feed me good," he said, "I feel fine." Later the
daughter came again and found him dead from the cold—or perhaps the excitement.

That this camp was spread out is indicated in a Manly letter to Colton (March 26, 1890). At least by inference Colton had questioned not seeing Manly there. In reply Manly wrote that he had only been at the Doty camp and had come and left in the night.[42]

That "messes" were intermittent as far as Midway Well, where Young camped, seems substantiated by an exploring party of the 1861 Boundary Commission. An article by one of those members appeared in the *Sacramento Daily Union,* July 13, 1861, tells of:

> ... riding along the border of the plain (salt pan) we observed the faint tracks of the emigrant wagons of '49 ... we came to a spot where they had camped . . . strewn with the relics of their wagons—the spokes, tires and hubs of their wheels and the iron of the running gear, chain, broken pots and other remains of camp equipage marking the abandonment and destruction of part of the train.
>
> We continued up the creek some three miles . . . keeping on the north side in the sand hills . . . and pitched camp in a mesquit grove on the flat . . . thinly covered with salt grass and . . . a shallow well of very salt water. We dug a new well above the old one. . . . Here again we find traces of the emigrant encampment—bones of cattle in plenty, and the less perishable parts of their abandoned wagons, trace chains, broken pots, etc.

Manly does not mention meeting the Briers, but as with Colton, they could have been easily missed. But on his way back, the morning of the 28th, he tells of meeting "two of our camp companions . . . a Mr. Fish and another named Gould. . . . (I had a) feeling I should never see the middle-aged men again."

It was probably not Gould,[43] but Fisch and Isham. Both of these were traveling with Nusbaumer, who noted upon reaching Travertine, "Here on the 28th our traveling companions left us. . . ."

In his "Vermont to California" version (serialized in the *Santa*

---

[42] He had arrived early at night and left before daylight.

[43] Gould is one of the shadowy '49ers, linked with the Jayhawkers and Young. A Charles Gould is identified with the San Francisco Mining Company that reached Salt Lake City. He may also have started out on the trail south with Stover's contingent, which also included the Earharts and Briers at that time. Rev. Brier says a "Mr. Gould of New York" was with them in Panamint Valley. Historian Ellenbecker mentions Gould being in the Doty mess, and that he died in New York in 1850, apparently having returned East with no delay!

Clara Monthly from 1887 to 1890, before his 1894 published book)
Manly notes only Fisch by name:

> . . . on my way met Mr. Fish and another man with their packs on
> their backs. They were both of our party and nearly out of grub and
> their cattle being poor and weak they had given them to their travel-
> ing companion Capt. Culverwell . . .

Manly continues with:

> It was almost night before I reached our camp . . . during my absence
> for the two days (27th and 28th) the Indians had shot arrows into
> three of our oxen . . .

A welcome confirmation of the incidents and dating is supplied
by Nusbaumer who had left the Amargosa the morning of the 26th
and struggled for two days up Furnace Creek Wash until:

> . . . we succeeded in catching up . . . found the Indians had shot three
> of their oxen in one night. Here on the 28th our traveling companions
> left us . . . [44]

How long did the party remain at Travertine Springs?

We are to subsequently learn that the Bennetts-Arcans attempted
to cross the Panamints January 13-14, with Manly and Rogers leaving,
rescue bound on the 15th. If they had left Travertine December 29 it
would tally 16 days to the abortive Panamint try. Yet a literal reading
of Manly indicates only 5 or 6 days from Travertine to the rescue
departure.

We also know that for Nusbaumer's reduced group the "29th, 30th
and 31st we passed in drying meat and other preparations" at Travertine Springs where they remained "for about ten days." And:

> On the 7th of January we started once more and traveled on for about
> eight miles without water and not anticipating that we would find
> any. As viewed from the top of the mountain, the whole valley seem-
> ed to be filled with it but on approaching the same it proved to be

---

[44] Nusbaumer's original party of six had been reduced to five by the departure of Smith earlier.
Hadapp and Culverwell are to continue across Death Valley with Nusbaumer, leaving Fisch
and Isham as those who left to join the Jayhawkers at McLean. While his name was more correctly spelled "Fisch", most used the phonetic "Fish." Despite the inconsistency, the latter is
used in quoting Manly, etc. Much in the same manner with Nusbaumer's "Calverwell" and
the more widely known "Culverwell."

clear salt water. We even had to march through salt puddles and dry salt.

He also provides two clues that the Bennetts-Arcans had left by then. Four days later he notes reaching a campsite of those who "had gone on ahead." The other clue also includes a puzzling new note:

> Happy New Year! The first of January, 1850!
>
> Two Alsatians took pity on our condition and provided us with boiled beans. Thus we began the New Year quite cheerfully. . . . We exchanged a pistol for beans and coffee and are now living in comparative affluence. Today (on the 2nd of January) we had excellent soup. We boiled ox feet and snout with beans, etc., for a whole night and as a result we had a fine mulligan this morning. . . . Blessed New Year, dear wife and perhaps child.[45]

Who were the "Alsatians"? How many? Nusbaumer mentions two but there may have been more. In all of the compilations of the '49ers there are gaps that never will be filled beyond all shadow of doubt. As "foreigners" some were omitted from references or simply generalized as "The Germans," "the Frenchman," etc.

Did the Alsatians, like Fisch and Isham, turn north to follow the Jayhawkers? Manly did not meet them. And the Jayhawkers, well into the Panamints by January 1-2, do not note the belated joining of others than the Bennett-Arcan teamsters. When did the Alsatians arrive at Travertine? If they had been in camp, it is unlikely that Fisch and Isham would have splintered off from this helpful two (or more).

Are unmarked Alsatian graves the basis for the naming of Death Valley—a singularly sordid name for a locale in which only one known '49er fatality occurred?

Assuredly the Alsatians did not remain at Travertine Springs with the decimated Nusbaumer party or these Good Samaritans would have been referred to again. Leaving this blank until it can be brought into better focus, we find that on January 7, Nusbaumer, Culverwell and Hadapp left to follow the Bennetts-Arcans who had obviously not been part of the "Happy New Year!" occasion. Or if they had were strangely silent about it.

That Nusbaumer does not mention sighting others ahead, only their trail, indicates the Bennetts-Arcans may have left as late as the day before (Jan. 6), perhaps two or even three days.

---

[45] This would have been his second son, Albert, born after his father's departure for California.

Very likely a few days had been spent in discussions, decisions and preparations, as well as recuperating and reconnoitering. With Manly's deeply ingrained habit of scouting they were not apt to strike out blindly.

Both clouding and clarifying this is John Roger's controversial and oft skeptically viewed account, that while at Travertine he and Manly:

> . . . traveled about ten miles and struck a bunch of willows[46] and a spring of fresh water. In prospecting ten miles farther we struck a lake after which we retraced our steps to camp. . . . We moved camp to the spring at the willows. The ground was covered three or four inches deep with something like salt petre or borax. We then traveled down the valley till we struck the lake and down the lake some 15 or 20 miles where we concluded to cross.

Just where they could have "struck a bunch of willows and a spring of fresh water" in about ten miles is frustratingly unknown. Yet springs do come and go and the willows may have succumbed to time and early day borax activities. Eminent geologist Dr. Thomas Clements says, "Regarding the mystery of the spring of fresh water with willow trees on the east side of the valley, we have never come across it. However, this does not mean that it could not have been there when Manly and Rogers were there. There was a very strong earthquake in the valley in the early 1900's, with downdropping of the valley side along a fault on the east side. This could have destroyed the spring, after which the willow trees would have died. There is an old Indian trail on the east side of the valley, just a little south of Mushroom Rock. These trails are said to have gone from spring to spring, so perhaps there was one somewhere in that area."

Thus, according to Rogers, there was a 20 mile scouting to the south; and that later the party went to the "willows camp" (about 10 miles distant) and some 15 or 20 to where they decided to cross. But 30 miles would have taken them to the valley's narrowing near Mormon Point, incompatible with the Bennett-Arcan crossing and descriptive sequences.

Twenty guesstimated miles for the initial scouting, *might* have taken them to the area west of Greenwater and Furnace. Discounting

---

[46] Possibly mesquite rather than willows. Later Manly tells of cutting a piece of mesquite about the size of his arm and four feet long to test the salt pool area for their wagon crossing.

the possibility of a spring and willows in the flat, they may have explored the side canyons on the western slope of the Black Mountains and found a spring such as in the Willow Creek area. Assuredly Manly felt water was more likely to be found in the hills rather than the flatlands.

Having gone this far, close to the Badwater area, they would also be aware that a route in this direction would be squeezed in between the marshy salt pools and the slopes; practical for those afoot but not for wagons.[47]

However faulty Roger's recollections it does point to Manly and Rogers being away on a two day scouting December 31 and January 1, returning to camp the morning of the 2nd. With one to three days allowance for reporting their findings and preparing to move out, the Bennetts-Arcans seem to have left Travertine January 4, 5 or 6.

While all of this may seem needlessly weighty, the datings are important to counter Manly's very erroneous recollection that he and Rogers reached the San Fernando Valley on their rescue effort (page 176, Manly 1929 edition) on ". . . either one of the very last days of December 1849, or the first of January, 1850." Having been at the Brier's camp December 25, and taking two days to visit the Jayhawkers, plus the crossing and camps in Death Valley itself, his datings are an impossibility, which fortunately he later corrects.

Also, to establish datings and locations now helps to form a basis for that to follow. As with similar occasions there is always uncertainty of days partially in camp, partially on the move; of camps not specifically noted, and of "meetings until late at night" to leave one wonder if they had gone on through the day as well.

Heading south from Travertine Springs, Manly says, ". . . we had not gone long on this course before we saw that we must cross the valley and get over to the west side. To do this we must cross through some water. . . ."

The decision to change direction was not impulsive but one they

---

[47] It has been theorized they might have taken Greenwater Valley as their exploration route. However they would have had to backtrack about 10 miles up Furnace Creek Wash, and invariably any such turnback was unthinkable. Also the passage from Furnace Creek Wash into Greenwater Valley is not that promising to entice them and they had already passed it up. In hindsight, the Greenwater Valley route, one of those later used by borax wagons, would have been better than crossing Death Valley, but little did they know at the time.

must take or be mired in the muck nearing the Badwater salt pool area. And an attempt to squeeze between the pools and the talus slopes risked being blocked with too little turn-around room for the wagons.

The way across was one of a strange mixture of water, muck and rough eroded salt encrustrations. Manly cut a large mesquite branch to sound the uncertain bottoms. And Rogers indicates the slow, rough progress in noting one wagon broke through the crust, a laborious task of extrication.

"The second night we found a good spring of fresh water coming out from the bottom of the snow peak almost over our head," Manly says.

Despite the assumption he was referring to the second night from Travertine, he may well have been speaking of the second night *after* the crossing. And probably was, for it is about 20 slow miles from Travertine to Badwater, more of a two-day ordeal across rough terrain over which they precariously picked their way with lumbering wagons and slow-footed oxen. So, too, with the crossing of the incredibly encrusted serrations of the maliciously honeycombed salt flats where each mile and hour would seem like two.

Along with Nusbaumer's account, following the Bennetts-Arcans tracks, it points to the first night from Travertine being spent at an unnoted camp before reaching Badwater, the next at Badwater in preparation for the crossing. The obvious and necessarily slow crossing undoubtedly found them reaching the west side that night, perhaps between Eagle Borax and Bennetts Well, with the darkness precluding sighting or searching for water in the mesquite groves stretched out along the western edge like loosely strung beads. Continuing in the morning the spring of water would be encountered the second night after the crossing, on their new route south—January 9th.

In the meantime, Nusbaumer had left on the 7th. The next day, seeing the Bennetts-Arcans crossing in the distance, they angled to intercept:

> On the 8th . . . Hadapp and I had such an overpowering thirst we even tried to drink the salt water. It was here I tried to exchange my coat and two shirts for a drink of water. We had overtaken two

wagons where there was plenty of water, but we failed to obtain any. The man who refused to give us water was forced to abandon an ox account of sickness. We shot him and caught his blood in a vessel and drank it down, only regretting that there was not more of it to quench our thirst. This only made us more thirsty. We continued on our way until one o'clock at night when we lay down under a bush and tried to forget our miserable condition by sleeping.

Any thoughts, however facetious, that the "we shot him" may have referred to a human rather than bovine object are dispelled by the next day's entry about "overcoming the result of drinking the blood of the sick ox yesterday."

But who were the water spurners of the two wagons? It is inconceivable that they were the Alsatians who had earlier displayed their compassionate generosity. Nor would it be the invariable tag-ender Wade who had only one wagon; nor in his later comments did Nusbaumer ever tie Wade in with the incident. Chances are the two wagons were those of the teamsters who were to soon decamp to join the Jayhawkers.

On the 9th of January (Nusbaumer records) at the break of dawn we marched on, but thank God, after about two miles we came to a warm sweet spring where we have just now boiled coffee[48] for the fourth time to overcome the result of drinking the blood of the sick ox yesterday. The next day we went on and came to the place where one of the companies which had gone on ahead had camped. They had burned one of their wagons,[49] killed an ox and dried his meat. They are also in a precarious condition and yet (no) prospects of finding a way out of these mountains.

In crossing the valley a day behind, the Nusbaumer trio had fallen further behind, having stopped to kill and partake of the ox. Hurrying on they probably reached the outskirts of the tules in the wee hours to the north of the Bennetts-Arcans.

Manly does not state how far they continued on their next leg along the west side. It may have been two miles—or twenty. The distance can only be determined by the location of springs along that

---

[48] The tense of this passage, indicating it was written at the time of the incident, points up the importance of Nusbaumer's on-the-spot entries vs. the years later recollections of other '49ers.

[49] Unnoted by Manly, this is the first, if only, indication that the Bennetts-Arcans lost at least one wagon before the "Long Camp."

Approaching the soft "salt pools" area near Badwater
"we saw that we must cross the valley to get over to the west side."—Manly

Near Mesquite Well, about 8 miles
south of Bennetts Well
"a mound about four feet high and
in the top of this a little well
that held about a pailful of water
...quite strong of sulphur
...wire grass seemed to prevent
its caving in."—Manly

Bennett's Well in its
windmill days

route. Based on subsequent events, Manly's "good spring" on the second night was, controversial as it may be, at Bennetts Well.

That same day, Nusbaumer, after traveling two miles, also arrived at a spring. But they did not overtake the Bennetts-Arcans here so it was not the same spring. Nusbaumer, having crossed above the Bennetts-Arcans and with no directional indications to preclude it, had seemingly stopped near Tule Spring, which the Bennetts-Arcans missed in angling just to the south of it.

Some 8 miles or so of slow sandy travel still separated the two groups on the 9th.

On the 10th, taking advantage of the good spring of their "second night" the Bennetts-Arcans devoted the day to meetings until late that night. And on this day Nusbaumer reached the Bennetts-Arcans camp where they found the burned remains of a wagon. Here they remained in camp on the 11th.

This day Manly ruefully reports:

> Bennetts two teams(ters) and the two of Arcans concluded their chances of life were better if they could take some provisions and strike out on foot.[50]

Following the departure of the teamsters, Manly writes:

> Leaving this camp where the water was appreciated we went over a road for perhaps eight miles and came to the mouth of a rocky canyon leading up west to the summit of the range. This canyon was too rough for wagons. . . . Out in the valley near its mouth was a mound about four feet high and in the top of this a little well[51] that held about a pailful of water that was quite strong of sulphur. When stirred it was quite black. . . . We spent the night here and kept a man at the well all night to keep the water dipped out as fast as it flowed in order to get enough for ourselves and cattle. *The oxen drank this water better than they did the brackish water of the former camp.*

---

[50] He names Silas Helmer and S.S. (or C.C.) Abbott as Bennett's teamsters but could not recall Arcan's. These may have been the Atchison brothers. According to L. Burr Belden's *The Wade Story*, the Wades report their ox driver was "a Frenchman whose name was recalled as Charles in later years . . . (who) marooned the family in Death Valley and struck out on foot in company with the Arcan drivers." Be they 4 or 5, they struck out to the north to follow the Jayhawker trail.

[51] Often called "wells." With an implication of being man-made, they were usually pools, seeps or signs of subsurface water which were "dug" out by animals and/or Indians. Some have disappeared, others developed later such as in the borax days.

The italics are editorial. Unless the oxen had a peculiar craving for black sulphurous water, in preference to the good spring at their previous camp, there is an obvious conflict in the last sentence. The confusion is simply one of omission, for he later supplies at least a partial answer:

> We related (to the Jayhawkers) how our train could not go over the mountain with wagons, how they had returned to the best spring.

But the return to the good spring occurred *after* Manly and Rogers left to seek help. According to Bennett's speech the night after an abortive attempt to take the wagons up the rocky canyon and selecting two men to go on ahead, it was decided that the others ". . . will go back to the good spring we have just left and wait for their return."

Thus Manly and Rogers left from the small sulphurous well, but were to return to a good spring about eight miles back along the trail.

But where were these springs, which in turn key the routes they were to follow?

Within the span of a dozen or so miles there is a string of water "holes" along the valley's southwestern fringe. Yet in relationship to the canyons and wash-laced alluvial fans, each presents distinctly different possibilities for the historic escape from the valley of death.

INTERMISSION

In a needless interruption to some, but hopefully helpful to others, the importance of the springs to the historic "Long Camp" and rescue trek routes, seems sufficient to warrant a descriptive explanation.

Desert springs do come and go. Those today may not have been flowing in 1850 and conversely flows of that date may have long since disappeared. Generally, tules or bullrushes are indicative of water, usually of good quality, at or near the surface. And while mesquite can be an unreliable guide, sizeable growths and girths bespeak of proportionately ample and steadily nurturing water if at some years past. Even where they have disappeared except for skeletal clumps, or have been buried by the shifting sands leaving only mounds to mark their passing, there is evidence that any number of small "springs" may have existed from time to time along the southwestern side.

In all likelihood, the site that sustained the Bennetts-Arcans for almost a month was a fairly good water source, large and long lasting enough to be tangibly evidenced today.

The first of these possibilities, north to south, is Tule Spring, now marked by the "Last Camp" plaque. A fair sized, if fluctuating pool ringed by tules it undoubtedly existed in 1850.

At Shorty's Well, just beyond, Indians and prospectors long knew that water was available for the digging. Whether it was apparently so in 1850 is uncertain but within the realm of possibility.

The high water level at Eagle Borax, the relative verdancy and large trees make it improbable that it was not flowing at the time.

Bennetts Well has been seriously questioned because of the depths of the present water level, yet the tules and mesquite thickets show unmistakable signs of water sumps and channels. Early photos showing a windmill here indicate sufficient water to justify the effort, cost and long haul to erect it.

Gravel Well was dug in the 1930's after geologic studies indicated the likelihood of water although there were no evident surface signs.

Of Mesquite Well, variously located on old maps as $4\frac{1}{2}$ to $8\frac{1}{2}$ miles south of Bennetts Well there is no longer any obvious sign. There are reports, notably by Spears in his 1892 *Illustrated Sketches of Death Valley,* that it was a water supply or water tank storage stop for the borax wagons preparing for and/or recovering from the dry and dusty Wingate Wash route.

At first blush the determination of which spring it was may border on topographical hair splitting. Yet because of the relationship of one to another, the spring determines the canyon, and the canyon, each distinctly different, determines the emigrant escape route.

According to Manly they had reached two water supplies: the first, a good spring of fresh water; the second, a small sulphurous "well" about 8 miles beyond.

Were Tule Spring the former, the chain of tule and mesquite oases strung out for over 15 miles to the south like a loosely knotted necklace, their greenness at least hopefully indicative of water, would have kept the company continuing in that direction. The easily traversable terrain southward and the flattening ridges also promised far more practical wagon crossings than cutting west into the Panamints at this point. Too, if Tule was the "good spring," they could scarcely have missed, or at least mentioned, the intervening water holes.

While the existence of Shorty's Well at that time is questionable, Eagle Borax would hardly be described as the small brackish "well." Much the same would apply to the good spring being either one with Manly's mileage carrying them past Bennetts Well with its mesquite grove basins—an equally improbable locale for the mounded "well."

It is possible, of course, that the "eight miles" is an error of memory. But if only by process of preliminary elimination for later substantiation, the clues make Bennetts Well the prime suspect as the "good spring."

From here, near the end of the mesquite chain, amid the last scattering of green growths, however scrubby, lay Mesquite Well— "about 8 miles away"—its exact location now lost in an area of anonymous mesquite and wire-grass covered mounds.[52] Silently, tenaciously it fought the smothering sands only to be eventually buried beneath a dune of countless counter-parts.

So long as there had been even signs of water to the south they would have gone on. But here they might well ponder whether to continue south or cut west. To the south, though the elevations were lower, they were as bare of hope. Westward, always the choice when in doubt, now seemed the only alternate even though the Panamints still barred the way.

Yet even in this they took heart with the reminder:

Some who had read Fremont's travels said that the range immediately west of us must be the one he described, on the west side of which was a beautiful country, of rich soil and having plenty of cattle and horses, and containing some settlers; but on the east all was barren, dry, rocky, sandy desert as far as could be seen. We knew this eastern side answered well the description and believed that this was really the range described, or at least it was close by.

Too, a westward try, if at all possible, contained the hope that:

We had been in the region long enough to know the higher mountains contained most water, and that the valleys had bad water or none

[52] U.S. Geological map, 1910, places Mesquite Well just between Six Springs and Galena canyons and about 8½ miles south of Bennett's Well. It is not to be confused with a Mesquite Spring near Scotty's Castle.

at all, so that while the lower altitudes to the south gave some promise of easier crossing it gave us no promise of water or grass without which we must certainly perish.

To those delving deeply into the Manly story there is a puzzling discrepancy in the distance from camp to mountains on the Manly-Rogers trip out, on their return, and the eventual trek out with the others.

While there are omissions and seeming contradictions by Manly in the haze of his recollections, a solution can be sorted out from a series of rather loosely related clues:

The brackish well was at the mouth of a canyon leading to the summit.[53]

Although it appeared "too rough for wagons" the men still decided "they would take this canyon."

Returning from the abortive attempt, Arcan drove one of his exhausted oxen to a spring.

Manly and Rogers were to leave via the same canyon.

On their return "down the same (canyon) in which we had turned back with the wagons" they again reached the small sulphurous well but "still had to travel many hours to the appointed camping place."

On the final trek, with the others, they took a nearer route to reach more quickly the water he and Rogers camped at on the first trip.

(Since this trek started from the good spring, not the sulphurous well, they still had to go south before taking this "nearer route" to avoid the innumerable gullies fanning down into the valley; at least until they got closer to the canyon area).

With this setting of the stage, let us return to the actors in their roles, as the next act begins for the "Long Camp" at which the Bennetts and Arcans were to wait for almost a month, hoping against hope.

---

[53] While "mouth" has been interpreted as the actual cleavage into the mountains, the canyons have long "tongues" reaching to the valley floor. There are no springs on the talus slopes. Manly also notes the "well" was "out in the valley." For a greater descriptive detailing of the canyons and springs along this route see appendix C.

AN ESCAPE ATTEMPT

As if magnetized, the Bennetts and Arcans, straggling Wades, trailing Nusbaumer trio and mystery Alsatians were drawn together for their fateful moment of truth—for some 25 to 27 men, women and children.[54]

On January 12 the Bennett-Arcan wagons started up the slopes toward what appeared to be a canyon opening into the Panamint Mountains. As was his custom, Manly went ahead and found:

> ...the canyon spread out into a kind of basin inclosed on all sides but the entrance, with a wall of high, steep rock, possible to ascend on foot but which apparently bar the further progress of the wagons.

Of the several canyons criss-crossing the Panamints south of Telescope Peak, none has so distinctive a basin or bowl-like entrance as Galena Canyon. The others, with their cleft openings and continuing passage are not blocked by back-walls creating an enclosed "basin." Moreover, just as no man is an island, entire of itself, so too with a canyon. In addition to descriptive eligibility, it must tie in with all of the events to follow. Leaving these to fall into place as they occur, let us rejoin Manly.

As Manly turned back from scouting the canyon, he fell and broke the stock of his rifle; symbolic perhaps of the heartbreaking news imparted to the wagon train that now had to turn back. It was dark when he rejoined them so a dry camp was made on the slopes. In the morning they started back toward the valley floor.

That night there was a fatefully decisive meeting. It was proposed that two of the youngest and strongest try to find a settlement ahead. Manly and John Rogers were chosen.

The next day was spent in preparations. An ox was killed and the meat dried. Indicating the gauntness of the cattle, 7/8ths of the meat was packed into two knapsacks. New moccasions were made of the

---

[54] See appendix A.

hide and the women made each man a knapsack. They were also given a couple of spoonfuls of rice and as much tea, and all of the money in camp—about $60.

Manly had half a blanket in lieu of a coat and Bennett's rifle to replace his broken one. Rogers had a thin coat, no blanket and was given Bennett's double barrel shotgun. Each had a sheath knife, a tin cup and a quart-size camp kettle.

They were also given a variously reported 10, 15, 18 days, or three weeks according to Rogers, for their mission. Little did any suspect they were to take 26 days.

On the morning of the 15th of January they were bid farewell with "all sorts of advice" including that of "Captain Culverwell (who) was an old seafaring man and was going to tell us how to find our way back."

In the meantime, back on the 12th, Nusbaumer's trio had been following slowly behind, and on the 13th spotted the wagons starting up the slope.

On the 14th, his entry reports a surprising development. They were now joined by a wagon:

> The owner of this wagon was an Alsatian by the name of Anton Schlogel from Engersheim, District of Molsheim near Strasbourg, who had settled in Quincy, Illinois.
>
> He had three yoke of oxen but after traveling together for several miles one of his oxen took sick and was unable to go further. We therefore decided to join our lots and promised never to desert one another, but to help each other and to divide our provisions. We killed the ox, took his tongue and heart and liver and followed after the company when suddenly we saw them returning and we also turned back.

Where did Schlogel come from, to suddenly appear like a desert mirage complete with wagon? A solitary straggler? All of the parties had now been in Death Valley for three weeks, surely sufficient time for any strays to join a flock. Was he the man they encountered on the 8th, who refused them water and whose abandoned ox was killed? Hardly, in view of the friendship now displayed.

The plausible explanation is that Schlogel, from the Alsatian city

of Strasbourg, was one of those who befriendèd Nusbaumer's group
at Travertine Springs and who probably trailed circuitiously in the
wake of the Bennetts-Arcans, separated from his own companions
for some unknown reason.[55]

Obviously taking a dim view of Manly's and Roger's chances and
of an escape route in an area already tried and failed, Nusbaumer's
group did not linger in camp for long. Soon after Culverwell was
named by Manly among those left behind, he, Nusbaumer and at
least Hadapp were to make their own abortive effort to seek a more
southerly exit.

However distracting flashbacks may be, they are dictated by the
separation of the parties by route and events. While each might be
followed as separately from start to finish, the vital dovetailing in
confirming dates and places when and where they periodically rejoined makes it equally important to follow them by time divisions at key
points. Having taken one major grouping to, indeed into, the Panamints, let us now do so with the others who had camped to the north.

---

[55] In all probability, before Travertine Springs the Alsatians followed the Jayhawkers from
Papoose Dry Lake, bonded by language but separated from the others for much the same reason.

1849	BENNETTS-ARCANS	NUSBAUMER
Dec.25	Manly arrives Travertine Springs, meets Briers at dusk	Abandon wagon near Death V. Junction
26	Manly guides Bennetts-Arcans into camp	Load possessions on 3 remaining oxen and follow company ahead
27	Manly to Doty (Jayhawker) camp; oxen shot by Indians at Travertine Spg.	At Furnace Creek Wash; 2nd day and night without water
28	Manly returns to Travertine late; meets Fisch, Isham enroute; at camp learns of oxen being shot	Arrives Travertine Spg.; learns of oxen being shot; part of his party(2) leave to join Jayhawkers
29-30	At Travertine camp	At Travertine camp
31	Manly & Rogers explore south to "willows", spring, salt marsh area	" "
1850 Jan. 1	" "	" " (Happy New Year!)
2	Manly & Rogers return to camp	" "
3	At Travertine camp; discussions, decisions and preparations	" "
4-5	" " (leave ?)	" "
6	(Leave?); camp enroute to Badwater	"Have been here 10 days"; Alsatians probably leave - or earlier?
7	p.m. near Badwater salt pool area	a.m. Nusbaumer 3 leave Travertine, following Bennett-Arcan trail
8	a.m. start across valley p.m. unnoted first night across valley, between Eagle Borax and Bennetts Well. Probably dry camp	a.m. see B/A crossing, angle to intercept; overtake 2 straggling wagons p.m. delayed by killing ox; hurry on in dark; sleep under bush; 1 a.m. near Tule Spg. on a more direct course than Bennetts-Arcans
9	a.m. start down west side; unknown distance p.m. good spring, grass (Bennetts Well) "second night"	a.m. 2 miles to spring (Tule Spg.) p.m. encamped; sickness
10	Meetings, untian late at night	At B/A #1 camp of 8th; find burned wagon
11	a.m. teamsters leave; continue south p.m. at brackish well (Mesquite)	Encamped
12	a.m. head up wash into Galena Canyon with wagons; Manly goes ahead p.m. Manly turns back; meets wagons near dark	a.m. follow B/A route along valley p.m. slowed by ailing Culverwell, stop short of Mesquite camp
13	a.m. wagons turn back p.m. meeting	Travels part of day; sees wagons up Galena Canyon; camps to rest
14	Preparations for Manly & Rogers rescue trek	Joined by Schlogel; start to follow wagons; see them turn back; remain in camp
15	Manly & Rogers leave; Culverwell among those bidding farewell; Bennetts-Arcans turn back to "appointed camping place" at good spring (Bennetts Well)	Nusbaumer scouts route to south

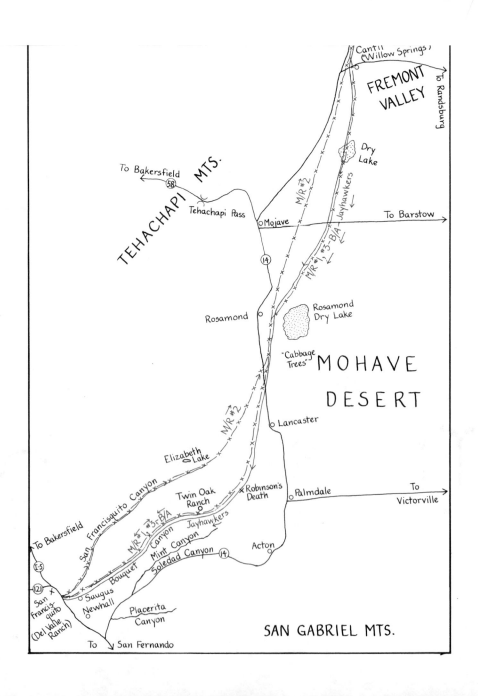

Cantil
("Willow Springs")

FREMONT
VALLEY

To Randsburg

Dry
Lake

To Bakersfield

58

TEHACHAPI MTS.

Tehachapi Pass

M/R #2

B/A Jayhawkers

To Barstow

Mojave

14

Rosamond

Rosamond
Dry Lake

M/R #1, 3-B/A Jayhawkers

"Cabbage
Trees"

MOHAVE

DESERT

M/R #2

Lancaster

Elizabeth
Lake

San Franciscquito Canyon

Twin Oak
Ranch

Robinson's
Death

Palmdale

To
Victorville

M/R #1, 3-B/A

Jayhawkers

To Bakersfield

Bouquet Canyon

Mint Canyon

Soledad Canyon

Acton

14

I-5

121

San Francis-
quito
(Del Valle
Ranch)

Saugus

Newhall

Placerita
Canyon

SAN GABRIEL MTS.

To   San Fernando

Escaping the Dragon's Lair

The Exodus

THE JAYHAWKERS AND BRIERS

A contingent of "Georgians" were the first to leave the McLean camp, on December 29.[1]

Haynes, arriving at McLean on the 25th, and laying over four days to leave on the 30th, makes no mention of arrivals. But Stephens tells of three:

> Here (McLean) Rev. J. W. Brier and family came up to us and wanted to travel with us. At first we objected, as we didn't want to be encumbered with any women, but we hadn't the heart to refuse. So they joined the Jayhawkers and the little woman proved to be as plucky and brave as any woman that ever crossed the plains ...

> There were others who came to our camp. One was a company of Georgians, about fifteen of them. The next day we saw snow on the mountains in the distance and we knew if we could reach the pass through the mountains we would find water, so we started straight for it. But the Georgians hugged the foot of the mountain in hopes of finding water in the canyon. They found no water, but did find a silver mine. I saw a piece they melted and made a gunsight of ... Captain Townshend, who seemed to be the head man of the Georgia company, took the company through another route.... They packed their provisions on their backs and were better supplied than we were as they still had some flour of which they gave a portion to the Brier family.

> Another party of eleven men passed ... out of the eleven there was but two to finish the trip, the others having died in a pile. These two would have died also had it not been they disagreed on the route to travel and stole away in the night.

---

[1] Young notes on the 28th the arrival of the "Bug-smashers," by which some of the Georgians were known. And their departure on the 29th. They are tied too closely with commentaries by the Jayhawkers to have actually been at Young's camp. There was undoubtedly visiting between camps and Young observed their departure on one of these occasions. Fragmented, as were all of the groups, the Georgians-Bugsmashers were no longer an intact unit but enough stayed together to retain that convenient identity.

In addition to the flour noted by Stephens, Manly says "The Martin Party . . . gave all their oxen they had left to Mr. Brier." Perhaps "all" should have been "some of" for Colton says the Georgians gave his party "all of the cattle (they had) left" at the "snow camp" on the summit. And Brier Jr. recalled Town's party gave "some score of their oxen" to the Briers. In any event, the matter of oxen was to provide a bone of contention that bitterly split Rev. Brier and the Jayhawkers in later years.

The eleven men is, of course, another cryptic reference to the Savage-Pinney Party and the controversial versions of whether proposed cannibalism or a difference over direction called for stealing away from the others in the night. As noted elsewhere, no substantiation has ever been found for nine dying "in a pile."

Since Manly had been at the Jayhawker camp on the 27th, returning to Travertine the next morning, one may well wonder he didn't see or mention passing any of those arriving at McLean on the 28th. The answer may be in Manly reaching the Jayhawker camp at night and leaving before daybreak. In the darkness, with some traveling in the flat along Salt Creek and others higher on the slopes and low intervening mounds much of the way, they may have passed as ships in the night.

Colton says, ". . . we finished our pack-saddles at sunset and started on the trail for the snow bank (that the Georgians headed for)." This could have been at sunset on the 29th, although mindful treks rarely began at night, it may have been on the 30th.

He continues with:

> . . . expecting to reach it by morning . . . (but) deceived by distance and in our weak condition did not reach the snow until the second morning about 3 o'clock. . . . The Georgia boys built signal fires to guide us to camp . . .
>
> The Georgia men were old silver miners. They told us upon our arrival in camp that there was immense wealth of silver in sight where we camped. One showed me a chunk of black rock he held in his hands and told me it was half silver and if we only had provisions and water and knew where we were that there was all the wealth in sight we could ask. Before leaving this camp one of the Georgians cached five thousand dollars in gold . . .

While the amount of gold varies, the accounts are similar. George Miller, for example, who sought the Gunsight silver in 1869 with Jayhawker Bill Rood's guidance, writes:

> Rhodes (Rood) told me that two men named Martin and Townsend brought the ore in at the place now known as Summit Camp, or Emigrant Pass, between Death Valley and the head of Panamint Valley, the second camp after they left their wagons. Rhodes told me that before they separated at this place they divided up the money they had, each taking what he wanted, and dumped the rest in a blanket, about $2,000 or $2,500, and buried it under a greasewood bush. While we were there we made a good search to find the money but unforunately there had been a cloudburst on that side of the pass which obliterated everything where they had buried the money.

According to Ellenbecker, in close touch with the surviving '49ers and their families, it was non-Georgian Shannon who cached $6000 in gold coin.

The discoverers of the "Gunsight silver" are also as varied. One of the Turner brothers avowed, "I was the one who found it . . . and Martin brought some of it away and had a gunsight made of it at Mariposa Mines." Rood credits Martin and Townsend (Toun, Town, Townshend). Still others claimed or were given credit. Since neither the gold or silver were ever found it matters little except for the naming of some who followed this route, and for clues to the locale.

First is that they could *see* the snow from McLean, "Toward the west . . . within a distance of ten miles, upon the high peak of a mountain of volcanic formation, a gorge filled with snow and protected from the sun, which had laid there a long time," which precludes it being seen up Emigrant Wash due to the projection of Tucki Mountain.

Further, it was in a crevice, sheltered from the sun and that it had been there a long time. Not only does this preclude newly fallen snow —and snows do not last on Death Valley's lower levels—but indicates it was on the east or sheltered side of the mountains, shaded from the warm afternoon sun.

From McLean snow peaks to the west can be seen in the Cottonwood and Marble canyons area, past the hump of Tucki Mountain, but this would be about 20 miles away and seemingly farther in the haze of distance.

But there is a closer sight of creviced snow. One familiar to winter months visitors. That on 6,732-foot Tucki Mountain. True, it is more to the southwest, but again one is reminded of sunbased bearings and that the sun set in the southwest at this time of year. The broad alluvial fans that lead into its heights are long, slow and laboriously climbed although they were well used in Skidoo's heyday by miners trapsing twixt that camp and Rhyolite via McLean and Old Stovepipe Wells.

That they took longer than anticipated to reach the summit may be due to following the Georgian's trail hugging the foot of the mountain to the most promising route up Tucki Wash.

Haynes records "15 W" the first day (Dec. 29) and "SW 24 miles to snow canion" the next. Via Towne Pass, 39 miles would have taken him well into Panamint Valley, scarcely the locale for any snow canyon.

More than ever one must make allowances for distances estimated by the way their feet felt, whether over flats or steep terrain and serpentine bendings where miles are more apt to be measured by time. Too, if there had been any rodometers before, contributing to some accuracy of mileage, they were now with the wagons left at McLean.

As Manly well put it:

> It seemed there were many men from the various parties scattered all around the country, each one seeking out the path which seemed to suit best his tender feet or present fancy, steering west as well as mountains and canyons would permit, some farther north, some farther south . . .

Manly also writes:

> The Doty party, or Jayhawkers, when they were ready, started first a northernly course . . . soon came to some good water . . . turned westward . . . while climbing the steep mountain side they came across a dead ox left by some party that had gone before them . . . when it was getting dark . . . almost at the summit . . . they saw a small firelight . . . finding a poor lone camper taking care of himself . . .

The ox and camper have been the subject of much conjecture. It has even been theorized that the ox may have belonged to an even earlier party than the Jayhawkers or Georgians. And a northerly start, to which Manly was not a witness, is at variance with a westerly route.

But one need not press unduly for a logical explanation of all three.

The Jayhawkers, in skirting Salt Creek and salt crusted surface and sand dunes just beyond, may well have started north, reaching Old Stovepipe Wells. However, since Manly's information on this is hearsay and neither Colton, Haynes, Stephens or others report finding water (an item above all to merit mention) in their drive to the snow, it is scarcely admissible evidence to offset a Tucki routing. For that matter, in then turning westward/southwestward, they could have still done so.

In following the Georgians, it would be their ox that was found. In rejoining the Georgians the second night, "guided by fire*s*" . . . "*they* told us . . ." and "one of the boys" showing them the silver specimen, a straggling Georgian may have been encountered the first night on the way up the slope.

Assuredly, in following the winding washes and skirting deeply cut gullies it was slow travel. After a hard way of soft and circuitous going, it could easily be guesstimated as 15 miles, per Haynes, by the time they halted for their first camp near the slopes of Tucki Wash.

The next day, December 30, they worked their way up Tucki or an adjoining wash, to the "snow canion camp" near the 6,000 foot level. It was a steep meandering climb and few could fault Haynes for it seeming like 24 miles. Heading uphill and with slow moving oxen, wending their way this way and that for the easiest going, made for a long day. But at long last, somewhere in the vicinity of 5,680-foot Skidoo, they made their "second camp" guided by the fires of the Georgians.

According to Brier Jr., they ". . . went into camp where they had water from a spring and their oxen saw the color and tasted the flavor of grass." Colton's account of melting snow for water and Brier Jr.'s spring and grass are not completely incompatible. The springs in this area are invariably small with patches of half frozen grass, making feasible the use of both melted snow and meager water.

To tie up a few loose ends left dangling—one would be remiss not to note Brier Jr.'s varied versions.

For example, in his July 26, 1884 *Inyo Independent* account:

> ...we skirted up the valley ... passed over the hillocks of sand, along
> the deeply furrowed and stony table lands until we reached the lofty
> pass which conducts into Panamint (Valley).

Because of their obviousness, the dunes northeast of Stovepipe
Wells Village are popularly taken as those referred to. Yet there are
also dunes, be they smaller, just across Salt Creek from McLean
Spring. And a "lofty pass" is as descriptive of the heights of Tucki
Mountain as Towne Pass.

In his *Out West Magazine* article of March 1903, he states they
steered "... north of west ... for twenty miles to a pass between the
Panamints and Telescope Peak from the summit of which we were
in plain view of Mt. Whitney and the Minarets." He seemingly
identifies this pass by name in his *Grizzly Bear* article of June 1911,
saying they "steered their course for Town's Pass."

But Brier Jr., cannot have his cake and eat it too. He either had
a summit sight of the Sierra or was at the top of Towne Pass. But not
both. The Sierra, including Mt. Whitney, can't be seen from the
4,900-foot crest of Towne Pass due to view-blocking terrain as it twists
and turns into Panamint Valley. And he certainly didn't see the
Minarets, close to 150 miles northwest.

Yet—his view of the Sierra at least is possible from a point 1.2
miles south of the present road. And in Lt. Wheeler's 1871-5 mappings Towne Pass is shown *south* of Pinto Peak rather than where it
is known today. Too, the Sierra may also be sighted along the descent
into Panamint Valley, but this is a view from the summit only by
semantic stretching and faulty recollection.

As in any projection, a base however tenuous must be established.
In this case, somewhat arbitrarily, it is in the Skidoo flats.

Here three basic courses were open to them. One, to the south,
via Wildrose Canyon. A second, via such as Telephone Canyon, into
Towne Pass. And a third, between these two, via one of the grades
down into Wildrose Canyon near the old Journigan Mill ruins.

So far as the first, any exit south from Wildrose Canyon would
result in less than 10 miles to the "Muskrat" (Mesquite) camp, con-
tradicting Rev. Brier's 20 miles to that camp from where the Mississippi boys left at the "head of Panamint Valley."

Choice #2, via Telephone Canyon, would drop them into the Towne Pass road near the present checking station. Inviting as this might have been, it would have also resulted in commenting upon the heart-breaking sight of the valley from which they had just fled.

However iconoclastic, credence is given to route #3.

Long "guided only by the fact we knew the Pacific Ocean was to the west" they had stubbornly clung to that bearing when possible, even though it had cost them dearly in not turning south at the Amargosa and in Death Valley.

To the west of Skidoo the slopes dropped downward into Wildrose Canyon. Continuing westward a winding wash and trail lead up towards Pinto Peak, leveling out at some small springs including Greer, Burro and Malapai. Here was space for a camp, some grass and water and high enough for snow.

Here, too, an old trail leads north and down into what has become known as Jayhawker Canyon—a long, narrow defile that opens onto the flat near the junction of the Emigrant/Wildrose road (#178) and the Towne Pass road (#190). Midway it bulges to enclose a spring and some large boulders covered with petroglyphs and inscribed names, including Weston and Hitchens of the 1860 Dr. French expedition.

On one of the smaller boulders is "1849 W.B.R."—acceptably that of Jayhawker William B. Rood. On another that of "LI ER." A crack and scuff mark between the I and E leaves uncertain whether there was a period or a trace of a "leg" on the I to make it "LL ER." While it has been theorized the name was BRIER, this was undoubtedly by those who have not actually seen it.

Discovery of the site has led to increasing acceptance that Jayhawker Canyon, not Towne Pass, was the '49er route. And the spring, formerly known as Hitchens Spring has been renamed Jayhawker Spring.

Any '49er leaving Death Valley via Emigrant Wash would find themselves in a broad bowl-like flat just beyond the Emigrant Ranger Station. Straight ahead would be a steep grade, from 2,000 to almost 5,000 feet, over Towne Pass. To their left, hooking southeasterly, the partially hidden Emigrant/Wildrose Canyon. Between was the opening to Jayhawker Canyon.

Rock inscriptions in Jayhawker Canyon

Adjoining inscriptions
in Jayhawker Canyon
include W. B. R(ood)

A second W B Rood
inscription on the flats
north of Emigrant
Ranger Station near
Cottonwood Canyon

Yet—much of this new thinking is based on the "WBR 1849" rock and another, inscribed "W. B. Rood 1849" near the foot of Lemoigne Canyon across the rocky alluvial fan towards Cottonwood Canyon from the ranger station. Obviously it would seem, these mark the route of the Jayhawkers including Rood.

But while there is little reason to doubt that Rood inscribed them, with a McLean departure on December 30th permitting a just under the wire dating of 1849, he may well have done so twenty years later! Returning to this area in 1869 with George Miller, seeking the Lost Gunsight silver, he may have post-dated his recording of having been there earlier. Certainly it would be understandable that in seeing the names of those who had come along later, he could feel, "I was here before them, so it is only fair to show it." He wasn't falsifying anything; simply post-recording he had been there ahead of them.

That any of the Jayhawkers descended into this canyon, even by scouting, is most unlikely, since it obviously led back toward Death Valley.

Instead, looking ahead, there are two encircling washes around Pinto Peak. At their descent into Panamint Valley both have memorable sightings of the Sierra. Which of the two they might have taken conjecturally depends on which was closest. With a few hundred yards scouting, the one to the south of the peak would likely offer the best of optional descents. This gains support from Lt. Wheeler's mapping of "Town Pass" just south of Pinto Peak. Later, for those on horses, mule or afoot it was an early route between the Darwin-Coso-Lookout mines and Skidoo-Wildrose-Panamint City mining activities.

With hindsight one knows where the '49ers should have gone. But this familiarization was not theirs and, ruefully, they often picked the poorest choices. As Brier Jr., added:

> We were only two days journey from Owens Lake, but we turned to the south and prolonged our journey by hundreds of miles.

Fatefully, had they angled northwesterly from Panamint Valley, they could have soon been at Owens Lake. But staring at the high Argus Range directly ahead and with the flat Panamint Valley extending far into the distance southward, the latter seemed best even though they had to, temporarily at least, abandon continuing west.

That they prolonged their journey by hundreds of miles is more of discouragement than accuracy. The route via Owens Lake to Los Angeles would be longer, although easier.

"New Year's day was hardly noticed," Mrs. Brier was to write, "We spent it resting at the head of Panamint Valley."

In a January 17, 1876, letter to Mecum, Rev. Brier retraces their trail eastward, that is in reverse from Panamint Valley to Death Valley:

> ... Panamint Valley, where Capt. Town and Company left me ... you all remember the Muskrat Swamp,[2] Indian Springs and wickiups ... from the Muskrat Swamp to the head of the valley where the Mississippi boys left us is twenty miles ...

That only *some* of the Mississippi boys left here is apparent in a January 20, 1898, letter to Deacon Richards:

> ... we were members of the Mississippi boys until we reached the head of Panamint Valley. There most of my company packed their backs and left us.

He then adds, in a helpful enlightenment of names:

> Now my family, Capt. Town, Mr. Martin and Compton[3] and the two Turner boys went with the Jayhawks down to Mesquite Swamp. There these 5 men left us and struck off west. . . . My family now fell in with the Jayhawks. We traveled with them a part of the time and generally camped with them ... but were no part of their Company.
>
> My family was composed of myself, wife and 3 boys ... Father Fish of Lima, Indiana, and Isham of Michigan, Mr. Gould of New York, though not in my family, camped with us ... further on Patrick and Lummis St. John overtook us ... I remember Capt. Haines and a boy that I supposed was John Colton ... I remember the Atchison brothers[4] ... Captain Doty ... Carter and Groscup. . . .

Since some of these are listed as "Mississippians" it is apparent that

---

[2] That "Muskrat," a creature incongrous with the area, was a slip of the pen is apparent in a Jan. 16, 1896, letter clarifying it was a "Mesquite Swamp" where they camped by a number of wickiups. And that they "went down some 5 or 6 miles south to other springs (Post Office Spring) where we tarried a few days longer."

[3] A probable misspelling of "Crumpton."

[4] No other mention by name is made of the Atchison brothers. As much as it may be argued as a slip of memories, it may also be they were the two Arcan teamsters who, with the Bennett teamsters, left that group in Death Valley.

The "snow camp" site near Greer Spring, near the crest into Jayhawker Canyon

The entrance to Water Canyon, which Rev. Brier preferred to the Jayhawkers' steep trail westward

From Pinto Peak, the route from near Greer Springs into Panamint Valley

only some left at the head of Panamint Valley, others farther south.

Who were the first Mississippians to leave? For one thing, despite inclinations to divide the Georgians, Mississippians and sub-groups of Bugsmashers into separate groups, the constant intermixture, secondary descriptions and free-wheeling identifications make attempts at categorization more confusing than consistent.

At best, lumped together, the conglomerated Mississippians numbered 14. Of these, six (Town, John Martin, the two Turner brothers, Masterson and Crumpton) left later. Two others, Coker and Smith (who had earlier been with Nusbaumer) are accounted for at Providence Springs. This leaves six who, by no small coincidence, do not appear in any incidents from here on: James Martin, of Mississippi; James Woods, of Mississippi; Joe, a negro ("Jim Wood's man"); Tom, a negro; "Little West" (not "Lew" West); Nat Ward.

Six, of course, is to be used as guide, not gospel. Savage and Pinney, however far fetched, may have been with them. And the shadowy figures of Morse and McGowan/McGrew could change any set figures.

Two of these are confirmed by name in Rev. Brier's letter to Richards and comrades, January 20, 1879:

> . . . we descended into Panamint Valley on New Year's Day . . . some of the Mississippi boys, with Little West and Town and Joe the darkie left us and steered for a canyon on the west side of the valley . . . the canyon is now called Darwin's . . .

Typical of the confusion of names and memories is his inclusion of Town whom he also later names as among those who continued to their next camp. Called "mesquite swamp camp" and "horsebones camp," it has been advocated as being in the center of the valley. But mesquites, Indian springs and wickiups points to the edge of the Panamints rather than its barren center. And Indian Ranch (Reservation), home of venerable 105(?)-year-old Indian George who reputedly witnessed the first white men to cross Death Valley in '49, still shows the verdancy that would entice the Jayhawkers.

Here they found water to warrant a two or three day layover, but six more of the intermixed Georgians-Mississippians—Town, John Martin, the Turner brothers, Masterson and Crumpton—apparently had second thoughts and decided to follow their compatriots who had headed for Darwin Canyon.[5] Unfortunately all that is known is that they struck off to the west, and the rumor that they reached Owens Lake and that Town was later killed by Indians.

On the 10th of January the Briers and Jayhawkers moved on to a similar verdancy sighted a few miles to the south of Ballarat at Post Office Spring.

A water source known as long as the memory of man, Post Office Spring was to be another of the major pivotal points in their odyssey.

The Briers and the Jayhawker segments that remained milled about uncertainly. To the south Panamint Valley narrowed and began to angle southeasterly between the curvatures of the Panamints and Slate Range. More to the southwest the valley ended at a joining of the two ranges. To the west the Argus Range, culminating in 8,850-foot Maturango Peak, seemed to block the way.

Rev. Brier recalled, in a January 16, 1896, letter:

> . . . while here, Capt. Town (he may have erred, having inferred Town's earlier departure and means Doty[6]) and I explored the west rim of the Panamints (they would not have turned back into the Panamints and is referring to the Argus Range in the sense of the "Panamints" encircling them) where we found an Indian trail over a very steep pass which I condemned as impassible.
>
> The Capt. differed and turned back to camp. I went on south many miles from there and discovered a very large canyon. I then returned to camp which I reached about 10 pm. I found my wife baking up the last of the flour which belonged to my companions. We had no ownership in it whatever. Old Capt. Haynes sat by looking wistfully on, and a boy, I think his nephew or grandson, was all the evening gathering fuel.
>
> Capt. Haynes took out a five dollar gold piece and offered it to one of the men for one bisquit but they refused. The Capt. wept and said to me, "I have the best 160 acres in Knox County, Illinois; 100 stock hogs and 2,000 bushels of old corn in crib and here I cannot get one bisquit for love or money . . .

[5] In doing so they may have veered instead into the pass since named after Town, or canted into it via Stone Canyon to near the present town of Darwin, with easy continuance to Owens Lake, and reportedly over Walker Pass.

[6] As noted in Manly's report of the Post Office Spring crossing it was Doty, not Town, who differed from Brier in the route to take from here.

Next morning the Jayhawks packed up and started for the con-
demned pass but we remained until noon to assist our two comrades
to pack up. Not one word was spoken all that forenoon . . . when
ready they turned their faces away and reached out their hands . . .
we gathered up our oxen and packed up and wearily followed on. At
sunset we came to a part of the Jayhawks and other stragglers . . .
these were Carter, John Groscup, Harry Vance, Mr. Gould, Father
Fish and Isham . . .

Backing Brier's declaration that the Jayhawkers struck *west* from
Post Office Spring is Manly:

> Captain Doty's mess crossed between the lakes (the shallow saline
> playas north and south of Ballarat, divided by a slight rise that still
> forms the roadbed to that site) on a strip of dried mud, while others
> went on where it was still soft and left marks of their footsteps. Both
> parties turned up a small canyon on the west side . . .

Noteworthy is that the Jayhawkers turned up a small canyon on
the *west* whereas Brier opted for a very large canyon further south,
yet both parties were to wind up together again two days later.

In leaving Post Office Spring there were the 5 Briers plus Patrick
and Lummis St. John who had overtaken them. Of the 6 stragglers
met crossing the valley, Carter, Vance and Gould had previously been
associated with Young's "independents." Apparently it was these
three who were those who shouldered their packs, per Young's entry
of December 9, to take the Panamint Valley route of the Jayhawkers
in preference to Young's deviating course (see page 154).

That all six stragglers followed the Briers as they turned southward is possible; that Fisch and Isham did is certain. Of their taking
a different route than the Jayhawkers there is no question. One can
be sure the difference was not great, for Brier was not a trail blazer.
Whatever pride had to be swallowed, he was a follower, not a leader.
At Mt. Misery he "would not stay put out but forced himself in" with
the Jayhawkers. At Papoose he followed, not led the Jayhawkers
westward. And at McLean they insisted on traveling with the others
although there were some initial objections.

So it was that on the 12th of January, 1850, the various parties were
positioned like fatefully animated chessmen for the next and deadly
phase of the game.

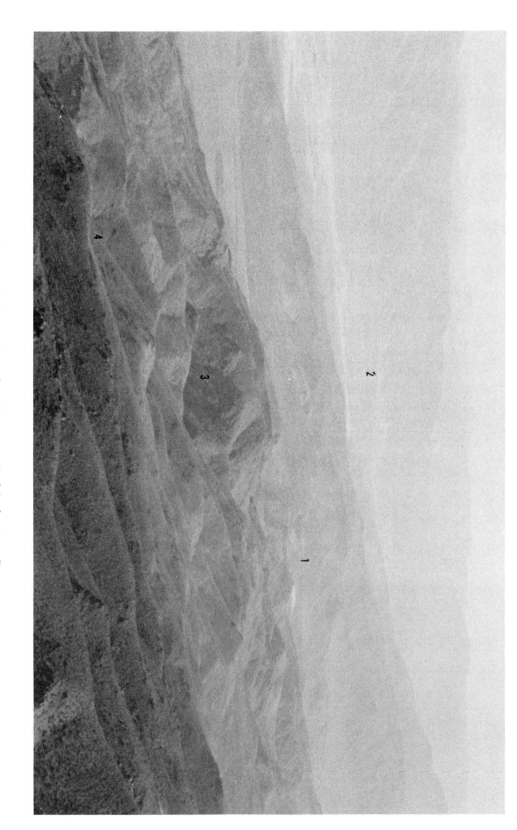

Panoramic view southeast from Maturango Peak in the Argus Range.
1) Searles Valley; 2) South arm of Panamint Valley; 3) Water Canyon; 4) Shepherd Canyon (just below ridge)

The Bennetts-Arcans were still encamped in Death Valley. Doty and his followers had left the day before, heading west over an old Indian trail[7] up a very steep pass to the west. And Young's independents were completing a 26-mile trek down a long valley containing a lake.

But the Brier trail, which had been holding together quite tolerably, now begins to part a bit at the seams.

The narrow arm of Panamint Valley that extended hazily to the south between the Panamints and Slates was enticingly flat, but a route that called for careful circling of shallow saline "lakes" and soft mire.

Where the two ranges joined, approximating the crossing of the old and new roads to Trona and Searles Lake, the way was barred. But there were signs of passes on the east side of the Slates. One, rather indistinguishably to the south except by scouting, was the now named "Fish Canyon-Manly Pass" area. Another, closer and more inviting, was an unnamed saddle. Here a wide alluvial fan slopes up to the lowest and narrowest part of the range—about three miles across and topping at less than 2,000 feet above its Panamint Valley approach; its contours softened by centuries of erosion with a notable lack of large canyons.

Yet Mrs. Brier vividly recalls:

> The valley ended in a canyon with great walls rising up—oh, as high as we could see almost. There seemed no way out for it ended almost in a straight wall. I know many of the company never expected to leave that narrow gorge.

Having committed themselves by crossing Panamint Valley to where they met the stragglers, the eastern slope Slate crossings were now behind them. Instead, they headed for the large canyon south of the Jayhawker trail and which Rev. Brier described as "many miles away," another time as "12 or 15 miles." However guesstimated, the distance is fittingly descriptive of Water Canyon near the foot of the present Slate Range highway crossing.[8]

---

[7] One of the rare occasions when they credited such guidance.

[8] However scornfully the stories of some desert rats may be viewed at times, a personal relationship with Ballarat's "Seldom Seen Slim" leaves little room to doubt the story told him by "Indian George" supporting the Brier-Doty split. As friends for some 35 years there is little

Indeed, earlier theorizations of a Slate Range crossing have been supplanted by credence to Water Canyon, be it with misgivings over its very high south wall as an exit.

Leaving this piece to fall into place, let us continue with Rev. Brier:

> I reached the mouth of the canyon about 2 pm, went 2 or 3 miles until it closed up to 20 feet in width with walls on either side, overhanging or perpendicular. A silent sepulchre. Here I found a little damp sand and scooping out a little hole a little water arose.
>
> Slaking my thirst I went on 2 or 3 hundred yards when I found the canyon walled in, but the kind wind of long ages had blown sand enough from the hills above, at a low point of some 50 feet, to make a windrow of sand to the bottom of the pass. With my hands I tore off the apex of this windrow and made a way out to good ground. I reached the top of the pass and seeing our way clear I returned and met the company at the mouth of the canyon. They (had) reached the seep of water and camped there . . .

Although Rev. Brier says he went into the canyon for 2 or 3 miles, climbed out of the canyon, back down and returned to camp that same day, his wife seems to disagree with his story. In her *San Francisco Call* article of December 25, 1898, she recalls that by the time they reached the canyon "Mr. Brier managed to keep erect with the aid of two sticks"—a condition scarcely compatible with his vigorously adventurous achievements. She also indicates the company was together when the sand seep was found:

> Seeping up from the sand, Mr. Brier found a little water and by digging the company managed to scoop up about a pint an hour.

But to continue with Rev. Brier—on the following day, he states they packed up by noon:

> (and) Father Fish took hold on the tail of his ox and was helped up the windrow out of the dismal canyon. He held onto the tail 3 or 4 hundred yards when he reeled and fell to rise no more. The boys were so excited they forgot to leave his blankets and sent back for him the next day but he was dead.

---

reason for Indian George to string Seldom along with tales normally reserved for cigarette and beer supplying greenhorns. Admittedly hearsay, it is nevertheless interesting to note Indian George stated watching two parties leaving the Ballarat area—one westward into Shepherd Canyon, the other angling farther south.

Again, somewhat contradictorily, Mrs. Brier indicates a dawn
departure rather than noon as well as a later hour demise for Fisch:

> At daylight we managed to reach the lowest branch of the cliff by
> holding to the cattle. Father Fish came up by holding to an ox's tail
> but could go no further. I made coffee for him but he was all worn
> out. That night he died.

In view of Mrs. Brier's compassionate recollections one can hope
her husband's was merely a matter of omission or unintentionally
poor wording in the seemingly callous abandonment of Fisch to die
alone in the darkness of a lonely and forbidding land and to un-
ministerially hurry on, belatedly sending someone back the next day.
Much in the same vein one winces at the "boys" (not his sons, but the
men of the party) being so excited as to hastily desert their companion
in such dire distress rather than doing all possible to be of aid and
comfort in what proved to be Fisch's last moments—as it might be
theirs further on.

Again returning to Rev. Brier, now at the summit of their wind-
row climb:

> After going down the western slope, in another canyon . . . about 3
> pm we found ourselves facing Borax lake[9] and right east of your
> (Jayhawker) camp. It looked to be about 3 miles away but it was mid-
> night when we reached the camp. Isham being weary stopped to rest
> some 4 or 5 miles back and did not come to camp . . .

Was the lack of concern over Isham another matter of wording or
omission? And were such incidents, justifiable or not, part of the

---

[9] Borax was an unfamiliar and expensive import until the first small discovery in Northern
California in 1856 (with a shipment of 12 tons), followed by the great finds in Nevada, at
Columbus Salt Marsh, Teel's Marsh and in California at Searles in the early 1870's, and Death
Valley's Harmony Borax and Eagle Borax works in the early 1880's. It is doubtful the '49ers
were familiar by sight or name with borax until 20 years later when they probably associated
the then newsy name with the lake beds they had seen.

As George Stewart so aptly noted of the Humboldt to Sacramento trail blazed by the
Stevens-Murphy Party in 1844:

> There is no good evidence that anyone traveled this route before 1844. In later
> years others claimed to have done so. By that time the "Truckee Route" had be-
> come famous on account of the railroad and anyone who wished to play himself
> up as a famous "old timer" would be likely to say he had traveled by it.

So, too, may it have been with the Brier's "borax lake," as well as their self-identification
with Town Pass; not to be wilfully misleading but simply an effort to relate to now familiar
locales that others could picture generally.

Overlooking the Jayhawkers' Shepherd Canyon route westward to Etcharren Valley in the distance. An old stage road angles from the right. The road from the left center approximately intersects the Brier route from Water Canyon

"After going down the western slope . . . we found ourselves facing a lake." Carricart Dry Lake. Here the Jayhawkers veered to the north to Providence Springs. Manly and Rogers continued west about where a road can now be seen.

strongly critical feelings and sensitive defense that later came to light between Brier and the other '49ers?

More pertinent is that after escaping from their dead-end canyon they continued *westerly,* to soon face a lake bed that seemed about 3 miles away but took from 3 p.m. to midnight to reach. Nine hours, even with rests, to go about 3 miles to reach the lake?! Something is radically amiss if one assumes the lake to be Searles.

Too, leaving Manly's detailing of his and Rogers' trek until later, there is his description of the Jayhawker trail at this point:

> Turning west again they had a down grade over a most barren and rocky road for many miles . . . to the left a lake could be seen . . .

A lake view *to their left* doesn't fit with a Slate-Argus highway area crossing where Searles would be visibly straight ahead, about 10 miles or so away. Nor does the time and distance match with the narrow crossing of a Slate saddle to the south, let alone the lack of a canyon with great walls as high as the eye could see.

Even those like historian Carl Wheat, who initially accepted Water Canyon for the Brier route, had misgivings over its sheer, high south wall as a means of exit. Even had they been able to do so after progressing far enough to where the south wall might be less of an obstacle it would then mean turning back southeast to Searles and any such retreat was repugnant.

But undoubtedly the Briers did take Water Canyon—to where a large rock slide blocked the way. And in turning back to their "seep camp," found the most feasible way out was on its north side over a series of undulating hills, near where the track of a mining road now leads to some small iron ore claims.

That Fisch had to hold onto an ox does not necessarily indicate sheerness of slope. As many a hiker has found, a constant upgrade can be exhausting. So it was that in working their way up the ascending slopes the elderly Fisch fell, age and deprivation having taken their toll.

Soon the slopes descend into upper Shepherd Canyon near Millspaugh[10] where it becomes less of a roadway winding westward between lowering slopes and tablelands.

---

[10] Only rubble and an old boiler remain of this mining camp, purportedly founded by spiritualists ethereally guided where to dig although this appears to be far more fancy than fact.

As it continues westward in dips and rises, it rounds a malpai ridge to overlook a surprisingly sizeable valley enclosing a usually dry lake bed. Deceptively it seemed only a few miles distant, and to their left. But while the grade was now down the soft sands made for slow going.

Meanwhile the Jayhawkers were also heading westward to the north of the Briers.

To the west, from Panamint Valley, the Argus Range presents a picture of an almost uncloven barrier from far to the north to its curving link with the Slate Range to the south. There are few practical crossings south of Darwin Canyon and Stone Canyon, with its clustered old mining camps of Modoc, Lookout and Minnietta, until one reaches Shepherd Canyon. This is, or was the old stage route from Ballarat to Junction Ranch via Millspaugh,[11] where it connected with the Darwin-Brown stage and continuance via Mountain Springs to the base of the Sierra Nevada.

Shepherd Canyon, a natural gateway, was long used even before. It was known to Lt. Wheeler in the 1870's, as well as to the earlier miners of Darwin, Coso and Panamint City. And long before them by Indians, traveling to the piñon pines, game and springs of 6,000-foot Etcharren Valley. For untold centuries this high mesa between the Argus and Coso ranges was a gathering place for tribes lost in time, as evidenced by an incomparably impressive array of ancient petroglyphs that line its washes and small canyons with mosaic displays that awe the eye and imagination.

However by chance or instinctive attempt to rejoin the others, the Briers' course triangulated into that of the Jayhawkers. The temptation to call it Fate, however, is tempered by awareness that where man had gone before, others will also do as surely as night follows day, when given any choice over the dictates of nature or blundering across country. So, too, did the Jayhawkers follow their trail to the west by intent and the Briers by luck.

Both now reached, not Searles, but little known Carricart Dry Lake in Etcharren Valley[12] in the high desert part of the present China Lake Naval Weapons Center.

---

[11] The old stone toll house and corral for horses added for the steep way ahead have, alas, fallen to landslides and time.

To the howls of protest that may arise, the writer can only admonish patience. However the shock, the time has come to shed the blinders of the past. As cautioned earlier, no single trail can be espoused without its relationship to that of the others in time, place and shared incidents. The pieces, including the Jayhawkers, Briers, Young, Coker, Manly and Rogers, do fit. Amazingly so.

Typically, the water at Carricart proved unpalatable. Rev. Brier called it "borax," a matter already covered. According to Young it was "salt." Mrs. Brier simply says it was undrinkable. To Manly it was wine colored and alkaline.

To varying tastes it is each of these. Its clay bed is sandy buff when dry, reddish when shallowly covered by rains, and definitely poor even to the thirsty.

Here Young had arrived on the 12th, the Jayhawkers during the 13th and the Briers about midnight.

According to Rev. Brier, Isham fell to rise no more about four miles from the lake. Manly also notes, although not a witness:

> The valley seemed about 8 miles across and before they were halfway over Mr. Isham, one of their party, sat down, perfectly exhausted and said he could not take another step . . . they could only look sadly at him and pass on in silence . . .

But others reports, as the story develops, indicate Isham's death may have occurred beyond the lake camp, having crawled some four miles along the trail to the life saving springs they were to providentially find and aptly name.

PROVIDENCE SPRINGS

Few geographical points are as critical to a retracing of the '49er trail as Providence Springs. Its location must fit with the approach and departure routes of the various parties who were obviously there, including its relationship to the lake where they camped. And be confirmed by Manly-Rogers treks to follow later.

To the advocates of Searles as the lake, "Indian Joe Spring," about four miles northwest of the rim of Searles Lake fits the distance.

---

[12]Modern mapping to the contrary, it is Etcharren, not Etcheron, named after Domingo Etcharren, an early sheep rancher of the area. So too with Carricart vs. Carricut, named after his partner John Carricart.

Others lean to "Peach Springs" in Bruce Canyon and about ten miles in the same direction. Both could allow westward progress, particularly via Wilson Canyon, across the narrow and low southern extension of the Argus Range. But both springs are only a short way into the range and it is difficult to picture them spurning continuing south over the flat passage past Searles to the easy Salt Wells Canyon grade, now the Trona-China Lake road, or the even flatter route past Spangler used by the Trona Railroad.

Leaving this to be pinned down more tightly by Manly, accept, at least for the moment, that the lake was Carricart, not Searles.

According to Young, his group found Providence Springs on the 13th:

> Jan. 13   This day went six miles north (from the lake) to a spring in a deep rocky canyon . . . the best water we have found in some time. Not much grass. Some browse. Killed a cow. Some of our men not in camp yet. Two we do not think can be got into camp. They were so fatigued out they cannot come in.[13]

> Jan. 14   This day went out in search of the two men. Found them both dead. Their names were Fish from Indiana and Isham from Michigan . . .

In Mrs. Brier's *Carson City News* account (June 8, 1913) she tells that after finding the water at the lake undrinkable:

> A Jayhawker named Richards wandered off up the highest peak of the Inyo Mountains[14] and in a canyon discovered what we christened Providence Springs and came running back to tell us. We camped by the spring and the next day two men went back for Isham. They found he had crawled along four miles on our trail on his hands and knees and then fallen over and died.

In a similar account (*San Francisco Call*, Dec. 25, 1898) she tells of being at the lake having been without water for 48 hours:

> At last we came upon two Germans of the company who had gone ahead[15]. They were cooking at a tiny fire. "Any water?" asked my

---

[13] Fisch and Isham were with the Briers, not Young's independents, but in the gathering at the lake all had become intermingled into one group.

[14] Her naming of "Inyo Mountains" was surprisingly correct. Technically the Inyos become the Cosos south of Owens Lake. But the almost continuous range is commonly called the Inyo Mountains in general.

[15] Perhaps Goler and his German speaking companion, possibly Wolfgang Tauber.

husband. "There's vasser," one said, pointing to a muddy puddle. It was awful stuff but it saved our lives. A little later we came to a beautiful cold spring. Oh, how good it was! I always believed Providence placed it there to save us for it was such an unlikely spot.

Apparently between the lake and the spring they had found a small sink of muddy water that shared in lifesaving credit. Less understandably is her recollection of having gone without water for 48 hours. They had found some water at the "seep camp" in Water Canyon, from which they left in the morning, reaching the lake that night. And had enough water with them to make coffee for Fisch, as she related, who fell before reaching the lake.

Be it as it may, Deacon Richards is generally credited with the finding of Providence Springs. In Rev. Brier's letter to Richards, January 20, 1898, he writes:

> I remember you well as the discoverer of Providence Springs . . . up a canyon . . . and as the man who climbed to the top of the highest peak of the Inyo Mountains and found there a camp of Diggers (Indians) who showed you our way out . . .

That Richards had climbed the highest peak of the Inyos is an obvious dramatic embellishment. John Ellenbecker, in his excellent detailed treatise quotes a letter he received from Richards' son expanding on the discovery:

> . . . father was still hunting water several miles away in the hills in a canyon. Looking up to a shelf 100 feet higher he saw five Indians with bows drawn ready to shoot him . . . he told them, by signs, he was hunting water . . . they took hold of his tattered shirt as if they wanted it. He discreetly gave it to them. Then in turn they threw a fine Indian blanket over his bare shoulders. . . . Mr. Richards went to where the Indians pointed. He could hear the water but could not see it. It was hidden by bushes. Without drinking he hurried towards the others and gave the happy signal that good water had been found.

This account also credits Colton, Doty and Stephens as those who hastened back to where Isham had fallen:

> They found Mr. Isham still alive, but his mouth, tongue and throat were so swollen and parched that he could no longer swallow. While they bathed his hands and body he expired.

Just where was, or is that spring?

Rev. Brier said the spring was found in a canyon or deep wash. Young said it was six miles north of the lake in a rocky canyon. Haynes also records, "N 6 miles. Water. Fish, Isham died."

Manly, who was to be directed to Providence Springs by the Jayhawkers when he and Rogers met them on the way toward Los Angeles, recommending their route because of that spring, tells of the Jayhawker-Briers, etc. experience from the lake to the spring:

> Those who bore farthest to the right (from the lake) in their course
> to the mountains, steering toward a pile of *tremendous rocks,* found
> a little stream of good water which flowed only a short distance and
> then sank into the sand.

The emphasis on *tremendous rocks* is deliberate, for it is a prime clue. While it is a region of rocks, those of impressionably large size are surprisingly rare. Isolated, scattered boulders there are, but a pile of tremendous ones are a most unusual sight in that high desert area.

Mindful that the basic course to the lake was westward, those bearing "farthest to the right" indicates a search to the north. Within a radius of about six miles in that direction there is "East Spring," which supplied the old Indian camp near Junction Ranch. Next in line northward are Pipeline, House and Wall Springs as well as Tennessee Spring. But these are all up on the slope of the Argus Range and in the open rather than in canyons or deep washes. And none are noteworthy for big rocks in the surrounding expanse of weathered talus.

To the west there are no contending springs, as Manly and Rogers found as they turned west after abandoning the Jayhawker trail at the lake, not knowing the latter had found water to the north.

This leaves a north to northwesterly arc as the target area. But for those who have not been in this restricted access area it might be well to picture its peculiarities.

Etcharren Valley, enclosing Carricart Lake, is an elongated ampitheatre about 8 miles wide and about 12 miles long. Some ten miles to the north it gradually rises to hide its continuance as the far reaching extension of Darwin Wash leading to the old town of Darwin. Along its western side, a volcanic malpai forms an almost continuous

North in Etcharren Valley, about six miles from Carricart Dry Lake,
through a gap in the malpai to Providence Springs.

Providence Springs, about six miles from the "alkali lake."
"a pile of tremendous rocks . . . a little stream of good water which flowed
only a short distance and then sank into the sand."—Manly

Leaving Providence Springs "we reached the summit and camped in a valley. This being at quite a high elevation . . . we had a good view of the country."
— Manly, with the Bennetts-Arcans

Today the water of Providence Springs is intermittently used by cattlemen

The terrain north of Providence Springs toward Coso, the route used by Coker

low ridge. Here and there it is split by ancient cleavages that afford passage into a long narrow flat towards Cole's Flat, Coso and Darwin —an area, to those who have wandered it, that is notable for the geological occurrences of great granitic rocks.

From Carricart the first and most inviting malpai opening is about three miles from the lake, leading over a rise to drop into a deep wash about another two miles or so away. Here, unnamed and unknown today, save for its still flowing use as a corralled water supply for cattle, lies a spring—in a small stream bed, at the base of not just a great pile of rocks but of great rocks. Along the base charred remains of old campfires may be seen. While inconceivable these were of the '49ers, and likely that of latter day miners and cattlemen, it is a singularly rare campsite to which men have been drawn over many years.

Here is not only *a* spring, but *the* spring in that locale. Approximately six miles from Carricart Lake, at the base of tremendous rocks, and with sloping exits both to the north and west to fit the Jayhawker and diverging Coker routes that followed.

That Coker (aka Croker) was with them is undeniable yet confusing. Although related as told to Manly, Coker's references to Isham are first-hand testimony:

> It was at this camp (either the lake, springs or a stop between) that Mr. Isham died. The night before our departure he came wandering into camp and presented an awful appearance, simply a living skeleton of a once grand and powerful man. He must have suffered untold agony as he struggled on to overtake the party, starving and alone, with the knowledge two of his companions had perished of starvation in that unknown wilderness of rocks and alkalai.

The confusion lies in two preceding paragraphs. In one, seemingly unrelated at first, he ties in the colored man named Smith who was originally with Nusbaumer but joined the Jayhawkers at Papoose Dry Lake:

> One other of the party was a colored man who joined us at the camp where we left the families, he being the only remaining member of a small party who had followed our wagon tracks after we had tried to proceed south. This party was made up of a Mr. Culverwell . . . a man named Fish . . . and another man whose name I never knew. He, poor fellow, arrived at our camp in a starving condition and died be-

fore our departure. The other two unfortunate ones died on the desert and the colored man reported he simply covered their remains with their blankets.

The "poor fellow" was probably his similarly described Isham. One of the "other two unfortunates" could be Fisch. Which leaves the third known death that of Culverwell—and Smith definitely was not at that Long Camp incident.[16]

Adding to the confusion is Coker's reference to the camp where they left the families. And he compounds this by adding:

> I well remember that last night in camp before we started with our knapsacks and left the families; for it was plain the women and children must go very slowly and we felt we could go over rougher and shorter roads on foot and get through sooner by going straight across the Sierra Nevada Mountains. It was at this camp that Mr. Isham died . . .

Since there was only one family at the lake-Providence Springs camps, and the locale of the Fisch and Isham deaths, the association of the camp where they left the families is unquestionably an error of recollection or a garbling in its retelling by Manly, who admitted he was relating it "somewhat as follows."

However flawed, Coker was at the Providence Springs camp for his account of Isham's death is too first-hand to be hearsay. Apparently after leaving the families at Papoose, and the Briers nearing the Amargosa, he again merged with the Jayhawkers in leaving Death Valley.

But at Providence Springs he was to again leave them, for he tells of reaching Owens Lake, crossing Walker Pass and reaching an Indian village in "Tulare Valley . . . a few miles south of where Porterville now stands." Continuing to the San Joaquin River, just north of Fresno, and Mariposa to arrive at a camp of Mexicans, he intriguingly adds:

> I can well believe that a company of 21 starving men was the cause of some disquietude to them. . . It is strange that I have never met a single man of that party of 21 since then.

---

[16] While Nusbaumer noted hearing that Smith was "killed by Piutes" he does not say when or where. In any event, it was not an incident noted by others.

In his *Mexican Gold Trail—Journal of a Forty-niner,* George Evans tells that near the Mariposa mines a party of 12 men arrived, January 29, who had been with the Death Valley group. And that they had reached Owens Lake, where they were directed to Walker Pass by Indians. And on February 10 records another 10 of that same contingent arrived. A total of 22 is no small coincidence with Coker's tally of 21.

Admittedly there is an almost irresistible temptation to play a "numbers game" although the constant shiftings, conflicting accounts and shadowy unnamed persons preclude any accurate count. Still it is of helpful guidance to picture how many were at Providence Springs and what happened to them.

The best head count that can be determined is that 69 left Death Valley with the Jayhawkers.[17]

Jayhawkers	30
Young's group	9
Isham, Fisch, Smith (from Nusbaumer's party)	3
Bennett-Arcane teamsters (Abbott, Helmer, and possibly Atchison brothers) and the Wade teamster called "Charles"	5
Briers	7
Mississippians-Georgians	15
	69

But not all reached Providence Springs. Fisch and Isham perished approaching it, and 12 Georgians-Mississippians had left, in two groups of six each, in Panamint Valley. Which leaves 55. Eight apparently left Providence Springs with Coker. Since he tells of "21 starving men" reaching Mariposa, he probably met the 12 Georgians-Mississippians nearing Owens Lake. Coker's 9 from 55 leaves 46. According to Brier Jr., 42 reached the San Fernando Valley after two losses enroute: a Robinson who died nearing Bouquet Canyon and "a Frenchman" who "wandered off." The discrepancy of two can be attributed to a number of things, including Brier Jr.'s possible miscounting, the uncertainties of who and how many went where, and

---

[17] This does not include the Long Camp contingents nor the Savage-Pinney party of 11 who remain too nebulous to be accounted for.

the possible exclusion of Manly and Rogers who were not only a unit unto themselves but angrily discredited by the Briers.[18]

For those patiently wading through this head-count there is an informative bonus. An explanation of why and how Coker reached Owens Lake to the northwest while the others continued west and southwest.

At Providence Springs the '49ers were in a high desert north-south trending valley cradled between the Argus and Coso/Inyo ranges. From this elevation the Sierra were enticingly in view. Unwittingly perhaps, those angling northwesterly toward that sight, probably took the better route.

Traveling northerly across broad Cole's Flat and the site of the Coso mines of a dozen or so years later, they wended their way along the old supply, stage and army exploration route into lower Centennial Flat, its easy going terrain beckoning to its terminus at Owens Lake.

But in the meantime, the Jayhawkers clung to their almost obsessively westward goal.

Colton simply says, "Crossing the Inyo mountains we struck Walker's trail." Since they did not take Walker Pass he is referring to the main trail along the Sierra base, which others called "Fremont's trail."

A little more helpful is Rev. Brier in his January 20, 1898, letter to Richards, recalling that they left Providence Springs up a small canyon and that when they reached a summit found a small valley— "the most fertile we had seen for a long time." From here they could see a plain that seemed 30 miles wide and guessed it to be at least 50 miles to the base of the great snow mountains ahead of them.

Once again we can turn to Young's rather reliable "log" and corroboration by Haynes:

---

[18]Picking up a final loose end, not of Coker's but from Young's entry of Jan. 14: "Six men came up to camp this evening from 4 wagons that were behind." Who were these six?

They could have simply been the result of a reshuffling of the Providence Springs parties. More likely, mindful of the coincidental 4 wagons at the Long Camp that Manly and Rogers found upon their return, these late arrivals were the Bennett-Arcan teamsters and Wade's driver "Charles." The sixth may have been an unnoted teamster or a straggler picked up along the way. With the teamsters leaving the Long Camp early on the 11th, hastening to overtake the Jayhawkers, a four day forced march, with little time lost along the now marked trail, could reasonably see them at Providence Springs late on the 14th.

	Young	Haynes
Jan. 15	In camp	In camp
Jan. 16	12 *west* . . . crossed in a deep canyon . . . had a dry camp near the top. In sight of Sierra Nevada. They look very lofty.	W 16
Jan. 17	10 SW into a valley of salt and alkali.	S 8
Jan. 18	10 SW. Left Old Brin (ox).	SW 12
Jan. 19	16 SW. Camped at a spring. Now near pass on elevated ground.	18 S of W
Jan. 20	16 . . . struck a large trail	S 15

Contributing to these clues is Stephens:

> From Providence Springs we crossed the range of mountains and going down the other side, one of the best oxen went over the cliff and broke his back. We had to stop and make him into jerky.[19] It seemed only a short distance across to the snow mountains that loomed up in sight but the remainder of that day and the next went by before we came to water, which has since been known as Indian Wells, owing to the water being in holes or wells.

Not to be forgotten is Manly. He wasn't with the Jayhawkers at that time, but he and Rogers overtook some of them at Indian Wells. In sharing experiences they told him about Providence Springs, which he and Rogers had missed by continuing west from the lake. On their return to the Long Camp they were to follow the Jayhawker recommended route, and also did so in bringing the Bennetts-Arcans out.

Leaving the details to be expanded upon later in covering the three Manly-Rogers treks, Manly tells of leaving Providence Springs on his final trek:

> . . . following the trail made by the Jayhawkers . . . by night reached the summit . . . a short distance down the *western* slope we camped

---
[19] Probably Young's "Old Brin," left or lost by the accident.

in a valley ... this being at quite a high elevation we could see the foot as well as the top of the great snow mountain and we had a general good view of the country ...

However pieced the fragments, the "Jayhawker route" from Providence Springs to a large trail paralleling the Sierra was *to the west*. Also, that it took two days, with an intervening camp in a high valley, to reach the base of the mountains they were crossing. And that there was to be another 30 miles or so until they reached the main trail.

Leaving the last word to Brier Jr., he tells of leaving Providence Springs by a trail "long used by the natives in their plundering expeditions coastward ... (the) well worn trails made going easy...."

It may not have been "easy" but it was likely very well used for centuries by Indians as evidenced by ancient petroglyphs that line it. Rather than a plundering route, although horse raiding was certainly not unknown in later years, it was probably a trade route between tribes as well as one for securing piñon nuts and game in the lower Sierra.

SHELDON YOUNG

There has been a general acceptance that Sheldon Young's "Independents" left Death Valley with the Jayhawkers. But in view of the differing descriptions, routes and events to follow, it is a too casual assumption.

Becoming even more pronounced later, the signs of separation start to surface the first week:

	JAYHAWKERS, BRIERS, HAYNES, ETC.	YOUNG
Dec. 30	Snow camp	Lv 3 o'clock. 12 miles
Dec. 31	[Descent into Panamint Valley]	24 miles to top of high mountain ... plenty of snow
Jan. 1	"New Year's Day ... resting at head of Panamint Valley"	In camp, melting snow for cattle
Jan. 2	(Some) Mississippi boys leave	Lv noon. 8 miles. Descend into another valley. *West*.
Jan. 3	South down Panamint Valley	8 *W* to bottom of a valley

		JAYHAWKERS, BRIERS, HAYNES, ETC.	YOUNG
Jan.	4	Mesquite/Muskrat camp	10 down valley. Water, no grass
Jan.	5	Camp	24 S by *E*. Dry camp. Rained some
Jan.	6	Town, John Martin, two Turners, Masterson and Crumpton leave	4 *E*. Wood and grass. Signs of Indian horses.

Camped well north near Midway Well, Young's group had a different view of the Panamint passes possibilities. There was no need to round or climb any mountain such as the others faced at McLean Spring. Nor a need to tackle the long arduous alluvial fan of Emigrant Wash. Ahead of them was a flat direct route to a canyon opening through which the setting sun beckoned toward water-promising highlands. And they were along an old water-to-water Indian trail between the Funerals and Marble Canyon.

Although they left in mid-afternoon on the 30th, the flat haul was easy enough to reach the canyon by nightfall.

By the time Young reached Providence Springs he is to log 134 miles from Death Valley. Rev. Brier, who returned over part of the route as a guide to some miners, per his January 17, 1876, letter to Mecum, says it was 70 miles from that spring *to* Death Valley (apparently to a point near the Emigrant Ranger Station), which is acceptably in keeping with modern mapping. Allowing another 20 to the Midway Well area comes to 90, about 40 less than Young. Along with this difference, Young logs westerly bearings, then southeast and east, then back to west and southwest. Seemingly the "independents" wandered back and forth like the Israelites in their wilderness of old.

Whether one follows Young by map plotting, or by foot for an even better perspective, let us pick him up after the 12 mile crossing from the vicinity of Midway Well.

On December 31, now unencumbered by wagons, they made 24 miles to the top of a high mountain near the Lost Burro Mine in the Cottonwood Mountains, extension of the Panamints. Why seek such heights? Much for the same reason the Jayhawkers headed for their "snow camp"—snow to be melted as a substitute for springs which they did not or could not see.

The entrance to Marble Canyon from Death Valley. Young's route from Midway Well.

The "Racetrack Valley." Young, Jan. 2

Lee Flat south across Highway 190 into Darwin Wash. Young, Jan. 10, elected this high-desert route to Providence Springs

Moreover there is an important clue for their route—a pecked-out "1849" inscription on a cliff wall in Marble Canyon, just beyond a forking into Cottonwood Canyon. Almost lost among ancient petroglyphs, typical of Indian water trails, it was probably inscribed during a rest stop as they ascended the canyon.

Remaining encamped for another day, melting snow for man and beast, they left at noon on January 2, traveling 8 miles *west to another valley*—Racetrack Valley.

The next day they went another 8 miles west to the bottom of *a* valley. This, too, was still another valley or he would have said "the valley" or "this valley"—i.e., the same one they had been in.

Instead, crossing north of Ubehebe Peak (not the crater of that name), they undoubtedly followed the grade which once provided the old rough road from the Lippincott Mine into Saline Valley.

Now he/they continued down the slopes into Saline Valley and on for another 10 miles. They found some water but it was obviously poor for he notes their cattle were failing and three had to be left behind. Typical of such valleys, seeps are found near the perimeters.

That they had made a poor choice is evidenced by his next entry, on January 5, swinging 24 miles south by east. In doing so they would have a choice of Grapevine Canyon or more traversable Lucas Canyon.

On the 6th they went only 4 miles east, found wood, grass and recent signs of Indian horses. "Wood" indicates higher elevations, and nearby Hunter Mountain was a landmark on what was later to be familiar as a main route from Owens Valley into Death Valley by cattlemen and explorers, such as Lt. Wheeler, following Indian trails.

On the 7th they were "in a narrow valley," or what is known as Lee Flat. They continued 8 miles southeast on the 8th, camping at a spring with good grass. That spring is too elusive to pin down, but there are intermittent springs throughout this area.

His entry of the 9th has particular significance, for he notes: "Part of our company shouldering their packs."

They were now at a point where they could look into Panamint Valley, after their circuituous wandering. And soon after this three of the "independents" become linked with the Brier-Jayhawker accounts: Carter, who was with Young at the Amargosa per his entry on December 18; Harry Vance and Gould. All three were to be among the stragglers the Briers found at sunset after crossing Panamint Valley from Post Office Springs.

Assuredly it is not within the realm of fantasy that these three, disagreeing with Young's meanderings, now decided to head to where the Jayhawkers had gone. It may even be that they spotted them or their campfires far to the south. Or in again seeing Panamint Valley felt they had been given a second chance to take the route the others had taken. In any event, shouldering their packs on the 9th they would have easily reached that point where the Briers met them at sunset on the 11th.

That Young did not follow his dissidents is apparent by his 4 miles *southwest* to camp on a divide. Changing from southeast to southwest was occasioned by the chasm of Rainbow Canyon. Here, at present highway #190, they saw another choice before them—a long, large valley extending into the distance.

Crossing the divide or summit, they found standing water at the foot. While this has been taken to be the more familiar locale and sight after crossing the Slate-Argus pass into Trona, it is typical of other such settings as well.

Noteworthy is Young's observation that "in this valley is a lake." Yet he continued 14 miles to a dry camp and another 12 before reaching that lake. The 26 miles from such a summit crossing cannot be reconciled with a Slate-Argus passage with less than half of that mileage to Searles Lake.

Rather, the valley (Darwin Wash) that Young followed, higher but parallel to Panamint Valley, passes east of Darwin, past Cole's Flat on to Etcharren Valley and Carricart Dry Lake. That they were able to sight a lake 26 miles away can be attributed to the heights of their crossing, desert clarity and by advance scouting.

The lake, which they reached and dry-camped at on the 12th, is described by Young as "salty" although likely simply in contrast to anticipated good water.

On the next day, the 13th, they switched from southerly to a definite north six miles to a spring—fitting the Brier-Jayhawker directions from lake to Providence Springs.

Any doubt is dispelled by Young's entries that on the 13th, "Two we do not think can be got into camp . . . they were so fatigued." And on the 14th, "went in search of the two men. Found them both dead. Their names were Fish from Indiana and Isham from Michigan. . . ."

Nothing connects Young with traveling with the Jayhawkers and Briers from Sand Springs until now. However one group took the high road, the other the low, they had fatefully rejoined at Providence Springs.

From here on there is nothing to contradict Young's re-alliance with the Jayhawkers.[20] Independence had run its course.

BACK AT THE "LONG CAMP"

With at least some of the scattered Jayhawker contingents at "Indian Wells," near the junction of Sierra highway #14 and #178 to China Lake, January 19-20, it is time to pick up the other players poised in the wings for their starring roles in the Death Valley drama.

As Manly and Rogers departed on the morning of January 15 to seek help, Manly notes they left "11 grown people in all, besides a Mr. Wade, his wife and three children, who did not mingle with our party but usually camped a little distance off. . . ." And tallies them as the Bennetts with 3 children, the Arcans with 1 child, 2 "Earhart" brothers and a grown son, Captain Culverwell, "and some others I cannot recall." Eight named adults out of eleven leaves three as the unnamed.

Just as Manly loses track of time, and understandably so during these most trying days, so is his memory flawed in the names and numbers of those in the Long Camp.

He names Culverwell, but not his close companions Nusbaumer, Hadapp and Schlogel, possibly because as "foreigners" they were relatively unfamiliar to him.

He tallies 3 Ehrhardts, although back at Mt. Misery he says there were four—"two Earhart brothers and son*s*."[1]

---

[20] On the 18th Young notes losing an ox. Stephens, in a Mar. 16, 1884, letter to Colton, tells of Young "jumping an ox from rock to rock," and that it fell and broke its back. However hazy it does indicate their rejoining.

[1] The Jacob Stover narrative names four: Henry, Jacob, John and Abe. Stover also notes hearing that John died in Death Valley. Although Culverwell was the only known such death, it has been said that John may have perished in the exit south, but it is unsubstantiated. The

Manly also exhibits a bachelor-like uncertainty about children. In one place he says "Arcane followed with his children," and three pages later, "Arcane also took his *child*." He also refers to the Wades with three children, although there were four: Harry, Charles, Richard and Almira.

But to err is human. One is grateful that Manly recalled as much and as well as he did.

As best as can be accounted for, there were 17 to 19 adults and 8 children comprising the "Long Camp":

	Adults	Children
Bennetts	2	3
Arcans	2	1
Ehrhardts	4	
Nusbaumer, Hadapp, Schlogel, Culverwell	4	
Manly and Rogers	2	
Wades	2	4
Schaub	1	
Alsatians?[2]	2 ?	

Only four adults, with four children, were to await Manly's and Rogers' return—the Bennetts and Arcans.

It is unfortunate that there is so little clear-cut information on the departures of the others; yet fortunately much can be pieced together.

1836-82 *Johnson County History* (cited by Theodore Ressler in his *Trails Divided*) lists "Jacob Earhart and family and John and Henry Earhart." Seemingly Abe was the grown son of Jacob and Henry the son of John.

[2] At the Long Camp, the Wade teamster who left earlier to follow the Jayhawkers was replaced by "a frenchman, hired for his board." Nusbaumer is to identify him as "Schaub;" compatible with being an Alsatian from the French-German border provinces of Alsace-Lorraine. Approaching the Long Camp, Nusbaumer had encountered "an Alsatian by the name of Anton Schlogel."

These may well have been the two Alsatians who befriended the Nusbaumer trio at Travertine Springs, yet rather strangely he doesn't mention any Schaub-Schlogel association with that incident. While Nusbaumer tells only of two Alsatians there may have been at least two others re his Feb. 7 entry of departure with six other men.

The Alsatians were probably a splinter group with the Jayhawkers until the Amargosa, then temporarily fell in with Nusbaumer at Travertine. How many is unknown. Indicatively two, possibly four, followed the Long Camp route. Some, other than Schaub and Schlogel, may have followed the Jayhawker trail in Death Valley.

To do so, accept momentarily that Manly and Rogers left January 15 and returned February 9—to be substantiated in later detailing.

Although Manly was not in camp when the others left, his acquired information from those he did find in camp is consistent:

> "Some staid in camp six or eight days and Captain Culverwell had been gone about two weeks." ("Vermont to California") indicating the first departures about January 21-23 and Culverwell's about January 27-28.

> "We had not gone for more than ten days when Captain Culverwell started with some others." ("Vermont to California") dating Culverwell's departure about January 26.

> "Some did stay more than a week after we were gone." (*Death Valley in '49*) approximating January 22 for the first departures.

> "They packed their oxen and left in separate parties, the last some two weeks before . . . Captain Culverwell went with the last party." (*Death Valley in '49*) dating Culverwell's leaving about January 27-28.

But as if to frustrate any easy solution, Culverwell and his companions were to leave twice!

LOUIS NUSBAUMER

Fatefully, Nusbaumer's usual methodicalness gives way to painful physical distractions as he writes:

> Before our departure on the fourteenth I had felt a swelling in my limbs and noticed that my hands were also much swollen, but I did not pay much attention to it as friend Hadapp was having the same trouble.[3] Today, the fourth day, we turned back because we were not able to get through. My feet were swollen to such an extent that I could not put on my socks and had to cut open my shoes to the toes and even then it was only with the greatest difficulty that I was able to walk. My whole body from my chest down was swollen to abnormal proportions. The cause of the disease is incomprehensible to me. Can it be the water, our mode of living or the air? It is doubtful whether I shall survive or succumb.

---

[3] This is a misphrasing. He was still approaching the Long Camp per his entry for that date and when they met Schlogel. He is referring to noticing the symptoms in leaving that camp. Normally his entries are made daily, but undoubtedly due to his physical disabilities, he does not do so again until Feb. 1, undoubtedly completing this section at that time.

I have dieted for two days and the swelling having gone down I feel much better. We reached a camp with a fresh water spring after having lost another ox. Before that on the road we met the wagon of Schaub[4] and Wade who told us that they found a trail to the west— also a lake and hoped to be at the diggings or settlements within six days.

Evidently Nusbaumer was suffering from scurvy.

Like high-grade ore sparkling in a small mound of tailings, there is a wealth of clues as to their aborted exit route.

One, that they were "not able to get through" was due more to increasingly difficult terrain than physical plight. A recuperative halt for a day or so before continuing would have been a more likely alternative to retracing their footsteps.

Two, they turned back on the fourth day. However slowly they were forced to move, it indicates they had gone a fair distance. Had they been wending their way southeasterly along the flat, sandy Amargosa river bed as it hooks into Death Valley it is difficult to picture abandoning it after so much effort.

Three, they had returned, not necessarily all the way to the Long Camp, but perhaps to Mesquite Spring in Anvil Canyon or Warm Springs in Warm Springs Canyon, both near the area where Manly and Rogers were to find the body of Culverwell.

Four, they had met Wade and Schaub with a wagon, bearing out the report that the Wades did manage to bring theirs out.

Five, the Wades had found a trail to the *west,* including a lake (bed), contrary to the theorization they had reached the Mojave River via Baker.

Despite the easy terrain in that southeasterly direction, there are equally enticing options. The most obvious of which is Wingate Wash, historically used by explorers, miners and later borax "20-mule-team" wagons. And midway, in Long Valley, there is a large dry lake bed, as well as one at Wingate's Panamint Valley entrance.

There is also an alternate route through a gap in the Owlshead Mountains leading to Lost Lake, another dry lake bed. And still

---

[4] This may have been the "T. Schaub" listed with the German California Mining Company of which Nusbaumer had been a member. However nothing more is known except this possible **tie-in.**

another, rounding the east flank of the Owlsheads to Leach Lake, along the old Randsburg Road through a very long valley once a mining and borax route between Pilot Knob and Saratoga Springs.

Any of these would swing the escapees west-southwest into Pilot Knob Valley and an old route south to the Mojave River near Barstow.

Returning to Death Valley and Nusbaumer's next entries:

> This evening, the first of February, we are awaiting a signal from one of the scouts who went ahead to see if the trail which Wade proposed taking was practicable and if water and grass could be found . . .
>
> Feb. 7, 1850 . . . six men decide to go with us and follow the afore-mentioned trail Wade had taken . . . we again struck out for the west . . .

They had taken three days (Jan. 26, 27, 28) on their first attempt, turning back on the fourth (Jan. 29). Allowing the same length of time to return (Jan. 29, 30, 31) they had reached a spring sometime during the 31st or early on February 1. Recuperating and scouting they remained encamped for a week.

The datings for the aborted try also fit with Manly's, who, on his return with Rogers (Feb. 9), had been told of Culverwell's departure "some two weeks before" (about Jan. 27-28). Since the Culverwell-Nusbaumer contingent did not return all the way to the Long Camp, their second attempt would not be known.

Manly also indicates some may have left as early as January 21 or so, seemingly referring to the Wades. But Nusbaumer reports meeting them sometime during the January 29-31 return. Evidently the Wades had left closer to January 30. Possibly a few days earlier allowing for sandy slow-going miles to the south from the Long Camp. Dismayingly there are now missing pages in his fragile journal. And having written across some double pages we now have fragmented lines that start on one side but are lost on the other. Still there are some tantalizing partial lines. Among them is one about "Calverwell . . . Feb. 8 . . . to my shock heard . . . had not arrived at the camp . . . all efforts to find him were in vain." And there are hints of "Indians" . . . "ice" . . . "kept to the Indian trail uphill" . . . "led to a plateau."

At least we know the renewed effort to escape was on February 7. And a very strong indication that on the 8th, in spreading out to search for water, Culverwell was lost. Returning to the Long Camp

February 9 Manly and Rogers were to find his body along the route
to the wagons. In his "Vermont to California," Manly adds, "He looked to us as if he had been dead but a short time. There was no sign
of swelling or decay in the least." While he attributes this to the
climate it was more a shortness of time. Ironically, a day or less might
have meant the difference between life and death, although Culverwell may have been too far gone for Manly or Rogers to save him.

An interesting related interruption is an article by Mrs. Edward
Burrel in the *San Jose Pioneer,* December 15, 1894, "from the lips of
Almira Wade":

> One evening in one of their dry camps they were overtaken by Mr.
> Colwell (Culverwell) who was almost famished. . . . As they (the
> Wades) could not help him he went on but failing to find water per-
> ished alone on the sands. [6]

Manly had prophetically sensed it would be every man for himself.
Still one cannot help but reflect that the Wades must have had sufficient supplies for that family of six plus Schaub who was "hired for
his board." Seemingly a little could be spared for a famished man
who, in failing to find water, was left to perish all alone.

The Wades also had at least four oxen, which could be used for
food be it as a last resort. Taking a wagon also hints of a need to
transport some carefully hoarded supplies—and all of the Wades did
survive.

Yet things are not easily so black-or-white. In the shadings of grey
there is room for understanding. That the Wades kept to themselves,
as Manly noted, may have been traditional English reticence. It was
also a practical matter of survival. Following in the wake of others
saved scouting and also allowed for small water sources to refill from
the demands of a thirsty throng of people and cattle.

Too, turning away Nusbaumer has its counterpart in similar
stories where there is so little for some that any lessening by another
portion could be fatal to all. With four young children, and unknown
days of travail ahead, one can sympathize with a heart-rending decision that was faced.

---

[6] According to the article, in leaving ". . . the wagon cover was made into pack saddles and
accoutrements and . . . the family started out on foot." The uncertainty of a wagon is dispelled
by Nusbaumer, and in historian L. Burr Belden's fine booklet, *The Wade Story.*

So it was that Captain Culverwell became the only known fatality among the '49ers in Death Valley, on or about February 8.[7]

Turning back to Nusbaumer's February 7th entry that ". . . *six men* decided to go with us on the trail Wade proposed" is puzzling, at least at first.

Out of 14 men at the Long Camp, 4 were Bennett, Arcan, Manly and Rogers. Nusbaumer had already met and left Wade and Schaub. The Nusbaumer-Hadapp-Schlogel-Culverwell unit leaves four.

There were 4 Ehrhardts. But Nusbaumer says six men went with them.

As noted earlier, it is possible that there were two unnamed Alsatians at the Long Camp, lending credence to a total of 19 adults rather than 17. However reasonable the supposition, the answer is unlikely ever to be known.

This much is known, the Ehrhardts were among the six, for in a fragmented entry Nusbaumer writes:

> . . . broke camp in the middle of the night in order to move on to where we could find water and fodder. Thank God, after about 4 miles we reached this, where we remained on the 19th and 20th of February. . . . On the 21st we started late, our oxen having run away, and contrary to the other days when we made twenty or twenty five miles we made only fifteen miles. It is well for us three—Hadapp, Schlogel and myself[8]—that we joined these people for had we been alone we never would have been able to carry our provisions and water.
>
> Hadapp and I intend paying them thirty dollars should we have the good luck to arrive at our destination. I will be grateful all of my life to Jack (Jake) Ehrhardt from Iowa, that he has been so kind and generous to us and I will try to reward him in every way possible.

It also implies the possibility of an Ehrhardt wagon. Certainly the gratitude that they would not otherwise been able to *transport* his trio's provisions and water is a strong inference of a wagon— unless one can picture it being backpacked by men already nearing their last legs, in addition to their supplies.

---

[7] In *Gold Rush: The Journals of J. Goldsborough Bruff* (1849-51) a large annotated map, notes "Death of Culverwell, Feb. 10." Since Bruff, reliable authority though he is, was not among the Death Valley '49ers one can only wonder where he obtained that bit of information and surprisingly close dating.

[8] By this time they had lost Culverwell.

Wingate Wash, possible if not probable route of the Wades and Nusbaumer who reported Wade had found a trail to the west in escaping by way of the southwestern end of Death Valley. The wood bracings to the left mark the "bed" of a later-day mono-rail for transporting mineral deposits out of this remote and desolate area.

Perhaps, like the Wade's, a second wagon survived the trek. Or was abandoned along the way where its ribbed remnants may yet be found bleaching in the desert sun—or more likely, buried in the sand or scavenged by miners and borax men traveling along the old Wingate Wash-Pilot Knob-Granite Wells trail.

Continuing Nusbaumer's account:

> Feb. 22 we reached a river, the first we have seen since leaving the Little Salt Lake. Here we found hoof prints of horses and saw the snowclad mountains of the Sierra Nevada. . . . I believe that most of us have changed not only in body but in mind, no longer wishing for wealth but content to lead a quiet life with our families . . .
>
> Hurrah for California!
>
> At this very moment Ehrhardt returns to announce that not far from us the road has been found that will surely lead us to our destination within a few days.
>
> Thank God the news turned out to be correct. The river proved to be the Mojave, the road Captain Hunt's trail and we reached the Spanish settlements in four days crossing the Sierra.[9]

How the words, "Hurrah for California!" ring out, just three to a line, written extra large and in English as if to emphasize that his Americanization had passed the crucible's test.

It lessens not the joy to observe they had actually been "Californians" since December 24, when they crossed the Nevada border to enter Death Valley.

Apparently in the 16 days it took to reach the Old Spanish Trail at the Mojave River (Feb. 7 to 22) they never caught up with the Wades but followed their trail, for the Burrel article says the Wades reached Rowland Mills, near Los Angeles, about February 10.

Touchingly Nusbaumer writes, of his original party, ". . . of the six of us, Hadapp and myself are all that is left."

Wryly, the loss of desire for wealth was to last only a few months, until Nusbaumer joined the gold rush along the Merced River.

---

[9] Actually the San Gabriel Range.

LONG CAMP WAGON COUNT

Not to be overlooked, for it has a bearing on the unraveling, particularly that of those exiting south and west, is the Long Camp wagon count.

Back in the Amargosa, on the approach to Death Valley, Manly says:

> Our train now consisted of seven wagons. Bennett had two; Arcane two; the Earhart brothers one; Culverwell, Fish and others one; and there was one other, the owners of which I have forgotten.

And on returning to the Long Camp: "We surely left 7 wagons, now we could see only 4."

Of the seven, the one with the owners he could not recall was likely that of the Wades whom Manly tended to slough off at times.

In crossing the Amargosa, the Nusbaumer wagon was lost. On the 9th of January, after crossing Death Valley, Nusbaumer found the remains of a wagon those ahead had burned. But the five remaining are increased to six by Schlogel's on the 14th. Of these, one was undoubtedly that of the Wades, the "first departures" about January 22.

One more may well have been scavenged by the Long Camp party during the weeks of waiting for Manly's and Rogers' return. But since there is no mention or even hint of this, it adds to the probability that the Ehrhardts did leave with a wagon although it may have been abandoned in the two week trek to the Mojave River.

This wagon tally while feasible is not infallible. With all of the uncertainties that abound in this epic one becomes a bit suspicious of pieces falling into place too easily.

Manly recalls leaving 7. There could only have been 6 at most. And was the wagon of unknown ownership at the Amargosa that of the Wades? Could it have been Schlogels? Hardly, for he was seemingly a surprise to all until the 14th. And what happened to his wagon? Very likely the Bennetts-Arcans burned another wagon for fuel during their long stay, either Schlogel's or one of their own, replaced numerically by the former's.

Unless further information than has turned up in over a hundred years casts additional light on the subject, the accounting noted stands —seven wagons to Death Valley, six at the Long Camp, four remaining when Manly returned.

The Manly-Rogers Treks

William Manly and John Rogers have been so identified with the epic story of the Death Valley '49ers that it may well seem anticlimatic to have waited until now to detail their heroic treks. And, although sometimes casually overlooked, there were three. Each of some 250 seemingly endless, hopeless miles.

On the first, to seek help, they knew not where or how far away it might be. On the second, the return, having used 13 days of about 15 allowed for a round trip, and aware it would be close to another 13 days before reaching the Long Camp, few could blame them if they did not return; that either their companions would have perished by then or given up to try some other route out. They were not to know that some had left until they did return, nor until much later that the Wades and possibly Ehrhardts managed to do so with their wagons. In their worst fears they could only return to bury their friends. Or deciding not to wait, the others may have left on another and unknown route with frustrating, hopeless searching of where they might have gone. Just as Nusbaumer had to accept the fatal disappearance of Culverwell, so too might Manly and Rogers have to face harsh reality. In a land where men could be lost to sight in labyrinthian gullies, in sandy wastelands where tracks could be hidden by the next wind, weeks of searching could be unrewarding. And possibly add two more bodies, however well intentioned and heroic.

But return they did, whatever the misgivings. That by the third trek, with the families, the route was familiar lessens not the uncertainties that they would survive, weakened by three months of hardship and deprivation.

The lore and legends of the West are filled, of course, with countless heroes of sung and unsung sagas of dauntless deeds of body and spirit. Further, all is relative, for who is to say that the pioneer who buried loved ones along the trail was less heroic than the mountain man, the "injun" fighter or shotgun rider on a bullion bearing stage?

Yet by an ages-old measure Manly and Rogers earned their niche in the Hall of Valor—that greater love has no man than to be willing to die for others. Moreover, they did so with neither certainty of accomplishment nor assurance of martyrdom.

As the Jayhawkers, Briers, Young and Coker were camped at "Providence Springs" on January 14, the Bennetts-Arcans were turning back from their abortive attempt to penetrate the Panamints. That night, according to Manly, a meeting was held and Bennett spoke:

> ... I propose that we select two of our youngest[10] and strongest men ... and ask them to try to seek a settlement and food[11] and we will go back to the good spring we have just left and wait for their return. It will surely not take them more than ten days ...

That Manly and Rogers were "volunteered" dims not the light of their dedication. Since no one else offered to go, Manly and Rogers were selected and consented.

At this point in his narrative, Manly throws a few frustrating curves. Annoying as it may be to have the results posted before the game starts it is far better that it be done so that the dated chronology with others can be put into perspective.

As noted earlier, a literal reading of Manly's book indicates only ten days in Death Valley, including six in the swing south. Yet he met the Briers at Travertine Springs on Christmas Day and Nusbaumer dates the wagon turn back at Galena Canyon as January 14—a three week span. To the casual Death Valleyite this may be a minor matter. But to the more seriously interested the accounting can reconcile the various and oft conflicting and confusing Long Camp departures.

Admitting that "in our troubles the accuracy of the calendar was among the least of our worries," Manly recalls the sequence of events

---

[10] Since Bennett was about 42, Arcan 36, both with families, and the Ehrhardts old enough to have grown sons, the fickle finger of Fate pointed to Manly (30) and Rogers (age not known but likely similar). Ailing Culverwell (48 or 49) had been left by his "Washington City and California Mining Company" party at Fort Kearney due to illness before he joined the Death Valley '49ers near Salt Lake, and was an obvious non-candidate. Fatefully the others seemed spared by their "foreignness."

[11] One can only muse that they did have oxen and were at a good source of water. Enough so that even Bennett's dog "Cuff" survived to eventually be taken to the goldfields.

better than the calendrical datings on which they fell. Nor is this
to be construed critically, for it is more common than not with most
of us to recall time in terms of experiences rather than the dates.

It is with this in mind that we note (page 176 on Manly's book)
the recollection that it was "one of the very last days of December 1849
or the first of January 1850" when he and Rogers arrived at the San
Francisquito Rancho. This could not be, of course, for it would have
only been a week's span from Travertine Springs.

It also points up that from December 25 to the rancho arrival with
the Bennetts-Arcans on March 7 is 73 days. Yet from the initial Manly-
Rogers departure of January 15 to March 7 at the del Valle ranch is
only 52 days. Obviously more time was spent in Death Valley and/or
on the trail than Manly indicates.

Much in the same manner, in one place Manly says it was "pretty
near February 1st" for their return to the Long Camp; in another, that
it was "the early part of February." The seeming contradiction is
resolved in that it was the first part of the month, not the first day.[12]

Manly's book also indicates 21 days used on the trek to the rancho
and return, yet he tells the Bennetts-Arcans that it took them 26.
Confirming the latter, on the day before their return to the Long
Camp he tells of stopping where they had started "25 days before."
His serialized version, "From Vermont to California," bears out the 26
day figure.

The merit of these calendrical gymnastics is four-fold.

One, it helps to establish the dates of departures within logical
allowances.

Two, it clarifies the individual loggings, including sometimes confusing and conflicting entries as well as gaps.

Three, it dovetails with Nusbaumer's three weeks in Death Valley, from December 25 to the January 15 departure.

Four, it correlates with the datings of the Jayhawkers at Providence Springs, Indian Wells and approach to the San Fernando
Valley.

However disjointedly, the pieces do fit. Perhaps, in view of all of
the problems, surprisingly so.

---

[12] Again, a reminder that Nusbaumer, with Culverwell, left the Long Camp area Feb. 7. Had
Manly and Rogers returned before then they could not have found Culverwell's body.

TREK ONE, TO SAN FERNANDO MISSION

(1st day, Jan. 15) (We) took our course again up the canyon we had descended the night before ... by night we were far up the mountain ... far above us on a slope we could see some bunches of grass and sage brush ... and found some small water holes. But they were so small no water ran from them. Here we stayed all night. It did not seem very far to the snowy peak to the north of us. Just where we were seemed to be the lowest pass, for to the south were higher peaks and the rocks looked as if they were too steep to be got over. . . .

Manly's and Rogers' next day departure after their abortive wagon attempt at crossing, has been questioned so far as allowing sufficient time for preparations, including killing an ox, drying the meat, making moccasins, etc. Yet Manly's statement is specific and the preparations could have been underway until late at night, after the meeting, and for part of the next day. Even a mid-day departure could find them well up near the summit of the Panamints.

Far more controversial is the canyon itself. As noted previously, in a general sense it could be any one of several, with Six Springs Canyon most popularized. Yet that canyon has been weighed and found wanting in a number of ways. For one thing it has several springs, including a prominent mid-way cliff-wall spring—and there is no reason to assume it has materially changed over the years—and hardly to be described as "small water holes." Nor is the canyon's opening the "large, bowl-like" head Manly describes.

It has also been theorized that Manly and Rogers stopped at the free-flowing, hanging-wall spring, and cut south into what has been named "Old Crump Flat." But this is most unfeasible, calling for a steep climb into a region of ridges beyond, whereas straight ahead would be a smoothly graduated slope cresting to the west. Under any circumstance the latter would be the most likely choice by far in the easiest and quickest exit route.

But Manly also notes, dramatically and unmistakably, "It did not seem very far to the snowy peak to the north of us."

What snowy peak among many could it be?

The Sierra Nevada or other remote ranges are ruled out as both too distant and to the west.

Obviously he was referring to the nearby snowclad heights of Telescope Peak, which had been their landmark in Death Valley.

But, strangely enough, Telescope is not visible from Six Springs Canyon due to intervening canyon walls, slopes, ridges and projecting shoulders that block the view. Nor is there such a view from Johnson Canyon. Yet the view was not a figment of Manly's imagination. It was, descriptively, far too impressionable.

To this point their canyon would be the same one used on their return. But from the summit they were now approaching the descent to the west was to prove dismayingly rough. So much so that on their return crossing they elected to "try a new pass . . . for the way we came could not be crossed by a dog let alone our horses (so) we tried a canyon further south." Yet at the summit on that return, "we could see the place where we had found a water hole and camped the first night after we left the wagons," and turned down the same canyon taken on the way out.

Thus their route was a triangular one, with the doubly-used summit-valley canyon as the key. A canyon where progress westward was logical yet where their first night camp could be seen returning via a different canyon to the south.

Whatever the misgivings, for the time being, accept Galena Canyon as the one that fits all criteria.

And more than any other its opening is bowl-like. As Manly says, "a kind of basin inclosed on all sides but the entrance with a wall of high steep rock, possible to ascend on foot but which would apparently bar wagons."

Galena's rock-walled basin now encloses some small talc mines. While there is a steep trail continuance almost due west it is doubtful that oxen, which they were to take on the final trek, could traverse it. Nor would there be a need to, with a better branch swinging southwesterly, leading to a small tableland and another forking. To the south a 4-wheel drive, or very low-gear way continues over a rise to drop down into nearby Warm Springs Canyon. That they should have taken it is a matter of hindsight, for little did they know that it would shortly lead into Warm Springs' fairly easy grade into Butte Valley.

And it is not impossible that they did for it would lead close to the same area they did reach. But descriptively they apparently took the steep westerly fork which he later describes as "a trail . . . more like a stairs than a road in its steep ascent."

Eventually Manly and Rogers broke out into a large flat ("Old Crump Flat") just below Gold Hill. Across the flat lay Arrastre Spring—a series of small water seeps nestled in a shallow ravine on the open slopes leading to the summit.[13]

In all probability they stopped to climb the short way up the slopes of Gold Hill as the handiest observation point for a look at the lay of the land ahead. And from here, as with no other site yet found, the Telescope Peak snowcaps break startlingly into view, clear of all obstructions. Truly it would seem "not far to the snowy peak to the north"!

Ahead, against the western sky, appeared to be the lowest "pass." To the north the range rose to some 10,000 feet. While it was somewhat lower to the south, the ridges were jumbled, jagged, broken and barren.

(2nd day, Jan. 16) In the morning we filled our canteens, which we had made by binding two powder cans together, and started for the summit. From this was the grandest sight we ever beheld.

Looking east we could see the country we had been crawling over since November fourth. . . . To the north was the biggest mountain we ever saw—peaks on peaks towering far above our heads. . . . Southward was nearly a level plain and to the West I thought I could dimly see a range of mountains that held a little snow upon their summits, but on the main range to the south there was none. It seemed to me the dim snowy mountains must be as far as two hundred miles away but of course I could not judge accurately.[14]

[13] Dr. John Wolff's excellent analysis of *The Route of the Manly Party of 1849-50 in Leaving Death Valley for the Coast* advocates Warm Springs to Death Valley as the route. But its verdant springs area at its Indian Ranch and talc mines would scarcely have been missed in the narrow confines. Too in reaching Butte Valley it is questionable that they would have then veered some two miles northwesterly to almost hidden Arrastre Spring, especially with a promising continuance almost directly ahead into Redlands Canyon. Conversely, Manly and Rogers would see Arrastre Spring ahead of them from Gold Hill but Redlands would be out of such sighting.

[14] It may be helpful to clarify that a range can and is likely to have more than one "summit." In a descriptive sense one can crest from a climb to a level area, then ascend again to another crest or summit beyond, somewhat like "landings" in climbing stairs.

"Old Crump Flat" west of Gold Hill

The entrance to Galena Canyon

The trail westward in upper Galena Canyon

Because of its descriptive details and importance in starting the re-trailing on the right footing, this second day is divided into two parts. First, to determine where they were, then as to where they went.

The way up Arrastre Spring ravine is not easy as it looks from a distance but the slopes alongside are switchbacked with well worn Indian and game trails leading to the crest, where old rock-circled campsites are clustered in a grove of piñon pines.

Northwesterly a trail, now a crude road, leads into Pleasant Canyon and Mormon Gulch. Southwesterly a trail forks into Middle Park.

From here the view was, and is, inspiring. Little wonder that Manly so movingly recalled it even after almost half a century. Even more, as no other single passage, it immortalizes the man. For over two months, they had wandered in a sand and saline wilderness. With leadened bodies and deadened souls they had struggled on in sheer instinct for survival. Eyes beheld no beauty, only desolation. They saw no glory, only a sandy grave. And in reaching the summit, with the faintly flickering hope it might be the long sought last barrier, they saw not California's verdant pastures but ridge upon ridge still blocking the way. Yet Manly's spirit soared above the discouragement, the despair, the deprivation, at "the grandest sight we ever beheld."

It was a view they were to see again, with the Bennetts and Arcans. Both times the details are similar however varied. Piecing them together provides the clues as to just where they were.

East (A) Looking east we could see the country we had been crawling over since November fourth. . . .

(B) . . . the range next east of us across the low valley was barren. . . . I believe this range is known as the Coffin's mountains.[15]

(C) . . . the slope to the east was soon met by a high ridge; between this and the main mountain(s) was a gentle slope scattered over with sagebrush and a few little stools of bunch grass.

(A) is self-explanatory. In (B) his description is that of Death Valley and the barren Black Mountains, a view that inspired them to voice, "Good-bye, Death Valley!" In (C) he is describing the more immediate view east—across the slopes from Arrastre Spring to a

---

[15] Coffin Peak, near Dante's View in the Black Mountains, east of Bennetts Well.

Telescope Peak, to the north from Gold Hill
"It did not seem very far to the snowy peak to the north of us."—Manly

Arrastre Spring, almost hidden in the small gully nearing the Panamint summit

low projecting ridge, on the other side of which is "Old Crump Flat"[16] and Gold Hill.

North The view of the snowy peaks that did not seem far to the north was, at the end of their first day, from Gold Hill. On the final trek, to show Bennett and Arcan the same sight, the men walked "three or four hundred yards" from the Arrastre Spring camp to a vantage point with an open view north.

> *West* (A)   . . . I could dimly see a range of mountains that had a little snow upon their summits. . . . It seemed to me (they) must be as far as two hundred miles away but of course I could not judge accurately.
>
> (B)   (See "south and west" below)

The crest of the Sierra appears through the gap of Pleasant Canyon and toward South Park Canyon. While actually only some 60 beeline miles away any distant haze could deceptively add to his guesstimation.

> *South* (A)   Southward was really a level plain.
>
> (B)   West and south it seemed level and low; dark and barren buttes rose from the plain. . . . I pointed out the route we were to follow. . . . This plain with its barren ranges and buttes is now known as the Mojave Desert.

Surprisingly perhaps, the Mojave Desert cannot be seen from this locale because of the intervening high ridges of the Panamints, Slates and Argus ranges. And it should be kept in mind that they were crossing at what appeared to be the lowest permissable pass and were not at the Panamint's highest elevations. Very likely he is "jumping ahead" in pointing out their route based on familiarity recalled from their earlier treks.

But, while not the Mojave, there was a plain to the west and south with dark and barren buttes.

Before them, in crossing the summit, was a large flat plain— actually twin flats, separated by a narrow short band of low hills— comprising the head of Middle Park and South Park canyons.[17] Darkly studded against the light clay flats the small hills bespeak of Manly's "dark and barren buttes."

---

[16] Named after Bennett's ox.

[17] Startlingly, large enough to have a bladed east-west airstrip!

It has been voiced that in crossing from Gold Hilll to the Arrastre Spring summit there could also be a somewhat similar sighting down Butte Valley, notable for its strikingly striped butte to the south. And seen in the morning, shadowed by the rising sun, it would appear simply as a dark butte. But from the north it is obscured by bends in the flanking mountains and a narrowing near its approach. Too, had they followed this route it would have automatically led them into Redlands Canyon, a singular choice dictated by high cliffs.

As it was they had three choices. That via Pleasant Canyon was dismissed as taking them too much to the north. Middle Park, which also trends northwesterly was probably skipped for much the same reason—plus the fact its opening is not easily discerned.

It is also to be noted that both Pleasant and Middle Park empty into the Ballarat-Post Office Spring area which the Briers and Doty had left January 11th after a five day camp. Had Manly and Rogers exited at this point it would be difficult indeed not to conceive of them noting some signs of that prolonged camp less than a week before. As it is they did not encounter any trail signs of others until across Panamint Valley and up the slopes of the opposite Argus Range.

Instead, they continued down the flat or plain, turning into the opening of South Park Canyon. And Manly mused, "to go over all these mountains and return within the limit of 15 days . . . would probably be impossible.[18] Still we must try as best we could, so down the rocky steep we clambered."

> (2nd day, Jan. 16, continued) When we were part way down the mountain a valley or depression opened . . . up which it seemed we could look a hundred miles. Nearby and a short distance north was a lake of water and when we reached the valley we crossed a clear stream of water flowing slowly toward the lake . . . as salt as brine.
>
> We now began an ascent of the next ridge, keeping a westerly course. . . . We crossed the head of a canyon near the summit about dark and here we found a trail which from indications we knew to be that of the Jayhawkers who had evidently been forced to the southward of the course they intended to take. . . . We stayed here all night.

Obviously Manly and Rogers had a long day. So much so that

---

[18] A few pages earlier it was noted as 10 days. In "Vermont to California" it was given as 18, and Rogers recalled it as a 3 weeks allowance. All fell short as they foresaw from the summit.

View southwest from the Panamint summit
Middle Park Canyon and playa at center, South Park at far left

View east and southeast from the Panamint summit
1) Arrastre Spring; 2) Galena Canyon
3) Gold Hill; 4) Death Valley

weight has been given to it being two. Particularly with Manly's later comment on the sixth day that "7 days had already passed", indicating the possibilities of an unnoted overnight halt. However, not only is the missing day better accounted for, but the distance traveled on the 16th is physically practicable. Especially mindful that for the most part it was downhill, however steep and rocky.

Noteworthy is that while still *part way* down they could not only look into Panamint Valley but seemingly for 100 miles (north). But, with one exception, the Panamint canyons openings offer little more than limited head-on views of the valley and those so close to it they could scarcely be recalled as "part way down."

South Park, on the other hand, actually breaks into the open high atop a series of ancient lake terracings. From here there is an unduplicated view of Panamint Valley extending an awesomely long way to the north as well as south.

Too, in the canyon they took they only found one place with a little water.[19] All of the westerly exits from the Panamints are given to steepness. But some, like Surprise, Happy and Pleasant canyons are well watered, as to even include flowing streams. While these may well reflect later developments in expanding springs as well as water flows from shaft sinkings they also indicate good water-table levels. And the happily pleasant surprise of finding water in the parched-appearing Panamints may have inspired their naming. But there are few if any signs of water in South Park Canyon.

Now below them was a barren expanse of sand and saline flats, a twin to Death Valley. Some maps indicate the sink of Panamint Valley as a single lake bed from Indian Ranch to below Redlands Canyon. In a way this can be so, for with good rains this depression could be shallowly covered. For the most part, however, the watery areas appear as separated small "lakes." Near the center of the sink they are separated by the Ballarat crossing, so mapped in that old supply center's early days. Southward there is another crossing nearly opposite South Park Canyon. Never developed as was the Ballarat passage this secondary causeway frequently has been mucky going,

---

[19] Possibly the seep known as Colter Spring.

North up Panamint Valley from South Park's high ledge (Ballarat bluff at right)
"Part way down the mountain . . . a valley up which it seemed
we could look a hundred miles."—Manly

Entrance to Shepherd Canyon
from Panamint Valley.
The Jayhawker trail up
the steep pass to the west

Valley floor at South Park.
Shepherd Canyon is to the west
beyond the low black butte.
"We crossed a salt stream flowing
north toward a lake."—Manly

although in drier spells it affords fair crossing. This may have been so then.

Rather elementary but meriting emphasis, the saline streams flow from the higher outer rims towards the lower centers of the sink. Thus to cross a stream flowing north places Manly and Rogers to the south of the Ballarat crossing.

Also keying their route, and dispelling a Searles crossing, is that they kept a *westerly* course. Had they gone south towards a Slate saddle they would have to skirt the southernmost "lake" for several miles before reaching solid ground. And it is far fetched to picture swerving south when almost directly across a route beckoned in the direction they had clung to so stubbornly for so long.

Keying the latter, late in the day in the winter months the shadowed wall of the Argus Range is cleft by the sunset-etched opening of Shepherd Canyon to the west. And singularly so. Even Water Canyon is lost in the high dark-walled background of its twists and turns.

Admittedly this is conjectural. But Manly's maps are not. Allowing that he wasn't the best of cartographers, that his routings were less definitive than explanatory, and that there are geographical and topographical flaws, credit must be given to their relative accuracy. And they consistently show a definite swing to the north after leaving the Panamints to cross the valley westward.[20]

Whether by intent or circumstance of terrain they were now on an intersecting trajectory with the trail of the Jayhawkers who had headed west from Post Office Spring.

At dusk, proceeding up into the Argus, they found that trail. How he *knew* it was that of the Jayhawkers and not some other contingent was presumably gained in later sharing accounts. At least it was sufficient to show that those who had camped to the north in Death Valley had not found an intended westerly escape route but had instead turned south in Panamint Valley.

In his "Vermont to California" version Manly says they found the Jayhawker trail and followed it until darkness. He identifies it as

---

[20] This also adds to the elimination of Pleasant and Middle Park Canyons which terminate close to the Ballarat crossing almost due west. And an exit from any canyons farther north would call for a mapped swing south, not north.

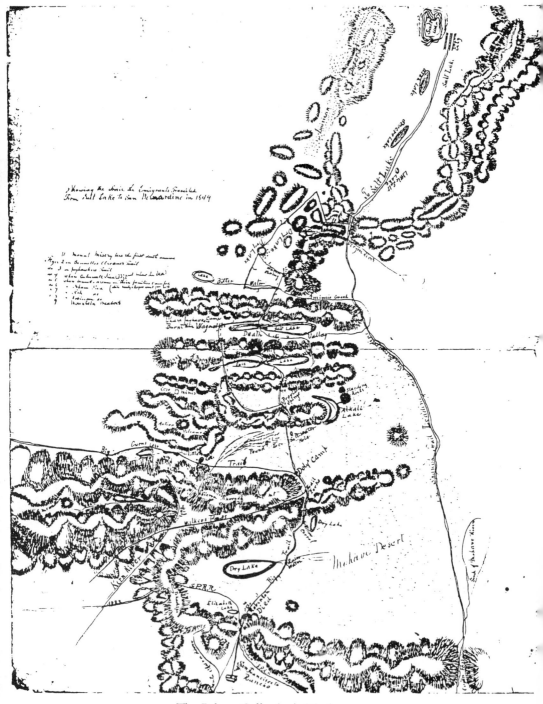

The Palmer Collection's Manly map

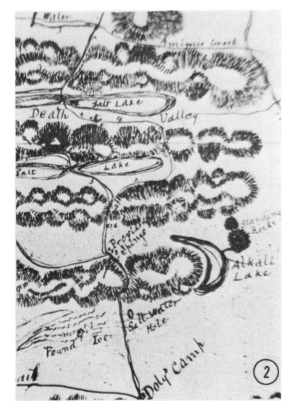

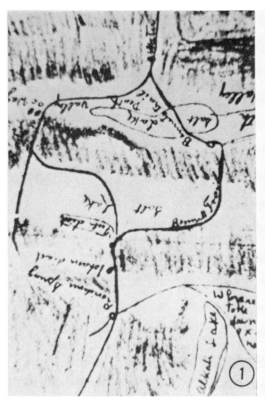

Excerpts from the Manly maps showing the consistency of his swing north in Panamint Valley, and the relationship of Providence Springs and "alkali lake"

1) From the Huntington map
2) From the Palmer map
3) From the Ardis Walker map

the trail of those "I had visited 15 days before and left them burning their wagons." Were this so it would now be January 11 rather than the 16th, having left Doty's camp December 28. And, in a rippling effect, would date the Manly-Rogers departure two days before as January 9, and their return twenty-six days later as February 3—five days before Culverwell's death. It would also add an unaccountable five days to the final trek with the Bennetts and Arcans. And it would date his meeting the Jayhawkers at Indian Wells on the 14th vs. Young's 19th. Since it has been corroboratively established that the Jayhawkers, Briers and Young were at "Providence Springs" the 14th, Manly's "15 days before" reference is viewed as a casual rather than factual recollection.

Now comes a more sticky part, where indulgence is needed to unravel a tangle of times. Because of the conflicting yet helpful nuances of difference between his book and earlier "Vermont to California," they are compared for the next few days.

In his book he indicates that it took one day to complete their climb to the summit, find Fisch's body, reach the lake, cross another summit and descend to the foot of the range, be it with night travel.

Yet on the final trek, with the families, his "Vermont to California" version says that from the point where they reached the body of Fisch, "We still had *two* short drives to, and one dry camp before, we could reach any water"—i.e. Providence Springs. He may have been anticipating the slower pace of oxen, women and children, but it is also an implication of more time-taking terrain and distance on his first trip than recalled in his book. Especially when a few days later he notes that "7 days had passed," although he seemingly accounts for only six. While the 7 may have been in error, and has been suspect as such, the tally of his trek from that day bears out its correctness.

Somewhere in the first seven days, with only six "camps" noted, a day is missing. While it might have taken two instead of one day from Arrastre Spring, across Panamint Valley and a start up the next range, this is downgrade for the most part and the distance feasible. This leaves the next, and a very long "leg" as the most likely gap. Especially since there is little to question on the coverage of the other days that followed.

3rd vs. 4th days (Jan. 17-18)

| *Death Valley in '49* | "Vermont to California" |
| *(3rd day)* | *(3rd day)* |

In the morning we started on and near the summit we came to the dead body of Mr. Fish lying in the hot sun. . . . As we came in sight of the next valley we could see a lake of water some distance south of our western course . . .

We went into a canyon to camp and look for water. When we reached the bed of the canyon we found a trail made by oxen. . . . We followed this trail until near dark . . . *stopped for the night.*

(4th day)

. . . found the body of Mr. Fish with some sagebrush thrown over him. . . . When we got out of the canyon we came to a valley several miles wide to cross before we could reach the next range . . . when we got fairly out into the valley we saw a lake to our left only a mile or two off. . . . We then turned south and went for the lake for we were now very much in want of water for the weather was warm and our road sandy. . . . Before we reached the lake we came to soft mud. . . . We waded on as fast as we could through the mud, but alas when we got to the water, to our disappointment it was a strong alkali, red as wine and slippery to the touch . . . we ascended (a) canyon (and) turned the summit of the mountain before night and could see

. . . having followed the Jayhawker trail this far . . . we decided to take a new route in the hope of finding a little water . . . the valley we now crossed *seemed to come to an end about ten miles to the north of us. To the south it widened out enclosing the lake* . . . we turned off to right angles to our course . . . long before we reached the water of the lake bottom because of a thin slimy mud . . . the water (was) a wine color (and) strongly alkalined . . .

We now turned west again, making for a canyon up which we passed . . . We traveled in it for miles and miles . . . We passed the summit . . . and on our way down the western side we

3rd vs. 4th days (Jan. 17-18)

Death Valley in '49 *(3rd day)*	"Vermont to California" *(4th day)*
came to a flat place where there was an Indian hut made of small brush. . . . The great snowy mountain(s) did not seem far off, but to the south and southwest a level or inclined plain extended for a long distance. . . . Our thirst became something terrible to endure. . . . Soon it became dark. . . . We tried to sleep but could not . . . we noted a bright star two hours above the horizon . . . pretty truly west of us. The moon gave us so much light that we went on . . . reached the foot of the range about sunrise.	a plain of at least 30 miles before us. When we got halfway to the foot of the mountain . . . came to an old Indian camp . . . built a fire . . . as it was moonlight we continued to search for water . . . we worked in this way all night long. . . . As soon as we could see the morning star to the west we started and worked our way along over the rough, rocky road. . . . We got to the foot of the mountain about sunrise.

Although the two accounts are very similar one evidences that the questionably long day was in fact two, supported later in both the return trek and the final exodus.

It also indicates a far greater distance from Panamint Valley to the foot of the next range than across the narrowing southern arm of the Argus from Searles.[21]

There are also several other keys to the locale. For example, referring to his maps, his "alkali lake" is definitely not in Panamint Valley or its Searles Valley extension. It is farther west and to the south of Providence Springs, fitting with the Brier and Young accounts.

That Manly notes the "alkali lake" being enclosed by the valley can be interpreted as Searles, although Searles' southern end is a very broad flat opening. In the case of Carricart the southern end is an unbroken ring of enclosing ridges.

---

[21] From Searles to the western foot of the Argus, via a Wilson Canyon routing, is about 10 miles.

Both could also be viewed as seeming to end about ten miles to the north of their lakes. From Carricart a gradual, imperceptible slope to the north crests close to ten miles away. Not that its enclosing Etcharren Valley ends there; it only seems to, with the slope simply cutting off a view of its continuance.

From the lake, Manly and Rogers unfortunately broke away from the trail of the Jayhawkers who did find their Providence Springs about 6 miles to the north. Instead, on the 4th day they headed up and through the beckoning canyon leading into what is now named "Wildhorse Mesa." A dry, barren "flat" it nevertheless has long been a habitat for Indian tribes as evidenced by its famous petroglyphs that mark an ancient route and rendezvous.

At this point, with blurring and blending valleys and summits keying their trail, it might be well to interject a short topographical note that their climb from Panamint Valley had taken them to about 6,000 feet. Descending the west slope to Carricart Valley they dipped to about 5,400 at the lake. In continuing west they faced another summit to climb back to 6,000 or so before descending into 5,200-foot Wildhorse Mesa.

In both accounts Manly tells of seeing a great level plain to the south well before their descent. Now, not before, they were seeing from the mesa an impressive view of the Mojave Desert, although this time he does not name it.

In his "Palmer Collection" map Manly shows "standing rocks" near his alkali lake. This has been taken to mean the lunar-like pillars southwesterly from Searles, likely because of their familiarity to those traveling the Trona-Ridgecrest highway. But even had they gone to the northern edge of Searles before continuing west (Manly and Rogers) or north (the Jayhawkers and Briers) the pillars could not be sighted in the distance and around the end of the Argus mountains.

But there are two optional explanations. One is that just beyond the southern edge of Carricart Dry Lake is a low malpai or volcanic ridge that once provided rough shelter for the Indians as evidenced by its petroglyphs.

The other, far fetched in its disagreement with Manly's mapping, is that the lake was actually China Lake where there is a large peaking of rocks sometimes used for rocket launchings. However this is completely at odds with all of the accounts.

A bit belatedly perhaps, but tied into the determination of one or two days travel from Panamint Valley is that they found Fisch's body lying in the hot sun. This was well up the range, following the Jayhawker's trail. Not being late risers, the '49ers were invariably up and on their way by dawn's early light. And in winter at this elevation it is close to noon before a "hot sun." Thus from Fisch's body to the lake was a greater distance than indicated, and in keeping with the Brier accounts of taking from 3 p.m. to late evening from sighting the lake.

After traveling all or most of the night to descend the range about sunrise, we now pick up Manly on that day:

> (5th day, Jan. 19) There was here a wide wash . . . down which water had sometime run after a big storm . . . we turned up the wash although its course was nearly to the north. . . . Rogers found a little ice . . .[22]
>
> We took our course west again . . . on and on we walked. . . . As the sun got further down we could see a small smoke curling up near the base of the mountain(s) . . . we set off towards it in the dusk and darkness . . . we found here, to our surprise, Ed Doty, Tom Shannon, L. D. Stephens and others . . . (some) having gone on ahead. . . . They said Mr. Brier and his family were still behind.
>
> . . . (we) related how our train could not go over the mountains with wagons, how they had returned to the best spring. They (Jayhawkers) were willing to give us any information we desired for our return (over) the best possible route. . . . They told us about the deaths of Mr. Fish and Isham and where we could find their bodies. . . .[23]

Tucked in the above, its significance almost lost in casual reading, is the pregnant phrase, "we turned up the wash although *its course was nearly to the north.*" It not only helps to key their locale but to set a Searles-Wilson Canyon theory at rest. Along that arm of the Argus the slope run-offs, as washes and gullies, inexorably flow west into the lowest part of the Coso Basin. Where the range hooks westerly past its Renegade Canyon entrance there are some north-south washes, but they are short, soon dead-ending into the abruptly rising

---

[22] In "Vermont to California" he says it was "perhaps a mile."

[23] While Manly and Rogers had found Fisch's body they did not know of Isham's death, having turned away from the trail to Providence Springs, indicating it occurred between the lake and that spring.

cliffs. But there is a natural descent down the terraces between Big Petroglyph and Little Petroglyph canyons. Here the washes extend northerly toward Coso Hot Springs.

Returning to their westerly course (actually southwesterly) they cut across the large, flat Coso Basin toward Indian Wells. In "Vermont to California" he adds that they took a bluff as their guide—the long, lava-flow bluff that parallels highway #6/395 along this area.

While the going was flat it was sandy and long. They had found the ice before the sun could melt it yet took until dark to reach what proved to be the Jayhawker camp.

Helping to substantiate the dating are Sheldon Young's entries:

Jan. 19 Went 16 miles SW. Camped at a spring. Grass, water, no wood . . . we are now near the pass on elevated ground.
Jan. 20 This day went 16 miles and struck a large trail (i.e. Walker Pass) . . . no grass.

While some of the Jayhawker contingents had forged ahead, others, like the Briers, lagged behind in a separation of more than trail and time. This is particularly observed in Manly's "Vermont to California" details of the Indian Wells meeting:

I asked if the Bennetts and Arcanes teamsters had been seen and they said, "Yes, they were ahead with others."
"Where is Brier?"
"He is behind perhaps a day or two. His wife has all the camp work to do as well as pack the oxen for he claims he is unwell." Tom Shannon said he was lazy. They did not seem to have much sympathy for him.

The seeds of discord nurtured by Shannon's comment and Manly's repetition of it in print were to eventually culminate in Rev. Brier's bitter renouncing of any connection with the Jayhawkers and a scathing denounciation of Shannon as ". . . that blackguard . . . he's paid me in full for my little unselfish act of kindness. This Tom of the Jayhawkers has paid me in vile slander, unmitigated falsehoods." And he lashed out at Manly with, ". . . this Manly's book, so called . . . and who is Louis Manly? He was one of Bennett's ox drivers. I did not know him, but I recalled that he and John Rogers passed us on the desert and that they filled themselves with my jerk(y)."

It is possible, however remotely so, that Manly and Rogers met and passed the lagging Briers on the way to Indian Wells. Yet Manly does not mention it, nor Rogers. Could it have been elsewhere, at another time, on the desert? Unlikely, for in singling out Manly and Rogers this is the only area where that encounter could have been. It is also far fetched to picture the two feasting on the Brier family's fare. The plight of Manly and Rogers was not that of hunger but of thirst. Both had a supply of dried meat from the Long Camp which was to last until they reached the San Fernando Valley.

Brier felt hurt, and angry reactions are often distorted and to be regretted. In the mores of the time, when women were to be helped rather than helping in physical tasks, the Jayhawkers may have judged too harshly and have been less than impartial. The truth may be somewhat between.[24]

> (6th day, Jan. 20) The next morning we shouldered our packs again
> ... by night we had overtaken the advance party of the Jayhawkers
> camped in a canyon where there was a little water. . . . Before us was
> a level plain . . . so broad as to take 5 or 6 days to cross. . . .

---

[24] Brier's reputation among the others may have been due less to laziness than too many oxen. In addition to their own they had been given "a score" by "Town" in Death Valley. Although Brier tells of reaching Los Angeles with "just 2 bits in pocket," Brier Jr. says his father "obtained a half interest in a hotel by disposing of 7 choice oxen out of a score." A score being 20, the Briers seemed to have struggled with a fair size herd, although it is not known how many survived the trek. In a letter to Richards, Rev. Brier says he sold Captain Doty 7 oxen for $115; apparently on a promissory note which he in turn sold to a "Dr. Earl"; probably shortly after arrival in time to buy into the hotel with Lewis Granger who had stayed with Hunt. The hotel "included a bakery, barber shop and blacksmith shop," with the elder Brier also "in charge of a fine old vineyard." This relative affluence among the impoverished '49ers was undoubtedly envied and rankled.

That Manly does not mention meeting the Briers enroute could not have been an intention of censorship or retaliation since both his "Vermont to California" and the book appeared long before Brier's scorching Jan. 20, 1898, letter asking that "our name no longer appear in the list of Jayhawkers."

Manly was, of course, far more than a mere ox driver. So far as the back of the hand crack at Manly's "so called book," the Briers were much given to writing themselves. Although most of their letters and articles appeared after Manly's book, a Jan. 25, 1884, letter to the Jayhawkers alludes to:

> My son has just finished the history of our suffering and it is ready for the press.
> I hope by next spring to publish the first edition.

Thus he may have been enviously miffed that Manly succeeded, on his own, in what he and the son did not.

Ironically, Brier was to hire Manly to work at the hotel for $50 a month. But about two weeks later Manly left with an opportunity to help drive some horses north and with half a month's pay as grubstake.

"Taking a bee line for a bluff," Manly and Rogers cross Airport Lake (China Lake) playa, crossing or rounding the volcanic bluff to the Jayhawker camp at Indian Wells

The distinctive grove of willows at Cantil
"We came to quite tall willows."—Manly

In following after those ahead, Manly notes passing a trail to the west over the mountains, which would be Walker Pass, but spurned as apt to lead into impassable snow.

Instead, they continued into the Red Rock Canyon area. Here several small canyons or large washes fan south. Manly notes theirs became very narrow, which has cast doubt upon Red Rock Canyon itself. But while its present width accommodates a modern highway it was not always so. There are still those who recall its pre-bulldozed days when its narrower passage was often clogged by debris and boulders cascaded down by heavy rains. Whether the '49ers took this or one of the side washes, such as Last Chance or Goler[25] matters little. The differences are slight, the entrances are close together and the exits all open to the same vista—a seemingly endless expanse of the Mojave Desert.

> (7th day, Jan. 21) In the morning . . . in a few more miles we reached the open level plain . . . (in) three or four miles, not far from the hills, we came to a bunch of quite tall willows. The center of the bunch had been cut out and the branches woven in so as to make a sort of corral. In the center of this was a spring of good water . . . took the trail again. . . . After walking all day we came to quite an elevation where we could stand and look in all directions.

A few miles from their starting into the plain would bring them to Cantil, now a rather startling stretch of high water table and irrigated greenness and where stands of willows are studded with old stumps whose datings were ended by axes of yesteryear.

In his following expansive detailing of the views, two are particularly helpful.

To the south were some snowcaps, including "probably what is known as Wilson's Peak." While his seeming naming of Mt. Wilson was likely one of identification by later association, there is little question of viewing the Big Pines area of the San Gabriel Range and distant San Bernardino Mountains.

To the north "was the same place now crossed by the Southern Pacific Railroad and known as the Tehachapi Pass, the noted loop in which the railroad crosses itself." While his memory erred in direc-

---

[25] Not the similarly named in the Panamints. This one is linked with a turn of the century miner who prospected the El Pasos and reportedly found gold in the Last Chance washes.

tion, the pass being more to the southwest from Cantil, he is speaking generally and unmistakably identifies the locale.

Despite a literal reading of his book indicating this was their 6th day, he now notes ". . . seven days had already passed." As deductively corrected, on the third day (and fourth) day, he had lost track of a day.

He now adds a small but puzzling note:

> . . . we went on . . . near our road stood a tree of a kind we had not seen before. The trunk was about six or eight inches through and six or eight feet high with arms at the top quite as large as the body, and at the end of the arms a bunch of long stiff bayonet shaped leaves.

On the next day he is to add that the old and deleafed stalks looked so much like overgrown cabbage stumps that they named them "cabbage trees."

Descriptively they would seem to be Joshuas. But it would have been impossible not to have seen them before this for they blanket major segments of the route and are as common in Nevada and California deserts as shells on the seashore.

In "Vermont to California" he de-arms the trees:

> . . . we came to a tree about six inches through and perhaps ten feet high. The leaves were a foot long and all dead except some at the top. This kind of tree we had never seen before.

Manly's strange trees are of more than idle interest, with thoughts that the '49er route might be keyed by a lack of certain species or encountering others linked with certain locales.

But there are many types of Yucca or Joshuas; some with "arms," some without, and Manly's inconsistency doesn't help. Possibly, if not probably, it was that common denizen of the Mojave Desert, *Yucca schidigera (Y. mohavensis)* which does occasionally "branch," is 12-15 feet high and has leaves a foot and longer. It also dries from the bottom, creating a green "crown." Or it may have been one of the "Spanish bayonet" family known as the "Candle of the Lord." Although armless, its clumped base and stalked center cane are reminiscent of a "cabbage tree." So, too, with the Agave or Century Plant, with its broad-leafed, cabbage-like base.

(8th day, Jan. 22) Starting on our course again . . . losing our trail
. . . about noon . . . neither of us had found (the trail) and we were
still about ten miles from the foothills . . . we pushed on . . . in the
rolling hills . . . about sundown we reached some water holes and
some old skulls of oxen . . . the night was quite cool. . . .

The trail they were following was not that of the Jayhawkers, who
were now behind. They were on the old main trail skirting the base
of the Sierra.

At first blush it might seem the distance traveled on the 7th and
8th days—about 40 miles from Red Rock Canyon to near Lancaster—
presents the possibility of another missing camp. Yet neither the book
nor "Vermont to California" even hint of an intervening camp. And
they did put in long, dawn to dusk days and were traveling over easily
traversable terrain.

The hills ahead presented a choice. Rogers had heard the pass
might be through the high mountains to the south. But deciding it
could also take them too far off their course, they opted to "try the
lowest place in the mountain first; if we failed we could then go and
try Rogers' route more to the south."

So it was they headed toward the hills forming the southwestern
flank of Antelope Valley.

While there are a number of routes penetrating this area, and innumerable cross-country variations, Bouquet Canyon survives the pro-
cesses of elimination as the prime probability. For example, Mint
Canyon to the south would necessitate a difficult steep crossing and
its entrance near Vincent, south of Palmdale, is more to be guessed at
from their direction. And San Francisquito Canyon, to the north of
Bouquet, as will be borne out later, was used for the return trip over
a definitely different route.

Leaving the events that follow to substantiate its selection, may
the plotting to this point suffice to allow temporary acceptance, to be
supported by the day-to-day detailing.

In the absence of more specific landmarks, their camp on the night
of the 22nd is placed near the present Leonis School and an ironically
named "Amargosa Creek."

Whose trail they were now following is hard to say. It may have been that of Indians or game. Or, in view of the ox bones, one used in the early Spanish settlement, or even of early emigrants veering from a southern overland route. Whatever the conjecture the trail was not an easy or well worn one.

> (9th day, Jan. 23) In the morning the trail led us to (into) the snow . . . we turned down the western slope . . . down (a) ravine many miles . . . this came out into a larger one . . . down the latter came a beautiful running brook of clear pure water, singing as it danced over the stones a happy song and telling us to drink and drink again.

Surely Allah never provided The Faithful with a more delightful glimpse of Paradise than the stream Manly and Rogers now encountered. Little wonder for their ecstasy after endless days of brackish seeps, alkaline water holes and no water at all. Clear, cold and copious, it sent their spirits soaring as it would be to the Bennetts and Arcans on the final trek.

It might be noted in passing that the stream is a singular identification of Bouquet Canyon. While the neighboring canyons also have water courses none are as fitting with the descriptive details that followed.

Proceeding no further, for who knew how long the dream might last, they camped, probably near what was later known as Twin Oak Ranch.

Since much has been made of the comparisons between Manly's accounts it is interesting to note, however unessential, that the book credits Rogers with killing a crow and a quail, Manly a hawk. In "Vermont to California" it was "*we* killed a crow," Rogers the hawk and quail. In Rogers' account he recalls that he killed two hawks and a raven (i.e. crow) and Manly, borrowing the shotgun, shot two quail.[26] This bit of trivia points up the variances of memory, some major and some minor, that run through the accounts.

> (10th day, Jan. 24) . . . (the next day) we went down the canyon (and) soon came to evergreen oaks and tall cottonwoods . . . about 400 yards distant we saw two horses . . . about ten o'clock I felt a sudden pain in my knee . . . as we went along it kept getting worse

---

[26] Rogers was armed with Bennett's double barrel shotgun and Manly with Bennett's rifle, replacing his own that he had broken.

... we worked our way through the tangled brush ... and camped in the dark brushy canyon.

Funneled down the narrow confines of the canyon, at times little more than a deep ravine, theirs was no primrose path. And in working their way through the impeding brush Manly's lameness also took its toll of time "to stop and rest quite often." As a result, the best one can allow is a camp in the vicinity of the "Falls" picnic area.

Of this day's journey there are two incidental highlights. The first, the sight of horses, a sign of man. The other, in his book, is quoting Rogers' refusal to abandon the lame Manly because "he could not do much better alone" vs. a more ringing declaration of devotion of Manly's "we will either die or go together" in the "Vermont to California" version.

> (11th day, Jan. 25) ... in the morning ... the tangle got worse as we descended. At noon we came to ... an excavation, a hole about four feet square ... and (a cottonwood tree) which had been cut down. This was the first sign of white men we had seen and it was evidently an attempt at mining. ...
>
> ... we came out into an open sandy valley ... our beautiful little brook that had kept us company soon sank into the dry sand. ... Before us was now a spur from the hills ... (from) the summit ... was a beautiful meadow of a thousand acres ... and a herd of cattle numbering many hundreds if not thousands ... tears of joy ran down our faces. ...
>
> ... it was either one of the very last days of December 1849 or the first of January 1850. I am inclined to think it was the very day of the new year, but in our troubles the accuracy of the calendar was among the least of our worries.

However shrewd the surmise over the excavation, little did Manly realize their nearness to the scene of California's first gold rush—in Placerita Canyon as early as 1842. The hole was probably part of the inevitable prospecting that fans out from discovery sites. While the horses only hinted of man, this was indeed a more conclusive sign, along with the cut down tree.

Descriptively they apparently had broken out into the open pasture lands near Vasquez Canyon where today the L-W Quarter Horse Ranch equines graze.

A view east from Shepherd Canyon across Panamint Valley to the Panamint Range
"Our wagons were nearly due east from this point . . .
we made our way down the rocky road."—Manly

Ranch scene near Saugus
"before us a beautiful meadow of a thousand acres . . . (with) a herd of cattle."

With all due sympathy and understanding of their calendrical troubles, it was definitely not the last of December nor the first of January. This startling but forgiveable slip of the pen is an embellishment of the earlier "Vermont to California" version which makes no such reference.

As noted earlier, Manly had been at the Briers' Travertine Springs camp on Christmas Day and many weeks had passed since then.

Killing a yearling steer, they spent the night roasting and drying the meat, "one sleeping while the other kept the fire." A feast it was, but one of fresh meat rather than acute starvation for Manly notes "the miserable dried meat in our knapsacks was put away and this splendid beef put in its place."

> (12th day, Jan. 26) The morning was clear and pleasant . . . as we went along a man and woman passed us at some distance on the left and they did not seem to notice us though we were in plain sight. . . .
>
> A house on higher ground soon appeared in sight . . . a man soon made his appearance. . . . We tried to inquire where we were or where we ought to go. . . . Passing on a mile or two we stopped . . . looking up the valley . . . several men on horseback advanced toward us . . . a white man who wished us good evening in our own language . . . told us to go across the valley . . . where we would find an American . . . we found (him) . . . I think (his) name was Springer. He had come by way of the Santa Fe route. . . .

It seems inexplicably strange that after so long and arduous a trek that the first Californians they met, and close enough to describe details of dress, should be passed without hailing them. As two armed men against a man and woman the hesitancy to at least call out hardly hazarded being overpowered. And although Manly infers a probable language barrier prevented their speaking, sign language had bridged such gaps before and could again.

The answer appears to be as simple as in "Vermont to California" when, mindful they had made moccasins from the yearling, Manly says, "As we were a little afraid to meet anyone with fresh rawhide on our feet we turned one side and let them go by."

The house, which Manly notes as built with sun-dried bricks about one by two feet in size, was the historic del Valle adobe[27] dating back to 1804 as an "assistencia" of the San Fernando Mission. About 107 x

23 feet, it was also used as a granary. Some small structures, such as storerooms, may have been subsequently added about the time it was occupied by Antonio del Valle about 1840.

Here Manly mused, "there was no way of getting back in fifteen days as we had agreed upon . . . very likely it would take us 24 or 30 days at best and while they probably had oxen enough to provide them food for so long a time they might take a notion to move on, which would be fatal."

Manly was correct. Starvation was not the spectre hovering over those left at the Long Camp. Unless disaster struck there was meat enough, on the hoof, for at least a month.[28] Nor was concern voiced over water, the stay-behinds having returned to the "good spring." The danger, as Manly so practically presented it, was in moving on into an untraceable maze of desert. Thoughts of a long rescue trip back to an abandoned camp and prospects of two more treks needlessly wasted are hinted at in a Manly letter of January 30, 1893: ". . . We said to each other, if no women and children was out there we would not go back. . . ."

It is an intriguing if halo-tarnishing reminder of his bitterness over being abandoned by Bennett a decade later on a Panamint mining trip.

But the next day, provided with two horses and accompanied by two companion-guides:

> (13th day, Jan. 27) We arose very early . . . started on a trip of 30 miles to the town of Los Angeles. . . . We passed the (San Fernando) Mission about noon and a few miles beyond met a man. . . . His name was French[29] and he had a cattle ranch at a place called Tejon . . . we turned back. When night came we were again at the Mission. . . . They let us sleep in the big house on the floor. . . .[30]

---

[27] Faint signs of it may still be found, near the Castaic junction of I-5/#99 and #126.

[28] Nearing the rancho on the final trek, Manly notes they still had five oxen. That they killed a cow and two yearlings from the cattle they passed is understandably attributed both to the poor fare from the gaunt oxen and an instinctive need to have something for the unknown days ahead.

[29] Dr. E. Darwin French, later closely identified with Death Valley history.

[30] Unfortunately, and probably due to its secularization by 1834 and a subsequent deterioration of records, there is nothing to evidence their stay at the famed mission. Manly notes they were told it was the Mission of San Fernando and a residence for priests and followers and were treated hospitably by an anonymous "they."

For those who may be curious, after 1837 the mission was occasionally served by a visiting

Much of the detailing of the events at this time and place by Manly are omitted in this writing in which the purpose is more that of re-tracing the '49er trails and accounting of related datings. It would be pleasant indeed to reflect that even this much would encourage a reading and re-reading of Manly's classic account.

In any event, let us continue with Manly and Rogers for their return to the valley of the shadow of death.

TREK TWO, THE RETURN

The first day, with no traveling to contribute to the routing, mere-ly marks the passage of the day itself:

(14th day, Jan. 28) (from the mission) we left leading our horses . . . reaching the house again late in the day. . . . We were given a place to sleep . . . the second house we have slept in since leaving Wisconsin and it seemed rather pent-up to us.

(15th day, Jan. 29) In the morning we were shown a kind of mill (to) grind flour for ourselves. We found it hard slow work . . . break-fast . . . we thought one of the best meals we had ever eaten.

From the sign-language bargaining that followed, Manly and Rogers were given two horses with packsaddles and ropes and provi-sions, including a sack of beans, a small sack of wheat and a quantity of good dried meat in exchange for $30.

By gestures Manly indicated they had left 3 women and 4 children at the Long Camp and were given 4 oranges, one for each child.

Three women would be the wives of Bennett, Arcan and Wade. But only four children would be half of the 8 left behind! In "Ver-mont to California" he tallies two women and four children.

In leaving the Long Camp, Manly notes the Wades, and could not have known of their subsequent departure. Was the count a slip of memory or a deliberate slighting? Certainly one cannot help but toy with the picture of four youngsters seeing or hearing of the or-anges for the other four. And while it may have turned out to be half

---

or "circuit" priest from the San Gabriel-Los Angeles missions. The last baptism was recorded in 1846, with no marriages, confessions or deaths recorded until about 1852, indicating infre-quent activities. The mission was leased by Pio Pico to his brother and a Juan Manso in 1845 for $1120 a year for nine years, a contract whose fulfillment is uncertain. It was also occupied by Fremont in January 1847 as a temporary station.

an orange each, one wonders why he didn't say there were eight youngsters. Hopefully the discrepancy is simply one of recalling the count in retrospect, corrected by what he was to know later.

> (15th day, Jan. 29, continued) We started on our return . . . the way we had come. . . . Toward night we came to a wagon road . . . and as we well knew we could not go up the tangled creek bed with horses we took this road to the north which took a dry ravine for its course and in which there was a pack trail and this the wagons were following.
> . . . and camped with them overnight. . . . We told them (of the) 2 women and 4 children[31] . . . one man sold us a little one-eyed mule (for) fifteen dollars. . . . Another man offered us a little snow-white mare for fifteen dollars, which I paid though it took the last cent of money I had. . . . The people gave us a good supper and breakfast and 25 pounds of unbolted wheat flour.

Although they started back over their same route, Manly and Rogers soon veered off into the next canyon north of Bouquet Canyon —San Francisquito Canyon. Somewhat easier and shorter,[32] it was still relatively slow going. The wagon train may have been creating a road out of the pack trail as it went along, or was following an early route to the northern settlements via Tejon Pass into the San Joaquin Valley, avoiding the "Grapevine" highway route of today.

Oddly, in view of the use of "Vermont to California" to correct some of the book detailings, the former does not note an overnight camp with the wagon train. However, there is no doubt over Manly's specific references to "camped with them overnight" and "they gave us supper and breakfast."

According to his book, the following day they passed Elizabeth Lake, reached the "cabbage trees" and water hole (where they had camped coming in), encountered the Jayhawkers' trail and reached the willow corral sometime that night. But even had they started at Elizabeth Lake it would be about 60 miles to the willows. And while the three horses and mule could mean easier, more sustained traveling, herding the animals along would hardly make for a much faster

---

[31] At variance with his earlier count of 3 women and in corroboration of his "Vermont to California" tally.

[32] Their inbound trip was about 39 miles to the ranch vs. 26 outbound.

pace. Not counting the slowed down days within the Bouquet Canyon of their inbound trip, they had taken three days to reach it from the willows. They were not likely to return in just one. Too, from ranch to the willows would be over 80 miles; an average of more than 40 for two days traveling through the San Gabriel Mountains and across desert sands.

The constant inconsistencies between the book and "Vermont to California" necessitates a weaving of both, and in this case the greater weight is given to the latter. Both for clarification and accounting of days, a comparison is helpful:

Death Valley in '49	"Vermont to California"
(16th day, Jan. 30) Still bearing north we soon came to a beautiful lake . . . now called Elizabeth Lake.	. . . passing Elizabeth Lake we watered our horses and filled our canteens . . . among the cabbage trees night came on and *we had to camp.*
We steered . . . among the cabbage trees . . . reached the rain-water hole where we camped as we came over about noon . . . here found the Jayhawkers' trail . . . pushed on and reached the willow corral . . . sometime in the night.	
(17th day, Jan. 31)	. . . after a night's rest we started on . . . soon came to the ox trail of those we had left behind (i.e. the Jayhawkers). We had missed them by coming over the mountain in a different canyon further north. We got to our little rain-water hole before sundown; *here we camped.*
(18th day, Feb. 1)	At the break of day we were off again . . . and reached the willow corral *near sundown* . . . we stood guard without fire to save our horses from the Indians.

As Manly surmised, as they were exiting from their San Francisquito route to the north, the Jayhawkers were entering Bouquet Canyon, probably following Manly and Roger's tracks. As Manly and Rogers started back on the 29th, Young was recording:

Jan. 27 ... lost the trail ... had a dry camp.

Jan. 28 ... went 16 miles to the mountains. Struck into a large canyon. Found grass and water. Horses and ox bones about here plenty. . . . Wm. Robinson . . . died in the evening.

Back to Manly and Rogers—

(19th day, Feb. 2) The next day we passed the water holes at the place we had so stealthily crawled up to Doty's camp . . . it was 30 miles from here to the next water Doty had told us and night overtook us before we could reach it so a dry camp was made.

Manly implies they camped after leaving the Doty campsite, but in "Vermont to California" says they stayed here before going on:

The next night (after the willows) we camped at the place we had crawled up to and found it to be E. Doty's camp . . . from here we had a good two days to travel with only a salt water hole (enroute).

Since it is a good 25-mile day twixt Cantil and Indian Wells, including uphill through Red Rock Canyon, it is indeed difficult to conceive of not stopping overnight at the willows where there was water to provide a recuperative rest for men and beasts to tide them over the next 25 miles or so.

Their journey now continued according to Doty's directions, not the route taken by Manly and Rogers on their first trek.

(20th day, Feb. 3) Our horses began now to walk with . . . slow tired steps. The water (at the salt-water hole) proved so salt(y) the horses would not drink it and as Doty had told us the next water was over the mountains ahead of us we followed their trail which went up a very rocky canyon. . . .

(21st day, Feb. 4) We reached the summit and turned down a ravine following the trail and about dark came to the water they had told us about, a faint running stream which came out of a rocky ravine and sank almost immediately in the dry sand.

That this was more than a one day trek is indicated by Manly's own comment that it was to be "a good two days travel" from Indian

Wells to Providence Springs. And at that easier said than done. While the route started out across the flats, they had more than twenty miles of sand to cross before reaching the very rugged Inyo/Coso range for a very steep uphill climb. And the animals, as he says, were beat.

Piecing together segments from both accounts, it appears:

1. The next "water", which proved to be salty, was close to 30 miles from Indian Wells, a distance approximating the approach to Black Canyon. The salty water indicates it was one of a number of shallow saline pools around the perimeter of the dry lake playas.
2. That they dry-camped near the salty water hole is borne out in "Vermont to California":

   "The next morning we had a canyon to go up."—indicating both their location close to the mountains as well as the start of another day.

Whatever their other differences both accounts are in accord that it was a very rocky canyon "well filled with boulders," descriptive of both Black Canyon and Big Petroglyph Canyon. Closely adjoining, it could be either. And the course might have been partially via canyon until the going got too rough, then, as opportunity allowed, reverting to the side slopes where going was easier than the canyon bottoms oft clogged with cascades of rock and debris from the top. At best it was a difficult route and resulted in the loss of the white mare from a fatal caroming into a rocky wall.

At the summit they would crest into Cole's Flat[33] where the Darwin Wash system starts as a shallow ravine, meandering and expanding to the north. Descending into this ravine, flanked by walls of rock and large boulders, was, and still is, a spring—although endeavors have been made periodically to conserve its dissipation into the sands by troughing for occasional cattle grazing. In following the Jayhawker trail, Manly and Rogers had reached Providence Springs, which they had missed on the first trip by leaving the Jayhawker trail at the "alkali lake."

---

[33] In a hopefully interesting aside, Manly was to return to this area in 1860 and again in 1861 with Charles Alvord and Dick Hickman. His June 15, 1895 article in the *San Jose Pioneer* vividly describes the Coso Hot Springs geysers and colorful boiling mud pots. Continuing to Crystal Springs and the Coso mines they heard the news, in late May or June, of the outbreak of the Civil War. For this and other Manly *Pioneer* articles, Arthur Woodward's superb *Jayhawkers Oath and Other Sketches* is a must on any Death Valley bookshelf.

(22nd day, Feb. 5) The next morning . . . there were now eight miles of clean loose sand to go over, across a *little* valley which came to an end about ten miles north of us and extended south *to the lake* where we went for water on our outward journey. . . .

Near the eastern edge of the valley we turned aside to visit the grave of Mr. Isham which they had told us of. Our next camp was to be on the summit of the range just before us and we passed the dead body of Mr. Fish which we had seen before. We continued on to a level spot . . . just large enough to sleep on. The whole range is a black rocky piece of earth. . . . We tied our horses to rocks and there stayed all night.

Leaving Providence Spring an angling course southeasterly was over a series of rises and through a break in the malpai into Etcharren Valley. Before them lay seven or eight miles of sandy valley to Shepherd Canyon, its well defined entrance rising in a long slope cresting at about 6,000 feet.

Several items merit particular attention.

One, Manly describes it as a *little* valley, which Searles definitely is not.

Two, he notes it extended south *to* the lake, indicating the valley's ending. Carricart Dry Lake is at the closed end of the horseshoe of circling ridges. The south, or open end, of Searles Valley extends far into the distance. True, the comparison may be argued semantically— whether the valley ended near the lake, or continued beyond. But along with his other descriptive clues there is little reason not to accept his literal description rather than interpolate what he meant.

Three, they traveled an entire day, camping that night at a summit, without descending into Panamint Valley; indeed, a good part of the next day as well. In time and distance this would be incompatible with about four miles from Indian Joe Spring (as Providence Springs), and even less from Peach Spring, across Searles Valley to a Slate saddle crossing of about another three or four miles.

Four, in leaving Providence Springs, just northwesterly of historic Junction Ranch, across some eight miles of desert flatland, they could see the singular opening of Shepherd Canyon used on their first trek. Looking back from up on that slope, Manly confirms his previous calculation of the valley seeming to end about ten miles to the north

—vs. half that from Indian Joe Spring, and even less from Peach Spring, to a Slate crossing.

That they had missed Isham's body on their outbound trip indicates it was to the north of the lake, perhaps near the ruins of the old Howard Ranch along the eastern edge of the valley.

Proceeding up the long Shepherd ascent, they camped where it crests in a series of small sandy interludes, just before the gullies began to finger their way eastward and downward to plunge into Panamint Valley. Here, still in the heights, they had passed the body of Fisch.

In closing off this day, mention might, and should be, made of the distinctive consistency and coloring of the Argus Range, especially in this area. Along one side of their route, jutting high over the surrounding terrain, is a large basalt mesa-butte, stark and dark against the sky. On the other side, rocky crags mark the Millspaugh mining activities. It is indeed a "black, rocky piece of earth." And notably so in contrast to the eroded dirt-sloped Slates at the north or "saddle" end.

> (23rd day, Feb. 6) In the morning an important question was to be decided and that was whether we should continue to follow the Jayhawker trail. . . . Our wagons were nearly due east from this point . . . it seemed to be the quickest way to camp to try and get up a rough looking canyon which was nearly opposite us . . . we made our way down the rocky road to the ridge, then left the Jayhawker trail . . . around a salt lake which lay directly before us . . . close to a steep bluff and cross a piece of ground that looked like a well dried mortar bed.

Bearing in mind that they were now following Doty's trail and directions, it is to be recalled that Doty had crossed Panamint Valley from Post Office Spring and had taken a steep pass that Brier spurned as impassible. On their return, Manly and Rogers were retracing Doty's trail in reverse. Now, from the heights of that "impassible pass" an impressive and enlightening panorama lay before them.

From their heights they could see far up the valley to the north, from whence the Jayhawkers had hooked their way out of Death Valley. And "nearly due east" were the Bennett-Arcan wagons.

How, in viewing the great expanse of the Panamints, did he arrive at his directional observation? Was he guessing or approximating? Over three weeks had passed. Such scenes can seemingly change in that span, especially viewed from a different direction, heights and time of day—which is why so many recalled "mines" have become legendarily "lost." How could he be sure, having returned via a relatively new route, that the wagons weren't more to the south—or north?

While there are a number of minor memory joggers, such as certain canyon contours, the saline "lakes" and perhaps the distinctive Ballarat bluff, he was also seeing them from a different perspective.

But there was one landmark that whatever the angle or approach would remain unmistakably identifiable—Telescope Peak. They had been guided by it into Death Valley. The camps along the southwestern edge of that valley had been related to it. It was a memorable sight in crossing the Panamints outbound. Whatever else may have appeared in a different light, snow-capped Telescope remained familiarly unchanged. In determining the positions of the wagons, from where they now stood it was simple and sure to orient it by that telltale peak. So it is that by no chance guesstimate that the "Long Camp" was nearly "due east" from their Shepherd Canyon viewpoint. And irresistibly injected is the assurance the wagons were not *east* from an upper Slate Range crossing.

Too, there is still another clue to their position in the noting of *black buttes to the south,* standing like black icebergs in the saline flats. While they can be seen to the south of Shepherd they are almost due east of a Slate crossing. And there are no other similar buttes in sight to the south of these.

These items in the Slate vs. Shepherd route are not to belabor an already well beaten point. But in endeavoring to offset deeply ingrained patterns and early theories formed into fact by repetition, one must necessarily marshal all possible ammunition. So it is that the long theorized Slate-Searles routing must be negated in order to give Shepherd Canyon and Carricart Lake their neglected recognition.

But Manly and Rogers were not to return through the Panamints via the same route taken on their trip out. In his book, Manly rather offhandedly notes a decision to try a rough canyon nearly opposite their viewpoint—which would approximate South Park. But he disdains the canyon they had used outbound; simply noting "a canyon." And in "Vermont to California" is more explicit:

... we had to try a new pass in the last range, for the way we had
come over could not be crossed by a dog let alone our horses. We tried
a canyon *further south*. This was all new to us . . . the canyon we
entered did not look very favorable. . . .

Manly does not mention camping at this point. Indeed, in a literal
reading of his book, they did not camp until well into the canyon,
including surmounting the obstructions they were to encounter—as
will be detailed shortly.

In "Vermont to California" he says that they left their campsite
near where they found Fisch's body "in the morning as soon as it was
light enough to see to travel." This would make for a long day's progress, yet he then adds, "The next day we had to try a new pass in the
last range."

In a close look at their 23rd day, we find they were still high in
the mountains for their panoramic view, worked their way down the
steep "Doty's trail" and crossed Panamint Valley—a distance, from
Millspaugh to Redlands Canyon for example, of about 25 miles.
While much of their route was downgrade, herding three horses over
the steep rocky declines undoubtedly slowed the pace. So it is that 25
miles, with at least a third of it spent picking a cautious descent, could
easily be a full day's journey. As such there is little quarrel with his
"Vermont to California" version of starting into their "new pass" the
next day—one that was to be filled with enough activities for a day
in itself.

At the risk of belaboring the point, had Indian Joe or Peach
Springs been "Providence Springs" and the camp near Fisch's body
been atop the Slates, it would be a short and easy 10-12 miles for two
days from the spring to the Panamint canyon, a strangely slow pace
for men hastening to a life or death rescue, especially over good traveling terrain. A careful reading of the activities for these days indicates
a greater span of distance and time, as did their 3rd and 4th days
outbound.

Before proceeding to the next day and the canyon they took, some
preliminary weeding out may be helpful in setting the stage.

As outlined earlier, all canyons north of South Park were well
eliminated from their westbound first trek. Now they were about
to try a canyon "further south." Obviously it was south of the one

A view southeast across Carricart Dry Lake
toward Shepherd Canyon (arrow) in the Argus Range. Panamint Range is beyond.
"To the south (the valley) widened out enclosing the lake" . . . "There were now
seven or eight miles of clean loose sand to go over."—Manly

The entrance into Redlands Canyon
The trails ascended more directly than the bladed mining road at left.
"The canyon was rough . . . heavy upgrade."—Manly

they had traversed afoot but deemed too rough to return over with horses. Less obviously, south from where?

Again, of necessity it pits a Shepherd route against a Slate crossing.

South from the latter there are three potential contenders: Coyote Canyon, Goler "Wash" and Wingate Wash. Wingate is ruled out as far too distant even for sighting. Indistinguishable Coyote Canyon heads an impassible way into the highlands along a descriptively incompatible route. Goler, although traversible, at least at times and to varying degrees dependent on run-off damage, also fails to fit the descriptive details to follow. And none of the three crest to Manly's subsequent view of the route used for their climb out of Death Valley.

From an Argus viewpoint the most evident canyon south of South Park is Redlands Canyon, an easily sighted dark fissure whose extent is indicated by a deeply etched "V" crest.

Dr. John Wolff, one of the first to delve into retracing the '49er route, analytically and physically, published his small but lengthily titled booklet, *Route of the Manly Party of 1849-50 in Leaving Death Valley for the Coast,* advocating Redlands for the inbound and final trek with the families. Despite its shortcomings, which can be attributed to the limited scope of too small a segment of the whole, Wolff's plotting was and still is a most meritorious effort. Certainly his coverage of Redlands for the inbound trip indicates he had part of the answer. Alas, his lonely death in the desert prevented any furtherance of that for which he grasped. Regrettably, too, his iconoclastic trail tracings find him among the unheralded and unsung pioneers in this field.

Accepting the "Vermont to California" supplied clue of starting into the canyon on a new day, and aware of the many times told tale of that eventful progress, only those highlights are noted that contribute to the identification of that canyon and the days and dates involved.

> (24th day, Feb. 7) The canyon was rough where we entered it . . . a heavy up grade . . . rough, yellowish rocky walls closed in nearer and nearer . . . a rise in the rocks was approached and there was great difficulty in persuading the horses . . . to get up and over . . . another obstruction of about 3 feet opposed our way . . . it was nearly night . . . we had to leave the horses and go on. . . .

We found the little mule stopped by a still higher precipice . . . of fully *ten feet*. . . . The north wall of the canyon leaned far over the channel . . . while the south wall sloped back . . . making a huge crevice in a sloping direction. . . . Gathering all the loose rocks we could, piling them against the south wall . . . putting up all those in the bed of the *stream* . . . we built a sort of inclined plane along the wall . . . a narrow shelf scarcely four inches wide and a space of from 12 to 15 feet to cross to reach the level of the crest. . . . I had to creep on hands and knees or be dashed *down fifty feet* to a certain death. . . .

(the mule) safely climbed to the top . . . only a little distance beyond this place we found a small willow bush and enough good water for a camp. . . .

There are only a few and minor variations in the details of this day between the book and "Vermont to California." In the latter he notes it was about half a mile from the first rockfall to the second. And notes that they camped at "a small patch" of willows vs. *a* willow bush. But he makes no reference to abandoning the horses at "nearly night" as he does in the book, which may have been a later embellishment recalling the early darkening shadows in the narrow canyon.

Since adjoining canyons in the same range are, to varying degrees, somewhat similar, it is not surprising that some of the clues are applicable to more than one canyon. But only two share the key clues.

Progressing by elimination—Surprise and Pleasant Canyon are well watered, relatively verdant and without claustrophobic narrowness. So, too, with Goler which has rock cascades but no difficult "drops." And Coyote and Middle Park are notably lacking in water, willows or passability. True, cloudbursts and erosion have changed the countenance of many a canyon, but it is often surprising how little basic change is wrought by the tides of time, especially when controlled by the strong geological factors that prevail in the Panamints.

So it is, by no small coincidence, two eligible canyons are left in this elimination—South Park and Redlands. Both have age-old stream-worn rockfalls and both have a midway spring—Colter Spring near the summit of South Park and Redlands Spring in Redlands Canyon. Both, too, have a steeply graded entry. The former high up on the ancient shore line buttes, the latter by the need to circumvent "Manly Falls" near its steep entrance.

But even if South Park had not already been acceptably set as the route out, leaving Redlands as the canyon "to the south" of it, there is the matter of narrowness.

South Park is relatively narrow in parts. Of this there is no question. But Redlands is particularly so distinctive. And while the general geologic terrain may be much the same, it is in Redlands that one is aware of its yellowed hue, heightened by the reflected light from the narrow patch of sky overhead caroming off the bare rock walls, filtering into the canyon's crevicing and probing its silent depths in a sharply etched contrast of lights and shadows.

The ascent into Redlands, steep and winding, to flank "Manly Falls"—a dry, sheer drop of perhaps 75 feet—is a slow one. The best passage, along the north side, is evidenced by a serpentine road now bulldozed part way for mining purposes.[34]

Ordinarily it would be difficult to picture a rockfall of only 3 feet as a sufficient obstacle to warrant abandoning the much needed horses. But this was not a tumbling of rocks where a way might be picked. Rather, a low vertical wall of solid rock with a slick, sheer water-worn drop.

About half a mile farther they reached a higher and more serious obstacle, one that has so resisted the petty changes of a century that it is essentially evident today. Here the fissure narrows with such precipitously inclined walls there are no side slopes up which the 10 feet or so drop can be by-passed. Nor, in a surface scoured smooth by countless sandy water coursing are there cracks and crumblings for hand and foot holds.

With an overhanging north wall precluding passage along that side, a crude narrow rock "bridge" along the opposite or south side still clings to its mute evidence of the route over and beyond.

Is this the remnant of *the* rock bridge Manly and Rogers used? Essentially, yes. However, it was doubtlessly used and rebuilt by later prospectors, including surface piping of the spring above to the mining camp below, evidenced by the rusted pipes that now lie scattered about like broken strands of spaghetti.

In checking the various canyons for their entire lengths, only

---

[34] Bulldozed, following an old trail, by Harry Briggs whose "Homestead Mine" properties and one of the abodes of the late Seldom Seen Slim are nestled at the foot of Manly Falls.

The narrows in Redlands Canyon
"the rough, yellowish rocky walls closed in nearer and nearer . . .
The north wall of the canyon leaned far over the channel while the south wall
sloped back about the same . . . like a huge crevice."—Manly

South Park was found to have a rock falls at all similar. But it is in a wide, non-hanging wall area that would permit slope by-passing be it with a bit of scrambling. Again, it is true that rock falls can be buried and resurrected by storm waters, but the well-worn Redlands rock falls little show the changes from centuries of survival.

Along with its distinctively ochered walls, narrow confines, a half mile distance from the smaller rock fall and a willowed spring just above, this second fall also supplies the answer to a rather puzzling contradiction between a ten-foot precipice and the danger of being dashed "50 feet" below.

The answer lies in the normally dry stream bed that carves its way through Redlands, gouging a path along the lowest end of the rock wall, undercutting the north side to dig deeply to bedrock. This left the stream bed of the canyon much lower than the remaining high ground along the south side. In so constricted an area, complicated by a bend at that point, it has left most of the rock "wall" overlooking the deepest drop. Thus the rise was 10 feet on its narrow side yet 50 feet above the stream-bed side.

But overcome it they did, as has oft been told, and a short distance beyond they camped at the still flowing, although now willow and tule clogged Redlands Spring.

(25th day, Feb. 8) Starting early we made the summit about noon, and from here we could see the place where we had found a water hole and camped the first night after we left the wagons. Down the steep canyon we turned—the same one in which we had turned back with the wagons . . . we hobbled along with sore and tender feet . . . and camped at the same spot from which we had set out *25 days before.* . . . Here was the same little water hole in the sand plain and the same strong sulphur water which we had to drink the day we left. . . .

Truly the confirmation of 25 days is rewarding for those who have patiently accepted much of this study, especially the accounting of days, with little more than faith in the assurances that all would eventually turn out well.

In continuing up Redlands, Manly and Rogers would crest at about 4,500 feet into Butte Valley. Although this valley has been weighed by others, it has invariably been found wanting for lack of

Redlands Canyon rock fall, the narrow rock shelf to the right over which Manly, Rogers and the mule worked their way up and over. The stream bed to the left had been gouged deeply so that a misstep could mean "fifty feet to certain death."—Manly

A comparable drawing from an illustration in Manly's book.

Manly mentioning its uniquely striated butte that dominates its center. To rationalize why he did not is conjectural. Possibly it was an oversight in his years-later writing. Perhaps painful feet lessened the concern with geological observations. Possibly, with the noon sun overhead and in angling toward the canyon used in leaving the wagons, the more subdued striped side was less memorable.

Indeed it may even have been that their attention was more focused on viewing a familiar sight—Arrastre Spring, the water holes where they had camped before. There, across the way, was acknowledgment that they had not erred in their return route and assurance they now had not far to go.

It also emphasizes their triangular route—out and back. They had not gone out Redlands for they would have been pre-warned of the rock falls. Yet they were now near the same seeps that marked their departure base point. Unfortunately once again, and fortunately for the last time, the eligibility of two canyons calls for the elimination of possible pairings.

Redlands, and Goler to the south, might be said to offer a rather stretched out triangulated course. But Redlands with its unanticipated rock falls was obviously not the exit route. This in turn negates a pairing with Goler to the south of it.

With Pleasant and Middle Park dropped from earlier contention as exit routes, a return via South Park, as the next canyon south, is eliminated. And Happy and Surprise canyons still farther north are out on all counts including any mutually shared spring just below the eastern edge of the summit.

While arguments can and probably will continue over the endless aspects posed by theorizations, invariably including support for Six Springs Canyon or the possibilities of impulsive ridge crossings rather than following channeled terrain, there is little need to pound square pegs into round holes. An exit via South Park and a return via Redlands descriptively drop into place like the well-oiled tumblers of a vault lock.

Having "freshly watered" at Redlands Spring there was little need to devote time and effort to turn aside to Arrastre's meager seeps. With the home stretch in sight, Manly and Rogers hastened down the canyon they knew. While they might have taken the better route

Redlands Spring. The metal pipe shows its use by many for many years.
Above the Redlands Canyon rock fall "we found a willow bush
and enough good water for a camp."—Manly

From Redlands Canyon, with Arrastre Spring off scene to the left
the descent was into Galena Canyon, "the same one in which
we had turned back with the wagons."—Manly

down Warm Springs Canyon they had just sweated out the untried in Redlands and could hardly be blamed for now preferring the familiar—one they knew posed no new problems. So, in turning up Butte Valley, in sight of the seeps they camped at outbound, they again swung down the small gap just south of Gold Hill, veering back into Galena and down to the little sulphurous water hole at Mesquite Well, in the sandy flat at the foot of the rock-crusted alluvial fan from where they had departed 25 days before.

> (26th day, Feb. 9) From this place, as we walked along, we had a wagon road to follow . . . seven or eight miles along (we found the body of) Captain Culverwell. . . . About noon came in sight of the wagons still a long way off. . . . Surely we had left 7 wagons . . . now we could see only 4. . . . I fired a shot . . . then as if by magic a man came out from under a wagon . . . and shouted, "The boys have come! The boys have come!"

The "wagon road" was, of course, the tracks of the Long Camp party wagons. But, as noted by others researching the Manly routes, there is a discrepancy in the mileage location of Culverwell's body.

Originally Manly had noted it was about 8 miles between the "good water" and the "sulphury well." If on their return they camped at that sulphury well, with the Bennetts-Arcans returning to the good spring, the distance should still be the same. Yet Manly now says they traveled seven or eight miles before finding the body and still had a way to go to the wagons. And later, in leaving the Long Camp he tells of going about 4 miles to where Mrs. Arcan's memorable incident with a bucking ox brought an early halt, with Rogers and Bennett going about a mile more to cover Culverwell's body. From the well 7 or 8 miles to where they found the body and 5 miles returning to it from camp, would add up to about 13 miles vs. the original 8.

Could there have been two similar sulphurous wells? Could the Bennetts-Arcans have moved up even farther north than Bennetts Well, perhaps to Tule Springs? Or had Manly and Rogers returned via a canyon farther south, such as Wingate Wash?

Fortunately, "Vermont to California" comes to the rescue wherein this earlier account records that from the sulphurous well they went "about a mile or so" to where they found Culverwell. That mile or so and about 5 from the camp reconciliably approximates 8.

THE FINAL TREK

Deductively, Manly and Rogers return the 9th of February was late in the day for it was about noon when they sighted the wagons still a "long way off."

How long did it take for them to break camp, and thus date their departure? Later, when they arrived at the San Francisquito Ranch, March 7, Manly relates they had been "22 days on the road." Was the day of arrival counted as a day on the road? Their first day in leaving the Long Camp was an abortive 4 or 5 miles. Having barely started, was it a day on the road? And in nearing the ranch the day's start was brought to a halt by Mrs. Bennett taking ill.

If 22 days was an elapsed time, they could have left as late as February 14. Literally 22 days of on the road travel could date the departure earlier. Admittedly arbitrarily, and aware it has minimal bearing in setting days and distances of campsites, the departure date has been rationalized as February 12. This could be debatable but assuredly it was between February 11 (allowing one day for readiness) and the 14th to encompass 22 days for a March 7 arrival.

Not knowing when, or even if, the "boys" would return, the camp was not apt to be ready to move out immediately. Two days for telling of all that had happened, making plans and preparations, seems reasonable.

Since the route of this final trek retraced the Manly and Rogers return it can be stripped of repetitive geographical detailing. So, too, with the need for specific extracts from Manly; the familiarization from two treks now allowing for a more simplified descriptive format.

TREK #3 (1st day, February 12)   It was close to noon, with the sun "high overhead" when the last of the Death Valley '49ers pulled out, with Manly, Rogers, the three Arcans, five Bennetts and 11 oxen (2 for the women to ride, 1 for the children, 1 to carry water; 5 of 16 having been eaten). They also took a shovel "so we might bury the body of Captain Culverwell and shovel up a pile of sand at the falls to enable us to get the oxen over."

Brought to an early halt by Mrs. Arcan's bucking ox,[35] a pictur-

---

[35] Mrs. Arcan was riding "Old Brigham", the children on "Old Crump". On his way to Moore's Flat in 1851, Manly found "Old Crump" near French Camp in the San Joaquin Valley, "now fat and sleek."

esquely many-times told tale, they camped only "about four miles" from Bennetts Well. From here Rogers and Bennett went ahead "about a mile" to cover Culverwell's body, "for some of the party feared the cattle might be terrified at seeing it." Wince as one may over the concern with the cattle rather than the sight of the body by the women and children, at least it helps to position the location in relation to Bennetts Well and Mesquite Spring.

Poor Captain Culverwell was the only known '49er fatality in Death Valley. He had left the Long Camp on February 7 with Nusbaumer and turned up missing apparently on the 8th. Lost, he had tried to return to the familiar Long Camp where there were people and some provisions, along a route he knew. He failed by but five miles, and perhaps by but a day of being helped by Manly and Rogers who found his body on the 9th. Manly observed that Culverwell "did not look much like a dead man," indicating a very recent demise.

(2nd day, February 13)   In the morning they decided to take a shortcut to the summit—an interesting deviation in an area for its single approach canyons.[36] Having already decided upon the route with which Manly and Rogers were twice familiar, they were not heading into a new and untried canyon but simply cutting "across the lot" into Galena. And this is one place where such a shortcut is visible and practical. Indeed it approximates a later road which, while it existed, provided a shortcut across the great alluvial fan from Bennetts Well to the Galena mines.

Continuing up the canyon, which was "more like a stairs than a road in its steep ascent," camp was made at Arrastre Spring that night.

(3rd day, February 14)   In the morning, Bennett and Arcan were taken to the viewpoint near the camp which has been detailed earlier (trek #1, 2nd day). That he says they "first made out the distant snowy peak, now so near us, on November 4th" is a slip of the lip. Impressive as Telescope Peak, the snowcapped Panamints and Sierra or even Mt. Charleston can be, they are not visible across the width of Nevada from Mt. Misery. However, the Charleston Peak area—"the only butte in this direction (eastward) that carried snow was the same

---

[36] In contrast, and as an example of the terrain, this writer achingly recalls scrambling up and down over a dozen 20-30 foot sheer sided washes in an attempt to cross the upper slopes from the mouth of Six Springs Canyon to adjoining Johnson Canyon.

one (near) where we captured the Indian and where the squashes were found" is, as he says, a visible landmark from here.

So far as his dramatization of doffing hats in bidding "Good-bye, Death Valley!" and this being "the party which named it," I leave to others. Arguments have long raged and will undoubtedly continue that also credit Mrs. Bennett and Asa Haynes with its naming.[37] Manly does not claim personal credit. And in noting he was "of" the party that named it, seems to be speaking collectively. In fact, it was a loosely descriptive naming applied variously to the vast general area as well as the heart of that saline sink.[38]

Following a route "along the foot of the high peak(s)," they soon turned south somewhat so as to enter the canyon leading down to the falls. In electing to take the Manly and Rogers return route, rather than working their way up the slopes from Arrastre Springs, they veered into Butte Valley to reach Redlands Canyon, camping at the willowed spring just above the high rock fall.

(4th day, February 15)   The next morning the oxen were "lowered" over the high rock drop by a combination of fastening a long rope to the oxen which Manly pulled from below while Bennett and Arcan pushed and Rogers applied "a Tennessee boost" at the rear to send the animals sprawling onto a shoveled mound of sand. The women were then helped more decorously down the narrow "rock bridge" ledge along the side wall.

As soon as the oxen could be reloaded they continued down the canyon, ". . . too deep and dark for either wolves or buzzards." Again this differentiates Redlands from South Park. West of its rock fall area, South Park is relatively wide, open and light; whereas Redlands is notably deep, narrow and shadowed. And since this was midmorning, the dark interior was indeed due to the canyon and not the time of day.

Reaching Panamint Valley they first turned south to flank a small salt stream.

---

[37] Ellenbecker credits Haynes as saying, in reaching the Del Valle Ranch, "We certainly came through the Valley of Death," and on the basis of the Jayhawkers having completed their trek before the Bennetts-Arcans crossed the Panamints, believes "the credit of naming Death Valley belongs to the Jayhawkers."

[38] Stephens says, "We finally reached Death Valley where we lost two men, Fish and Isham," events that transpired west of Panamint Valley. Being with the Jayhawkers he did not know of Culverwell's death.

On our left hand was a perpendicular cliff along which we traveled
for quite a little way. The range of mountains now before us . . .
was black . . . and barren.

At first blush it might seem that since they had been going westerly, traveling along a "cliff" to their left would indicate they were
heading south. The gap in his text is filled in by his maps,[39] all three in
consistent agreement that they turned north. The explanation lies in
that after crossing the stream they veered northwesterly to the "Jayhawker trail," used by Manly and Rogers inbound. In doing so the
black, barren range would be the Argus, now to their left.

In a perhaps repetitious refutation of a Slate saddle crossing into
Searles, about ten miles away, particular attention is focused upon
their camp distances as they continued, camping that night high in
the mountains, having had "the hardest . . . and probably longest"
stretch of their trek.

(5th day, February 16) There was a late start this morning,
especially for the bone-weary women, and Manly walked ahead to
Fisch's body. Returning to camp, soup was made for breakfast, the
oxen repacked and they continued "down the western slope (over)
hard broken rock . . . it cannot (be) imagined how hard it is to walk
with tender feet over broken rock . . . it was very slow getting along
at the best . . . and the oxen stumbled dreadfully in trying to protect
their sore feet."

In his book, Manly infers they reached Providence Springs that
night. However, in "Vermont to California" he states that as they
passed the body of Fisch "We still had *two* short drives to make and
one dry camp before we could reach any water."

This is supported by telling they went over several miles of soft
sand, that the sun was very hot and "we suffered dreadfully" before
reaching the grave of Mr. Isham. While Manly and Rogers had gone
from Providence Springs to Fisch's body in one day on their return,
they had started early, were well supplied with water and were unencumbered by oxen and families. Foreseeing their now much slower

---

[39] One is in the Huntington Library. Another, discovered by author-historian Ardis Manly
Walker, is now in the Death Valley National Monument Museum. The third, known as the
Palmer map, as "drawn for him by Manly (and) is remarkably accurate," according to T.R.
Goodwin, Death Valley National Monument Superintendent.

progress, they undoubtedly called a halt to camp near the dry lake bed.

(6th day, February 17)   Quoting "Vermont to California," Manly writes:

> Starting early the next morning . . . we passed Mr. Isham's body . . . it was now only a few miles to where there was water (Providence Springs).

But before they reached it, some of the men went ahead, ". . . reaching the camp place about noon and two of us hurried back with water for the women and children."

Although the book version notes that, encamped at Providence Springs, "five days had passed," this is reconcilable with their discounting the first and abortive camp only four miles from Bennetts Well. As such this would be the fifth day out of Death Valley.

(7th day, February 18)   "We now had a long canyon to go up to cross this our last range and another one on the other side."

They took all of this day to reach the "summit" by night, and "a short distance down the western slope we camped in a valley."

> This being at quite a high elevation, we could see the foot as well as the top of the great snow mountains and we had a general good view of the country.

It is to be noted that after all of this time and travel they were still high in the mountains. Had they been traversing Wilson Canyon,[40] from Searles, that relatively low and narrow canyon is void of panoramic views until it opens abruptly into the China Lake flatland. In comparison, a route westward from Providence Springs in the Argus would find them cresting about 6,000 feet where a series of terraced slopes start a long descent in the vicinity of Big Petroglyph Canyon. In doing so they would soon encounter a number of small high valleys.

In "Vermont to California" Manly informatively expands on the view:

---

[40] Mindful that the Searles-Wilson Canyon routing has been accepted by repetition over the years, it should also be kept in mind that if they did not cross via Wilson Canyon, then "Indian Joe" or "Peach" springs are out as Providence Spring. And if the latter is eliminated so too is Searles as the nearby alkali lake, which in turn eliminates any Slate Range crossing.

(from the valley camp) we could see ahead of us our road as far as we could travel in the next two weeks it seemed. To the north there seemed everlasting snow fields, all mountains and sky high.[41]

(8th day, February 19)   That they were still at a high elevation is confirmed by having "a long canyon to go down." And his description of the canyon being filled with great boulders over which it was very difficult to get the oxen through, points to rough, boulder clogged Big Petroglyph or Black Canyon.[42] However they may well have also used the high side slopes, cutting into the canyon lower down when the walls became less steep and the water coursed floor more promising however poor. This night camp was made at the salt water hole at the foot of the range, near where Manly and Rogers found "the piece of ice which saved our lives."

(9th day, February 20)   Although it was, as Manly notes, 30 miles to the camp where they met the Jayhawkers (Indian Wells) and the trail now familiar, they made a dry camp. In "Vermont to California" he more explicitly says, "15 miles" and "about halfway" for this day. As before, they were now crossing the large expanse of China Lake, or Indian Wells Valley, canted southwesterly by a long volcanic bluff.

(10th day, February 21)   This day they completed their trek across the playa, reaching Indian Wells—"the water holes at the place where Rogers and I had stolen up to the campfire in the evening, supposing it to be Indians but finding Captain Doty and his mess." His notation that they were "now nine days from the wagons" is, as before, justified as again excluding the aborted start from Bennetts Well, which was in fact a matter of about two hours and not a "day" in terms of travel.

(11th day, February 22)   Leaving at sunrise, with Rogers and

---

[41] A few miles from the summit just west of Providence Springs, is a small "hidden valley" containing a small shallow "lake" of muddy water. Along the shoreline are a series of ancient rounded stone rings, which may have been wickiup foundations or, as theorized, fish traps. Fragments of potsherds, arrowheads and chippings indicate a very old Indian encampment. As voiced before, although the '49ers rarely credit following Indian trails, there is little doubt that they often did so. Thus they now could easily have been following the signs or terrain of one of the ages-old trails and may well have camped at this little sheltered valley, or a similar vale in the vicinity. From the surrounding slopes there is indeed an impressive sight of the snow-capped Sierra and a view to the south as far as the eye can see.

[42] Where Young had lost an ox, a casualty to the boulders.

Manly in advance, camp was made this night on a "perfectly level plain" with "a branch near here . . . known as Walkers Pass." That they stopped not far from the landmarking "Robbers' Roost" rocks is supported by, ". . . to the north of us, a few miles away, we could see some standing columns of rock, much reminding one of the great stone chimney of the boiler house at Stanford University."

(12th day, February 23)   This day they entered Red Rock Canyon, camping at "the same place where Rogers and I had overtaken the advance parties of the Jayhawkers."

(13th day, February 24)   "In the morning we were off again down the canyon . . . now called Red (Rock) Canyon." But they made it only to the "mouth of the canyon and we were forced to go into camp." It was a miserably cold and wet night and in the morning about two inches of snow blanketed the ground.

(14th day, February 25)   In the morning after a hasty meal, they reached the willows of Cantil "about four miles away." It was such a "wonderful spot . . . of pure water . . . green willows and grass" they went no further.

(15th day, February 26)   With kegs and canteens filled with water, they moved on, camping this night in the desert. Since there is no indication of mileage or distinctive descriptions it can only be approximated as close to today's town of Mojave—accepting 15 to 20 miles as a good average for hoofing it in this type of terrain.

(16th day, February 27)   This day they reached the "cabbage trees"—rainwater pools near Rosamond Dry Lake at which Manly and Rogers had camped January 21 inbound and the 31st on the return. After noting that "It was rain water . . . there was evidence there had been a recent shower or snow to fill this depression up for our benefit," he adds, "The Jayhawkers had passed not more than a half mile north of this spot but no sign appeared that they had found it." This isn't surprising since Manly indicates that it was the luck of the weather that accounted for the water and not a spring whose verdancy would be apt to attract the Jayhawkers' attention. He and Rogers had been at the spot before and knew what they might expect.

(17th day, February 28)   Despite an early start and "no resting spell at noon," physical deterioration forced a halt before they reached their foothills goal. Again there are no clues as to where this might have been, save a guesstimated locale south of Lancaster. The trials of the trail were taking their toll. Whatever assurances Manly could give to spur them on, plodding one foot after another seemingly endlessly, each mile became slower and more of an effort.

(18th day, March 1) This day they began their ascent of the foothills and "reached our camping place in the lower hills." The identification of cattle skulls lying about indicates it being the same site at which he and Rogers had camped January 22, and his stating, in "Vermont to California" of reaching the "water holes in the foothills." Apparently they had decided to take Bouquet Canyon again instead of the San Francisquito Canyon return route. Perhaps they missed the entrance to the latter. Or it may be that the dancing water brook prospect outweighed the shorter route. One can only guess.

In any event, they did see signs of the Jayhawkers, ". . . their path was quite a beaten one . . . they followed the tracks made by Rogers and me as we made our first trip. . . ." This is a confirmation reminder that the Jayhawkers also used Bouquet Canyon and that Manly and Rogers missed them by taking San Francisquito Canyon on their return north to Death Valley.

(19th day, March 2) Crossing the range and encountering five or six miles of snow meant for slow going. But the snow was also welcomed as water, melted by a campfire of dry juniper branches.

(20th day, March 3) According to his book, they moved out at daylight and saw ". . . a grand view of the country to the south, and of the great snow mountain(s) to the north and east, the peak standing over the place where we had left our wagons nineteen days before."

One may doubt that even on a remarkably clear day Telescope Peak could be so distinguished 19 travel days away except in a general relationship to the terrain. What does jar a bit is the possibility of such a view after traveling a day into the hills where surrounding ridges block such extensive scenes.

But his dating slips smoothly into place, mindful of the view being at dawn on the 20th day, with 19 having passed.

Again we need turn to "Vermont to California" for an explanation of the view. In this he says they had their view after reaching the water holes camp (18th day) and had their snow camp that night. Having their panoramic view near the edge of the hills and then treking a day to their snow camp rings truer than the reverse. And in this his reflective view-inspiring comment of having left the wagons 19 days before would fit hand in glove. So it is that acceptance is given to the camp on the 19th day being near the summit, approaching the present Twin Oaks Ranch; the camp on the 20th day not far beyond.

And they did camp early that 20th day, for they had at long last reached "the little babbling brook Rogers and I had so long painted in the most refreshing colors. . . . It was not yet night but we had to camp in so beautiful a place as this."

While the others were savoring its delights, Manly went hunting and killed a cow and two yearlings. "We would not," he wrote, "be compelled to kill any more of our poor oxen. . . . So far we had killed six of them and there were five left." This tally, leaving Arcan with two and Bennett with three, is in keeping with leaving the Long Camp with eleven.

It was after midnight when Manly returned to camp. Tired and wet from his foraging he crawled into a blanket bed, awakening well after sun-up to find the others roasting the yearling meat over the campfire.

Postscripting this day is Manly's belated and casual, "And by the way, I think I have not mentioned our camp dog, Cuff." So far as known, this is the only dog of the Death Valley parties, at least which survived the trek all the way from the Platte River. He was even to make it to the goldfields where he became "lost, strayed or stolen" while Manly and Bennett were mining near Georgetown.

(21st day, March 4) This day's start was soon brought to an abortive halt by Mrs. Bennett taking ill. As to how far they progressed there is no clue. Only that they camped under a great live oak with a beautiful meadow nearby.

> We washed such clothes as we could do without long enough to dry and washed our faces over and over again to remove the dirt which had been burned and sweated in so completely as not to come off easily. We sat on the bank of the brook with our feet dangling in the water. . . .

(22nd day, March 5)   "The next morning . . . we had the trail of the Jayhawkers to follow, so the vines and brambles which had perplexed Rogers and me in our first passage were now somewhat broken down. . . . The constant wading and wet cold clothing caused the women to give out soon and we selected the first dry suitable place to camp."

Throughout this Bouquet Canyon passage, it is impossible to fix their campsites with any certainty. From the day they entered the foothills until their exit they averaged about six serpentine miles a day for the approximate 40 miles. Except for a few fragmentary clues, such as the viewpoint and the brook, all else is conjecture based on relatively short spans of travel.

(23rd day, March 6)   "The next day we did not wade half as much," he writes, and after noting they stopped to rest at noon, soon emerged from the brush, and found the stream bed dry of the water that had now subsided into its sandy bottom.

That little more is said of this day could imply continuing on, except he specifically says:

(24th day, March 7)   "*The next day* we came down to the point of the hill that nearly crossed the valley." Before them lay "a large green meadow of a thousand acres more or less. We tarried here perhaps two hours (and) soon prepared to move on toward the goal we were to reach. It was now the *seventh day of March,* 1850, and this date as well as the fourth of November, 1849, will always remain an important one in memory."

Whatever his haziness on some datings, this one was indelibly imprinted in his memory. Even much later, while overlooking San Francisco Bay, he musingly recalled Death Valley and of reaching the fertile fields "on the seventh of March 1850."

After reloading the oxen, "We reached our camping place at the foot of the hill, about a hundred yards from the house we had so long strived to reach."

The epic trek was over.

And to warm the heart of any historical researcher, all of the days have been accounted for, however confusing and conflicting Manly's accounts may have been at times.

Although Manly tells one of the rancheros that they "had been on the road 22 days," it was, as noted earlier, probably a matter of semantics. Discounting the very short distance the day they left the Long Camp, or the very early halt on the 21st day due to Mrs. Bennett's illness, could understandably be recalled as 22 days actually "on the road."

The details of their recuperation at the ranch are best left to Manly. But it may be well to add that, according to an article in *The Pioneer,* April 21-28, 1877, they continued on to reach Los Angeles March 11. In another article, of April 15, 1895, Manly says they reached the pueblo March 12 after four days of tramping. Ah, consistency was not one of his brighter jewels!

But acceptably it was March 9th that Arcan arranged to be taken to San Pedro, giving his gold ring to Manly and a silver watch to Rogers in a tearful parting. The others started on their way, passing the San Fernando Mission on March 10.

Reaching Los Angeles they met two old friends—Ransom G. Moody and Henry C. Skinner, who had traveled with the Bennetts along the Platte River. At Salt Lake City, Moody had stayed behind and later joined the Huffaker wagon train which left November 12, reaching Chino the end of January or early February. Skinner had gone with the Hunt train, turning back at Mt. Misery with Alexander Erkson, arriving at Chino about December 22.

The problem of name and spelling variances is again noted in that at Los Angeles, Moody found "Erickson (Erkson) and Skinner who told him that Louis Manly and R. Kane had reached the settlement," obtained supplies and had "nobly gone back" to their party's rescue.

To bring this saga to a fittingly descriptive close, mindful of all that they had endured and hoped for, it seems appropriate to turn back a few days and miles to where they feasted on the yearling, by the brook, and the end of their travails in sight:

> Our present situation was much appreciated, compared with that of a few days ago when we were crawling slowly over the desert, hungry, sore-footed and dry, when to lie was far easier than to take steps forward. We felt like rejoicing at our deliverance and there was no

mourning now for us. The surrounding hills and higher mountains seemed more beautiful to us. They were covered with green trees and brush, not a desert place in sight. The clear little singing brook ran merrily on its way, the happiest, brightest stream in all my memory. Wild birds came near us without fear and seemed very friendly. All was calm and the bright sunshine exactly warm enough so that no one could complain of heat or cold.

And, in Manly's touching last sentence of his book—"I rest in the midst of family and friends, and can truly say I am content."

Epilogue-The Later Years

The arrival of the Death Valley '49ers in the sleepy pueblo of Los Angeles was anti-climatic to all that had gone before.[1] What happened to them later is not within the realm of this trail retracing. But curiosity, particularly over those who played such major roles, warrants touching lightly upon them.

Scattering, some of the '49ers soon returned East, others later, with some returning to California. A surprising number settled in the Lodi, Merced, Santa Cruz and San Jose areas. Whether so many did so subconsciously seeking common bonds, or simply longing for greener scenery than they had experienced for so long, is speculative. Perhaps, too, after attempts to find their fortunes at mining, with less than notable results, they were attracted by the verdancy, weather and the ocean—a wonder to many of them. As ever since with many, "back East" palled in comparison with California.

In observance of February 4, 1850, as their "end of the trail," the Jayhawkers began to hold annual reunions on that date starting in 1872. The first was held at John Colton's home in Galesburg, Illinois. The last at Stephens' in San Jose in 1918. Except for a periodic continuance by their descendants, the reunions ended with the death, in 1919 at the age of 88, of Colton, the activist behind them. Stephens, "the last of the Jayhawkers" died in 1921 at 95. But he wasn't the oldest, for Mrs. Brier was to lack but three and a half months of her 100th birthday when she died in 1913.

As a reminder of the relative modernity of history, some of the '49ers, such as Mrs. Brier and Stephens, had crossed the plains by ox-drawn wagon, and lived to see the automobile and airplane!

The portraits with the biographical sketches in this segment of the book (with only two exceptions—Manly and Nusbaumer) ap-

[1] Although Manly and Rogers on their first trek reached the del Valle ranch January 26, it was not until March 7 that they returned with the Bennetts and Arcans. Between those dates the Jayhawkers arrived Feb. 4. Fatefully, those who kept to the main trail with Hunt had arrived on the outskirts the last week in December.

William Lewis Manly

Asahel Bennett

Jean Baptiste Arcan

Louis Nusbaumer

Harry Wade

John W. and Juliette Brier

Sheldon Young

Asa Haynes

peared in Frank F. Latta's *Death Valley '49ers,* Santa Cruz, Bear State Books, 1979, and are reproduced with their kind permission. Photos furnished for that book were from: The Huntington Library for Haynes and Young; Mrs. Fred Harder for the Arcans; Mrs. J. Q. White for the Wades; California State Library for the Briers; and Supt. T. R. Goodwin of Death Valley for that of Bennett.

MANLY

Manly tried mining, from the Merced River to Coloma. While prospecting near Georgetown, in partnership with Bennett, the dog "Cuff" who had been with them the entire trek, disappeared.

Manly returned to Wisconsin, but by July of 1851 was back in San Francisco—this time via the Isthmus, obviously having had his fill of overland travel. The lure of gold still glittering, he mined, with fair results, near Downieville and Moore's Flat, tucked in the Yuba River back-country, where he also ran a small store.

In 1859 he settled near San Jose. Three years later he married Mary J. Woods and they lived in the College Park section of San Jose. In mid-1901 he suffered a severe accident that confined him to a wheel chair. He died February 5, 1903, at 83, and was buried beside his wife, in Woodbridge, California, near Lodi.

• His book, which immortalized him, was not a commercial success. He had difficulty in selling copies at its $2 price, or $1.60 for 10 or more.[2] Although he had solicited information contributions from the other '49ers the response was rather sparse; a situation that seemed to change after its publication. Perhaps aware of a need for corrections and additions, he had talked of a revised edition until prevented from doing so by the infirmaries of age and his accident.

ROGERS

Woefully little is known of Rogers, save that he settled near Merced, tried mining and later worked in a quicksilver (Mercury) smelter. Its lethal fumes caused the loss of both feet at the instep.

In 1895, forty-one years after they last met, Manly found where Rogers was living and went to visit him in a touching reunion as they recalled their Death Valley days.

Thanks to Frank Latta's superb researching and book, *Death Val-*

---

[2] Currently copies of that edition sell for $150 or more, although there are some fine moderately priced reprints including Chalfant Press' reproduction of the original.

1891

(Dear Jayhawkers)

The task I now undertake is a dificult one for me to perform after so many years have passed by. I knew you once more tharn 40 years ago. & in a country I shall never forget, like the faces of many of us unfortunate travailers it does not change, our early troubles will soon be forgotten & we will all pass over the last _Desert_, when I try to write you a few lines I can truly say the reflection & thoughts of our early tramps troubles & hardships sends me back over that never to be forgotten road whare some of our unfortunate comerads bones still lie bleaching in the clareing desert sun they had not the vitality to endure such hardships & could not live like the stronger without water for days & on

W L Manly

College Park Santa Clara Co Cal

A portion of a Manly letter to '49er friends
"I had to have one assistant because I am not able to do such work and have it grammatical."—Manly letter to Colton. Just who assisted on Manly's book is conjectural. From the style and substance in this sample letter, the writing in the book is assuredly Manly's, and the assistance was more of editing for spelling, punctuation, and as Manly says, grammar.

ley '49ers, it seems that 6 foot 2 inch "Big John" apparently remained a bachelor, worked as a farm hand near Merced, and died without record, although he was listed as a registered voter in 1896.

BENNETT

As with many, Bennett's try at mining failed to pan out well and he eventually turned to farming near Santa Cruz. After Mrs. Bennett's death he moved to Utah and remarried. That and his relationships with the Mormons soured. Manly says he heard Bennett lived near Belmont, in south-central Nevada. Apparently Bennett died in 1891 in Idaho; and that the children, George and Martha, lived in Wilmington, California, and Melissa in San Bernardino where she died at only 24.

ARCAN

The Arcans slipped quietly into life in Santa Cruz, where his wife Abigail reportedly told him, "You can go to the mines if you want. I have seen all the God-forsaken country I am going to see and am going to stay right here."

Arcan died in 1869 and his wife in 1891.

NUSBAUMER

Nusbaumer joined the gold rush along the Merced River. But in April, 1851, his wife, whom he had left in Newark, rejoined him and they were to live out their lives in the Alameda County area, where he died in 1878 at the age of 59.

Touchingly his journal closed with the sad note that of his party, "Of the six of us, Hadapp and I are all that is left."

THE WADES

After mining along the Tuolumne River the Wades settled in Alviso, California, where he went into the freighting business, reportedly using the wagon they had brought out of Death Valley, later played in by the grandchildren.

Wade was to die a suicide, according to Stephens, in 1883; his wife in 1888. The Wade children—"Harry Jr., Charles, Almira and Richard, who all crossed the plains, and Mary (Ann) who was born in California, all married in comfortable circumstances (with) 24 (Wade) grandchildren."

THE BRIERS

There is a surprising lack of information on the Briers, including when and why they disposed of the hotel in Los Angeles in which Rev. Brier and Rev. Lewis Granger (who had stayed with Hunt) were partners, until the Briers settled in Lodi.

Presumably continuing as a clergyman, he died there in 1898; and his wife, the indomitable Juliette, in 1913. Brier Jr., following in his father's footsteps, became a well known minister. The son Christopher died in Oakland in 1907; Kirke at Sacramento in 1883.

YOUNG

Young returned to Missouri, although the date and any experiences in California are blanks. His obituary in the Moberly, Missouri, newspaper reports that he died August 18, 1892 at 77, and that he had:

> . . . lived in Monroe County, Mo., for almost ten years and had moved to Moberly, living there for six years. His wife died in 1887, after which he lived in his little house alone. . . .
>
> Having been an old sailor he could do his own cooking and housekeeping in a creditable manner. His stepson, Albert Hayden, lived close by and was with him almost every day. . . . His son from Galesburg, Ill., was present at the funeral.

HAYNES

Born in 1804, he was one of if not the oldest of the Jayhawkers at the time of the trek. Again there is a surprising dearth of information, particularly since his journal, like that of Sheldon Young, is so contributive to the '49er story.

What can be vaguely pieced out is that in later years he and his daughter went over the journal, apparently "strengthening" some of the faded writing and supplementing the diary with notes "at her father's dictation and approval." William Wiley, a grandson, recalled:

> . . . grandfather sitting in front of the big fireplace in the Haynes home in Illinois, watching the well directed tobacco juice make various portions of the logs crackle, and listening to the many experiences of the Jayhawkers while his mother (Asa's daughter) took notes from the old man's conversations.

Haynes was very active both physically and mentally until a short time before his death, in 1889 at the age of 85, as a result of a fall from a high porch at the home in DeLong, Illinois.

Appendices, Bibliography
and Index

Appendix A

A ROSTER OF THE NAMES

Group listings of the Death Valley '49ers are invariably confusing, conflicting and controversial. For example, the Briers are usually categorized separately, yet Mrs. Brier says, "Our company was from the southern states and called 'the Mississippi boys' " (although the Briers were from Iowa). And while the "Georgians" and "Mississippians" may have started as separate groups they gradually intermixed. As time progressed and difficulties increased there were countless partings, new alliances, rejoinings; some temporarily, others more permanently.

Variances in spelling are almost endless. Some were known only by their first name, or last. In one place Mrs. Brier refers to "two young men, St. John and Patrick made up our mess." In another she says Patrick and Loomis. And Brier Jr. refers to a Lummis St. John. The answer to this may well be in St. John being a surname—i.e. Lummis St. John and Patrick St. John.

For that matter, William Lewis Manly never refers to himself as William, but as Lewis; and divides the spelling of Manly and Manley rather equally. He is recorded in the family Bible as L. W. Manly and was known as "Uncle Lewis." His gravestone reads "Manly."

Some were known only descriptively, such as "Old Francis, a French Canadian", "the Dutchmen", "Goler's chum." Communication was a likely barrier with the "foreigners" who tended to keep to themselves in a shared bond of language and companionship. There were at least three blacks who were listed only as "Joe", "Tom" and Nusbaumer's companion "Smith."

Still others, listed in rosters and occasionally in later correspondence, remain shadowy participants throughout the trek—e.g. Woolsey, Cole, Morse, etc. Much in the same manner as the Atchison brothers, who may or may not have been Arcan teamsters. And there are vague references to a "Charles" (Coberly?) with the Wades as a possible teamster prior to the Long Camp. Some, like Louis Nusbaumer, Anton Schlogel and Schaub are never mentioned in '49er rosters.

Despite all of these qualifications, a listing of the participants may help to keep track of the names, however much they may bounce back and forth at times. And shift they did as the '49ers splintered—again and again.

JAYHAWKERS—30 persons

Allen (George)
Bartholomew (Ed)
Bartholomew ("son")
Byrum/Byram (Bruin/Brian)
Clarke/Clark (Charles)
Clay (Alonzo/Alonso)
Cole (John)
Colton (John B.)
Davidson (Urban)
Doty (Edward/Edwin)
Edgerton (Marshall)
Edgerton (Sidney)
Frans/Franz (Harrison)
Groscup/Grosscup (John)
Haynes/Haines (Asa)

Larkin (Aaron)
McGowen/McGowan (Ed)
McGrew/McGraw (Thomas)
Mecum (Charles)
Morse
Palmer (Alexander)
Plumer/Plummer (John)
Richards (Luther, "Deacon")
Robinson (William)
Rood/Rhodes/Rude (William B.)
Shannon (Thomas)
Stephens (Lorenzo Dow)
West (John L. "Lew")
Woolsey (Leander)
"a Frenchman"

INDEPENDENTS—9 persons

Carter
Funk (David)
Goler/Goller/Galer (John)
Gould
Gretzinger/Kritzner (Fred)

Tauber (Wolfgang)
Vance (Harry)
Young (Sheldon)
"Goler's chum"[1]

NUSBAUMER—14 persons

Culverwell/Calverwell
            (Richard)
Ehrhardt/Earhart (Jacob)
    ,,   ,,   (Henry)
    ,,   ,,   (John)
    ,,   ,,   (Abe)
Fisch

Hadapp (Adolph ?)
Isham (William)
Nusbaumer (Louis)
Schaub (T.)
Schlogel (Anton)
Smith (a colored man)
2 "Alsatians" (?)

---

[1] A "John Graff" according to John Baur's excellent biography of Goler. Manly does not give his name, noting only that the companion went to Mission San Luis Rey and was killed while operating a small clothing store. Newspaper reports of a robbery at nearby Mission San Juan Capistrano (about 30 miles away) give a "George Pfleugardt" as a German killed in the incident. And there is a "G. Pflagratu" rostered in Nusbaumer's original "German California Mining Company." Goler started a well known wagon shop in Los Angeles and served as Councilman in 1858-9 and again in 1868-9.

BENNETTS-ARCANS—14 persons

Arcan/Arcane (Jean Baptiste)
　　"　　"　　(Abigail Harriett)
　　"　　"　　(Charles)*
Bennett (Asahel/Asabel)
　　"　　(Sarah)
　　"　　(George)*
　　"　　(Melissa)*
　　"　　(Martha)*

Manly/Manley (William
　　　　Lewis/Louis)
Rogers/Rodgers (John Haney)
Abbott (S.S. or C.C.)—
　　　　Bennett teamster
Helmer (Silas)—Bennett
　　　　teamster
Atchison brothers—
　　　　Arcan teamsters ?

WADES—7 persons

Wade (Harry/Henry)
　　"　　(Mary)
　　"　　(Harry George, Jr.)*
　　"　　(Charles)*

Wade (Richard)*
　　"　　(Almira)*
Coberly ? (Charles ?)—
　　　　teamster

SAVAGE-PINNEY—11 persons

Adams
Allen
Baker (Mattison)
Moore
McDermot (Charles)
Pinney

Samore
Savage
Webster (Willie)
Ware (T.)
Ware (J.)

BRIERS—7 persons

Brier (John/James, Wells/Welsh)
　　"　　(Juliet/Juliette/Julia)
　　"　　(Christopher)*
　　"　　(John Wells/Welsh, Jr.)*

Brier (Kirke)*
St. John ? (Lommis/Lummis)
St. John ? (Patrick)

MISSISSIPPIANS—7 persons   and   GEORGIANS—8 persons

Martin (James of Miss.) (c)
Woods (James of Miss.) (c)
Joe (Negro) (c)
Tom (Negro)
"Little West" (Negro ?)
Coker/Croker (Ed) (c)
"Old Francis" (French
　　　　Canadian) (c)

Town/Townsend/Townshend
Masterson
Crumpton
Martin (John of Texas) (c)
Ward (Nat) (c)
Turner brothers
Carr (Fred) (c)

("c"—listed by Coker as his sub-group)

---

* An asterisk in these lists indicates children.

The eight groups compose a total of 107 persons.

There are also references to a "Town-Martin" party which may have developed from a mixing of the Mississippians and Georgians. ·

Some listings also include such names as Alexander Ewing, John Ewing, Deacon Arms, Robert Price, Norman Taylor, William Nesbit and Alexander Benson. The first five, however, took the Ft. Hall cutoff from Salt Lake City. The latter two may have done the same, or continued with Hunt.

THE "LONG CAMP": 17 or 19 adults and 8 children:

Manly	Wades (6)	Culverwell
Rogers	Schaub (Wade teamster)	Schlogel
Bennetts (5)	Nusbaumer	Ehrhardts (4)
Arcans (3)	Hadapp	Alsatians (2 ?)

AGES OF THE CHILDREN:

Briers:	Christopher	(8 or 9 in Sept. 1849)	
	John, Jr.	(7 or 8 in May	")
	Kirke	(4 in May	")
Wades:	Harry, Jr.	(14 in Dec.	")
	Charles	(11 in Aug.	")
	Almira	(9 in June	")
	Richard	(5 in Oct.	")
Arcans:	Charles	(2 or 3 ?	")
Bennetts:	George	(8 in June	")
	Melissa	(5 or 9 ?	")
	Martha	(1 ?	")

Appendix B

A DEATH VALLEY CHRONOLOGY

Not detailed lest it be a book unto itself this is to serve as a convenient reference for those who may wish to delve deeper into these fascinating facets of Death Valley history. It is also a reminder of the surprising activity in that then little-known area, not counting that of itinerant miners and adventurers who left no record.

1850[2] Mormon miners reported to have left a crude ore furnace in Furnace Creek Wash, inspiring its naming. Unfortunately there is no support for this, not even in the superb LDS archives.

1850 '49ers Turner (at least one of the brothers, perhaps both) and Toun (sic) return to search for the Lost Gunsight Lode in the Coso-Panamint area but evidently did not enter Death Valley.

1850 Four of the Turner-Toun party return to the Coso area with Dr. E. Darwin French, a cattleman at Tejon.

1855 Col. Henry Washington's survey. Maps "old wagon road" along Furnace Creek Wash.

1860 (Mar.) Dr. French party, including M. H. Farley, the first known group to descend into Death Valley, after again failing to find the Lost Gunsight.

1860 (Oct.) Dr. S. G. George, also searching for the Lost Gunsight, follows the French trail but continues into Death Valley and finds wagon remains.

1860 Two small parties with Bennett and Alvord search for the Lost Gunsight; Alvord left behind on second attempt.

1861 (April) The Rough & Ready Mining Company formed at Visalia, including Dr. George, and leave for the Coso-Panamint area but doubtful they went east of the Panamints.

---

[2] Too shadowed to be substantiated, Jayhawker "Lew" West is reported to have led a prospecting party back to Death Valley in 1850 as well as in 1859. The determination of this date is difficult, their penetration into Death Valley questionable and the details meager. Manly, in his *Pioneer* article of April 15, 1894, recalls they heard about the Gunsight while still working for Brier and Granger in Los Angeles in 1850. And that a party was formed, with West as guide although he had "scarcely recovered from the effects of the terrible trip (of the '49ers)." Frus-

1860-61   Manly mining trips. The first with Bennett to look for Alvord;
          the second with Alvord to look for his lost lead. Meet the Rough &
          Ready Mining Company.[3]

1861   Hugh McCormack enters Death Valley. Discovers and names Mc-
          Cormack's Wells "which may be found on some old maps." The site,
          six miles north of where they found emigrant wagon remains, ap-
          proximates that of old Stovepipe Wells.[4]

------

trated at not finding the rich silver lead, the party threatened to hang West, who admitted he
had never seen the exact spot where the silver was found, but thought he could locate it from
description.

    Since Manly only worked for Brier and Granger for half a month, it seems unlikely that it
took 9 years to motivate the West party. Noteworthy, too, Manly comments "West had just come
through," indicating an 1850 vs. '59 date.

[3] A report that Manly also retraced the Nevada portion of their trail with a Dyer Geer is
without any substantiation. In all of his writings Manly does not even hint of it.

[4] Few skeins are as snarled as that of Hugh McCormack. That which is known is from the
Hanks Report of 1883:

> In March 1861 Mr. Hugh McCormack visited Death Valley. He discovered and
> named McCormack's Wells, which may be found on some of the old maps. Six
> miles south of these wells . . . the old wagons of the emigrants were found. At
> Mesquit Springs he saw the shallow grave of a person supposed to be one of the
> emigrants, probably a woman, as a portion of a calico dress was found with the
> bones left exposed by the drifting desert sands . . .

No death of a woman was even hinted at by the '49ers, and all of the known women are subsequently accounted for. Remnants of a calico dress, but sans skeletal remains, can be attributed
to Indians finding some discarded material and discarding it in turn later on. Too, the story
may simply be one of those distortions in repeated hearsay telling — such as Hanks' — and as
fragmented as the calico dress, if indeed it ever existed.

    While a McCormack Well has been mapped near Tule Springs, the location of six miles
north of the notable finding of wagon remains would be that of old Stovepipe Wells. This site
is also mapped as "McCormick Well", possibly after a Dr. William McCormick who had
continued with the Stover packers from Mt. Misery and wound up mining in Grass Valley,
California. Despite his medical title, like Drs. French and George, he obviously had the "mining
bug" and may well have been one of the early Gunsight seekers.

    Adding to the mystery is an article published in 1872 by P.A. Chalfant, noting:

> . . . A party of young men, among whom were Dr. McCormick, Willie Webster
> and one or two others of our personal acquaintance, resolved to go back and see
> for themselves whether the story of that silver mountain was true. . . . In the Fall
> of '50 the writer, while prospecting around Rough & Ready, Nevada County,
> paid a visit to his former townsman and fellow emigrant of '49, Dr. McCormick
> above mentioned. In due course he related the story of that trip and of the silver
> mountain to which we have stated he and others returned . . . the doctor showed
> us a full handful of this silver . . .

Even overshadowing the rather wild possibility that the party did find the "Lost Gunsight"
silver, is Chalfant's pre-Fall of 1850 dating for the McCormick-Webster trip, not to mention

1861 Farley, who had been with the 1860 French party, drafts maps of "Newly Discovered Tramontane Silver Mines." First known map-naming of Death Valley. Also shows "Daylight Pass" and Amargosa Mines near Saratoga Springs.

1861 First appearance of "Death Valley" in print in *San Francisco Alta* April 12th; *Sacramento Union* July 11.

1861 Boundary Survey, under Sylvester Mowry and J. C. Ives, includes Hitchens and Lillard of French Party of 1860—and three camels! Find wagon remains at McLean Spring *and* to the north of it. Refers to "Furnace Creek."

1864 Bancroft's map of "California, Nevada, Utah, Arizona." Shows McCormick Spring at old Stovepipe Wells; also "Death Valley" and "Furnace Creek."

1864-5 David Buel and Joseph Todd, searching for the Lost Gunsight, find emigrant wagon remains in Death Valley, and meet a party of miners including the legendary Breyfogle. While their official report is lost, their exceptionally good map, particularly of the Nevada-California border mining districts, has surfaced. ("Map of the Reese River Mining Districts," N.Y., D. Van Nostrand, circa 1865.)

---

the inclusion of Webster who by all reports perished with the Savage-Pinney Party!

We have Stover's report that Dr. McCormick mined in Grass Valley, which isn't far from the old mining camp of Rough & Ready. And this is where, in the Fall of 1850, Chalfant talked to Dr. McCormick about the Lost Gunsight trip.

Chalfant, founder of the *Inyo Independent and Register,* was a knowledgable man on the Death Valley area and with a special interest in having been a '49er—although his contingent left Salt Lake City via the northern route while McCormick went south with Hunt's train.

Still, as a newspaper man, he could be given to reporting stories whose interest neither required nor were lessened by insistence on substantiation. They made good reading for his readers who lived relatively close to Death Valley and the Inyo-Coso mining activities. Yet here he was obviously not relaying a story from some unknown source, but was speaking from a personal knowledge of the persons involved.

Was '50 a typographical error for '60? Were "Dr. William McCormick" and "Hugh McCormack" one and the same? Was "Willie Webster" simply a remarkable coincidence of names? Alas, both P.A. and his fine Death Valley historian son, W.A. Chalfant, have passed on, leaving another deadend trail.

One further comment on State Mineralogist Hanks 1883 report to indicate that, however well intentioned and qualified in his field that he may have been, the addition to the McCormack story, that of Bennetts Well, should be taken with a grain of salt:

> . . . named after (Asabel Bennett) . . . He walked a day and a half and found water and he said, plenty of gold. At one time since, while piloting a prospecting party he brought a blacksmith's outfit. Anvil Canyon, on the west side of the valley, is supposed to have obtained its name from this, or a similar circumstance.

The Anvil Canyon story has validity since Bennett was in that area in 1860 with Alvord

1866   H. G. Blasdel, first Governor of Nevada (1865-70) with a party of "over 20" follows much of the Buel-Todd route, find wagon remains but contrary to '49er stories, no skeletons in the sand. They also encounter Breyfogle and find "a fine spring in a cave thirty feet long and ten wide" (Devil's Hole), reported by Nusbaumer with the Bennetts-Arcans.

   No map of this expedition has turned up, but the account is well detailed in the State Mineralogist Report and a series of 16 articles in the Virginia City *Territorial Enterprise* from April through June, 1866.

1867   Lt. Charles Bendire leaves Camp Independence with 25 men of Co. D, 1st US Cavalry and 4 civilian guides, entering Death Valley via Wingate Gap. Camp at nearby Anvil Springs where ". . . the Sergt. found an anvil, wagon tire and considerable old iron." Crossing the south end of Death Valley to Salt Springs (just east of Saratoga Springs), "I found here the remains of several adobe houses which had been built by miners and also an old quartz mill." Commends their guide, "Mr. Hahn."

1869   George Miller party searches for the Gunsight Lode, including W. H. Rhodes (aka Wm. B. Rood, Rude, Rhoods) one of the '49ers. Find wagon remains and signs that "some of the wagons had gone far west up the valley."

1869   Von Schmidt-Gibbes map shows Bennetts Well at approximately its present location.

1871-75   Lt. George Wheeler expeditions of exploration and mapping. That of 1871 included detachment under a Lt. Lockwood and Lt. D. A. Lyle (who, ironically, had just been recalled from Alaskan duty!). Lyle's guide, C. F. Hahn mysteriously disappears near Death Valley. In his excellent detailed map Wheeler shows "Town's Pass" south of Pinto Peak.

1870-72   Nevada borax discoveries at Teels Marsh, and Columbus Salt Marsh.

1873   Searles Lake borax discoveries.

---

and later with Manly in searching for Alvord who had been abandoned there. However, gold and "plenty of gold", is a tall tale indeed. Certainly Bennett never reported any. And in his treks with Alvord was searching for Alvord's "lead", not his own, one that he would have been more familiar with. There may be gold in them thar mountains, but not near Bennetts Well!

1874 Rev. Brier returns to Panamint Valley, and seemingly Death Valley. In letters to Jayhawkers Mecum and Richards describes his retracing of their route.

1870's Furnace Creek Ranch, called Greenland, established. Developed extensively in 1883 for borax operations.

1873-76 Co. D, 12th US Infantry maps of scouting throughout Coso and Panamint Districts and, slightly, northern Death Valley.

1874 Co's. B & D, 12th Infantry scouting and rough maps of Coso-Panamint-Death Valley area.

1875 Another map of scouting in "May, June, July, August" may be a duplication or of separate contigents.
       While somewhat repetitive, the 12th Infantry's scouting and mappings indicate the increased mining activity, particularly in the Darwin-Coso camps.

1875 Lt. Roger Birnie concludes the Wheeler explorations, traveling from Los Angeles to Searles Lake, westward to the Sierra, back to Coso and Darwin, on to Panamint City in the Panamints and into Death Valley via Johnson Canyon, camping two days at "Bennetts Wells", before proceeding to Furnace Creek "over the old emigrant road."
       Although by now Death Valley had been rather well traversed by a number of parties with and without wagons, very few went along the southwestern side. Thus the old road may well have been the tracks of the '49ers.

1875 Daunet finds borax at Eagle Borax, returning in '82 or '83 to start development.

1881 Coleman buys Aaron Winter's borax claims in Death Valley, establishing Harmony Borax Works in 1881-82.

Appendix C

THE "LONG CAMP" CANYONS AND SPRINGS

Much has been written and disputed over the various springs and canyons along the southwestern edge of Death Valley that might have been used by the '49ers. And none more controversially than the location of the historic "Long Camp."

Each possibility is governed by the '49ers spacings from water to water, intervening dry camps and canyons leading into the Panamints.

However else they may differ, most agree that Telescope Peak, an understandably memorable landmark, was the "snow peak" seen from the Bennetts-Arcans second-night camp in crossing the valley.

Progressing by elimination, the first canyon possibility south of Telescope is Starvation Canyon. As a route this has been discounted because of its heading into the still towering heights of the Panamints.

Next is Johnson Canyon, which leads far into the Panamints where a trail snakes to the crest and on into the site of Panamint City. An earlier forking swings into the head of Six Springs Canyon. However this forking is at the relative verdancy of what once was Hungry Bill's Ranch, which provided Panamint City with produce, and incompatible with the '49er's descriptions.

Six Springs Canyon has long been a popular choice. But its sizeable cliff-wall springs could hardly have been missed by Manly. And while there are some small springs at its easy-slope summit, the route is at odds with the Manly-Rogers triangular routing out and back. Too, its extremely rough rocky passage would deter any thought of oxen use.

Next in sequence is Galena Canyon. Below that, Warm Springs Canyon, Anvil Canyon and Wingate Wash are too far south to qualify descriptively and sequentially.

Galena Canyon has a singularly distinctive amphitheater-like entrance. Just beyond, a steep but passable ravine extends into Butte Valley and Gold Hill. An easier route forks southwesterly to a small ridge that drops into Warm Springs Canyon beyond its notable springs at the present day talc mines and hidden to sight by the canyon's bends. And here there is a choice of either crossing that small ridge or veering northwesterly up an arroyo to Gold Hill.

Uniquely, too, it is only at Gold Hill that this writer could find Manly's view of, "It did not seem very far to the snowy peak to the north of us." Surprisingly the bends and high walls of the other canyons, and intervening elevations between them and Telescope Peak preclude such sighting.

As to the "springs" near the foot of these canyons—

It is not without sympathetic understanding of the shortcomings of flesh and equipment that early observations and topographers are viewed as fallible. Death Valley was a maze of bewilderingly similar landmarks and illusive distances; its bareness so void of potentialities as to preclude painstaking accuracy over things of foreseeably little interest. As to site names, when given at all, old prospectors who had never heard of Shakespeare could well echo, "What's in a name?" It was sufficient to know where water was or apt to be, and how many miles, hours or days away. Besides, names changed with each passerby, each cursory report.

The arguments that have long raged whether Bennetts Well[5] was the "Long Camp" will undoubtedly never be settled beyond all shadow of doubt. Nor is it certain that the Bennetts Well of today is that of yesteryear.

For example, State Mineralogist Hanks' report of 1883 says, "The Eagle Borax Company have located at Bennetts Wells, 22 miles south from Furnace Creek." There should have been a qualifying "near" for it is actually at its own distinctively identifiable location 3½ miles away.

Hedging over the location of the famed Long Camp has even been evidenced in monument markers. Today at Tule Springs a brass plaque proclaims:

BENNETT's LONG CAMP
Near this spot the Bennett-Arcane contingent
of Death Valley '49ers . . . were stranded
for a month and almost perished. . . .

As writer-historian C. B. Glasscock ruminated, "Some folks do love an argument."

In his *Here's Death Valley,* Glasscock, who was in on the bubble-bursting boom of nearby Greenwater and publisher of its famed *Chuck-Walla,* includes an old photo of Bennetts Well showing a windmill and a slightly erroneous caption:

---

[5] Found spelled with and without an apostrophe, and sometimes singularly as "Well", other times pluralized as "Wells".

BENNETTS WELL
266 feet below sea level
Believed to be the campsite of the Bennett-Arcane party
from December 22, 1849, to January 16, 1850,
while awaiting the return of Manly and Rogers
who had gone on westward seeking a route
out of Death Valley to the coast.

Col. Henry Washington, in his 1855-56 survey maps only "A large spring of good water" on the west side—at approximately the site of Tule Spring.

The Dr. French Party of 1860 is credited by the eminent Phil Townsend Hanna, with the naming of Bennetts Well, although there is no evidence that the French Party, proceeding from McLean Spring to Travertine Spring, crossed over to the southwestern side. Certainly, Farley, a member of that group, shows neither route nor springs there on his 1861 map, the first known map-naming of Death Valley.

In 1867 a Lt. Charles Bendire, with a contingent of Co. D, 1st US Cavalry and four civilian guides from Camp Independence, crossed the Panamints near Wingate Wash. While they did not turn north, thus not observing any springs along the valley's edge, he does record some items of related interest:

> ... camped at Anvil Springs ... the Sergt. found an anvil, wagon tire and considerable old iron here ... after searching for a trail for some time, I found some old wagon tracks which I followed in an easterly direction and arrived at Salt Springs. ... I found here the remains of several adobe houses which had been built by miners and also an old quartz mill.

Presumably the spring was that at which the Bennett-Alvord party camped on their 1860 mining trek and are credited with the naming. But one wonders how Bendire knew of its earlier identification, or whether he now named it "Anvil." That it may have been known as such, along with the adobe ruins and mill he found at Salt Springs, not far from Saratoga Springs, does indicate a surprising if anonymous activity in the area by this time.

While the first appearance of the name "Death Valley" is credited to the Farley map of 1861 (and the first appearance in print that same year in the *San Francisco Alta* and *Sacramento Union,* publishing the reports of the 1861 Boundary Commission), that of Bennetts Well is first found on the Von Schmidt-Gibbes map of 1869, showing it close to its present location.

The naming of Bennetts Well has also been attributed to a "Bellerin' Tech (sic)" Bennett, associated with Furnace Creek Ranch back in the

1870's when it was called Greenland. This is supported by no less an authority than Carl Wheat, stating, ". . . apparently Bennetts Well received its
name not from Bennett of the '49 party, but one Bellerin' Tex Bennett, a
well known Death Valley character of borax days."

This, however, seems refuted by the Von Schmidt-Gibbes map prior to
that time. And while historian T. S. Palmer names him "Texas" Bennett,
Chalfant, equally a dean of Death Valley history, questions that he was
even surnamed Bennett:

> It is also alleged that "Bellerin' Teck" of Death Valley note, was sur-
> named Bennett, nicknamed Tex and described by the additional
> "Bellerin", and that the disputed wells may have been named for him.
> Inquiry has not developed any authentic support for this. . . .

Chalfant also discounts the naming after a borax teamster and Pahrump
Valley rancher, Charles Bennett, who didn't arrive until the 1880's.

Maps of "Itinerary of Scouts, Co. D 12th US Infantry during May, June,
July and August of 1875" show only a "Goodwater Spring," east of Tele-
scope and just north of the "road to Nevada" out of the Panamints via
Johnson Canyon.

During 1871-75, Lt. George Wheeler conducted a number of expeditions
of explorations and mapping throughout the area. On one of them, in 1875,
a Lt. Birnie left Panamint City, stopping at Hungry Bill's Ranch. Over a
route of few alternatives he descended into the valley:

> Entering Death Valley we turned northward and camped two days at
> Bennett's Wells, nearly on the edge of the great alkaline deposit of the
> valley but permanent and very good water . . . three or four holes
> scarcely more than 6 feet deep . . . coarse bunched grass furnished
> pasture for the animals and mesquite trees grew sparsely around. . . .

Lt. Birnie does not report any signs of an emigrant camp, but that they
did travel "over the old emigrant road to Furnace Creek." He also notes
that as they progressed north they found "two fresh water springs . . . but
the waters of both seem somewhat medicinal. . . ."

Coming out of Johnson Canyon, the route from Panamint City, Tule
Springs might have been that which he identifies as Bennetts Well, al-
though descriptively it better fits the latter. Too, depending on his angle of
descent into the valley, he may well have camped at present day Bennetts
Well, with the two springs north those of either Eagle Borax or Shorty's
Well and Tule Springs.

Basically the Wheeler maps are among the first to show four springs,
south to north, along the west side:

Bennetts Well—intriguingly also showing a trail south of the salt
pool area to the east side of the valley (Bendire's?)

Emigrant Spring—about 2½ miles north of Bennetts Well

Water Hole—about 2½ miles north of Emigrant Spring

Soda Spring—about 1 mile north of the "Water Hole"

approximating very reasonably that of Bennetts Well, Eagle Borax Spring,
Shorty's Well and Tule Spring.

Of the more modern recorders there is a potpourri of opinions.

Carl Wheat, in his *Trailing the Forty-Niners Through Death Valley,*
says:

> Bennetts Well is just that—a well—and apparently never had a liv-
> ing spring and a short running stream as described by Manly. Having
> camped at these various spots on several occasions, the writer believes
> that the Bennetts-Arcane camp must have been at a point north of
> Bennetts Well though the exact location, as between several possibil-
> ities, must probably remain indeterminable. The Indians have a tradi-
> tion that this camp was near the Eage Borax Works site.

Hanna adds his contradictory Indian tale with: "Tom Wilson, an Indian
living in Death Valley, quoted his mother as declaring Bennetts Well was
the spot."

Chalfant, in *The Story of Inyo,* 1933 edition, declares: "... the camp was
undoubtedly at Bennetts Well ... the water is brackish ... but is usable."

In his *Death Valley, The Facts,* three years later, he is less sure, questioning Manly's fixing the harness for the oxen in the shadow of the wagons
there being no other shade. "This could not have been the case at Bennetts
Well where there are numerous mesquite trees, some of venerable age."[6]

In his first (1930) edition of *Death Valley, The Facts,* Chalfant is definite
in separating and placing Eagle Borax Works ... "a few miles northerly
from Bennett Wells," adding:

> Bennett Wells, the last camp of the Manly-Bennett party, is a small
> pool a little below the surface. It was dug out and enlarged and sur-
> rounded by a rough fence to keep stock out. The Pacific Coast Borax
> Company ... erecting a windmill which still stands on a steel tower
> ... the water appears to be ample and for that region is fair in quality.
> Enough moisture comes from (is at?) Eagle Borax Works to main-
> tain a heavy growth of tules and considerable meadow.

---

[6] This writer agrees with both observations. There are large mesquite trees, but their low
drooping tangle of branches would make it awkward to work under and the partial shade
would be less desirable than that of the wagons and where the air could also circulate better.

He further expands on Eagle Borax with:

> We were told that water was obtained by digging. It would appear that they opened a spring which thereafter flowed, for today their abandoned site is an oasis of tule sloughs and marshy meadow.

Dr. Long, in her *Shadow of the Arrow* notes that, in 1921, they traveled "3 miles . . . from Eagle Borax to Bennett's Well" and over a "branch road toward a broken down windmill that rises above the mesquite trees at Bennett's Well."

Dane Coolidge, an advocate of Bennetts Well as the Long Camp, in his *Death Valley Prospectors* describes—

> Tule Spring—"a round patch of reeds about 10 feet across, from the middle of which good water wells up from some fissure leading down from the heights."
>
> Eagle Borax—"a similar spring but the pool itself is poison. It is only by going out on a plank and dipping down where the sweet water boils up that a man can get a good drink."
>
> Bennetts Well—"this water hole had long been used by Indians who scraped out the sand, filled their pitch-covered water baskets and covered the hole again to keep the water clean."

Glasscock, along with his pictorial record of the windmill, also avers the Long Camp was at Bennetts Well, succinctly adding:

> There has been some wasted effort to prove that Bennetts Well was not named for Asahel Bennett at all, but for "Bellerin' Tex" Bennett who came that way in 1870, or perhaps for Charles Bennett, who drove a mule team by in 1880-odd. Some folks do love to start an argument. . . .
>
> The argument about whether the exact location was at the harsh oasis still known as Bennetts Well, or at a point now called Tule Spring, a few miles north, was not to start for another fifty years. Long after the last of the wagon beds and frames and wheels had been burned by camping prospectors, and the last of the iron had been removed by Indians and others, thus removing the tangible identification of the site, the argument lovers rushed in with quotations from various emigrants of forty-nine to prove that Bennett really camped at Tule.

Interestingly, Elliott's *History of San Bernardino County,* 1883 notes:

> . . . Bennetts Wells, in Death Valley . . . is where a portion of the unfortunate party of 1849 remained six weeks until relief reached them

from Los Angeles . . . in 1873 David Henderson brought to San Bernardino a lot of relics of the party who perished in the valley in 1849.

However skeptical one may be of the uncorroborated authoritativeness of these early county histories, now popularly known as "mug books," the information was gained before memories and trails were too dimmed by time. Still there is the annoying question whether that Bennetts Well was the locale so named today. And whether the relics referred to came from there, or just someplace in Death Valley.

Just as one man's meat is another's poison, so do some swear by present day Bennetts Well. Others will buy that *if* Eagle Borax was in reality one of the mapped locales of Bennetts Well. Others side with Tule Springs. Each hinges arguments on the water supply and whether "well" or "spring." And of this one can pick and choose.

Hanks indicates Eagle Borax and Bennetts Well as one and the same. Glasscock, Chalfant, Coolidge and Long, knowing the area first hand, separate them.

Birnie, the first to detail it, describes Bennetts Well as 3 or 4 holes of very good water. Wheat says it was never more than *a* well. Chalfant describes it as a small pool and Coolidge as "water holes." Others, like Death Valley Ranger Matt Ryan, doubt there was any surface water in '49.

Reflectively one may wonder how literally, and varied, are the ways of a "well." To some the words connote man-made. To others, simply a hole in the ground, which may or may not be improved upon by man. Semantically a "spring" depicts flowing water as opposed to the stillness of a pool or pond, though they may be unobstrusively spring fed. What one may call a water hole, another may term a well. To still others, perhaps viewing it at different climatic stages, it may be a pool or barren basin.

To the tune of the old gambling cry, "Place yer bets and takes yer chances!" this writer stacks his chips on Bennetts Well and at its present location. Its expanse of tules, wire grass and mesquite are of sufficient scope. While no surface water is seen today, a network of old water channels and basins tucked in the mesquite speak of a less arid past.

It should also be kept in mind, that, as covered in the text, the continuance beyond the Long Camp site to a sulphurous sand-mound well. Then, after Manly and Rogers left, by agreement they returned to the better water at the Long Camp.

Tangible signs of this well, about 8 miles south of the Long Camp according to the '49ers, have been lost in countless counterparts of mounds built by the sands around mesquite and wire grass clumps.

Mapped near the foot of Galena Canyon is a "Salt Well (tanks)." Some say it was never more than storage tanks for use of the borax wagons. Yet Koch, in 1891, traveling north from Wingate Wash, writes, ". . . after 11 more miles of heavy pulling we reached Mesquite Wells, a large rectangular hole filled with salty and sulphury water, far from good but nevertheless eagerly swallowed by our thirsty horses." And that 4 hours and 6 miles later reached Bennetts Well.

A year later, Spears, in his classic book, tells of stopping at Mesquite Wells in the same locale enroute to Bennetts Well.

And in *Chasing Rainbows in Death Valley,* Sidney Norman, editor of the Los Angeles *Mining Review,* writes of:

> About noon we ate lunch at Salt Wells and drank up our scanty supply of water, pushing on to Bennetts Holes . . . there we found the water too foul to drink and were compelled to push on again to Eagle Borax Works Spring.

At some transitional time near the turn of the century, Mesquite Well slipped into Salt Well, first without and then with tanks. That it did exist as the former is gleaned from early post-Wheeler maps. Gradually succumbing to the sands and time, it apparently remained as a trail point identification, especially for those preparing for or recovering from traveling through Wingate Wash.

For those approaching from the north, Mesquite Well was the tail end of the staggered chain of mesquite groves and coarse-grass small oases. Only bare wastelands extended beyond. Here was, physically and psychologically, the turning point—either into Wingate Wash or easterly across the south end of Death Valley; and for those in need of water, a turning back to Bennetts Well, Tule Springs, etc., or into the Panamint canyons to springs at higher elevations.

Hopefully, as consolation to those who have patiently waded through all of this detailing of canyons and springs, there is a clearer picture of the pro's and con's for each.

After years of hoofing and huffing it in southwestern Death Valley and the labyrithian Panamint canyons, this writer is convinced that the Long Camp was at Bennetts Well, the sulphurous well at Mesquite Well, aka Salt Tank. As with no others they dovetail into the '49er routings, for Manly, Rogers, Bennetts and Arcans and those who sought an exit to "the south." But all of the evidence, including the contradictory, has been presented to you as a jury for your own decisions.

A Selected Bibliography

Rather than a formal bibliography, more comprehensively available elsewhere, this is a personal selection for those who wish to enjoy and explore more deeply the lore and legends of Death Valley, and especially the 1849ers.

Baur, John E. "John Goller (Goler), Pioneer Angeleno Manufacturer" in *Hist. Soc. of So. Calif. Quarterly,* vol. 36 #1, March 1954.

Belden, L. Burr. *Death Valley Heroine, and source accounts of the 1849 travelers.* San Bernardino, 1954.

————: *Goodbye, Death Valley! The 1849 Jayhawker Escape.* Palm Desert, 1956.

————: *Mines of Death Valley.* Glendale, CA, 1966.

Caruthers, William. *Loafing Along Death Valley Trails.* Palm Desert, 1951.

Chalfant, W. A. *Death Valley: The Facts.* Stanford, CA, 1930.

————: *The Story of Inyo.* Chicago, 1922; Bishop, CA, 1933.

Clements, Lydia. *Indians of Death Valley.* Hollywood (Death Valley '49ers Pubn. #1) 1967.

Clements, Dr. Thomas. *Geological Story of Death Valley.* Palm Desert, 1954.

Coolidge, Dane. *Death Valley Prospectors.* N.Y., 1937.

Cronkhite, Dan. *Death Valley's Victims.* Verdi, NV, 1968.

Edwards, E. I. *Desert Voices.* Los Angeles, 1958.

————: *The Enduring Desert.* Los Angeles, 1969.

————: *The Valley Whose Name is Death.* Pasadena, 1940.

Ellenbecker, John. *Jayhawkers of Death Valley.* Marysville, KS, 1938.

Glasscock, C. B. *Gold in Them Hills.* Indianapolis, 1932.

————: *Here's Death Valley.* Indianapolis, 1940.

Gower, Harry P. *Fifty Years in Death Valley.* Bishop, CA, Death Valley '49ers Pubn. #9, 1969.

Greene, Linda, and John A. Latschar. *A History of Mining in Death Valley National Monument.* 4 vols. Denver, Natl. Park Service, 1981.

Hafen, LeRoy R. and Ann W. *Journals of Forty-Niners, Salt Lake to Los Angeles.* Glendale, CA, 1954; and *Supplement,* 1961.

————: *The Old Spanish Trail.* Glendale, CA, 1954.

Hanks, Henry G. *Third Annual Report of the State Mineralogist.* Sacramento, CA, 1883.

Koenig, George (ed.) *Valley of Salt, Memories of Wine: A Journal of Death Valley 1849.* Berkeley, CA, 1967.

————: *The Lost Death Valley '49er Journal of Louis Nusbaumer.* Bishop, CA, 1974. Death Valley '49ers Pubn.

Latta, Frank. *Death Valley '49ers*. Santa Cruz, CA, 1979.

Lee, Bourke. *Death Valley*. N.Y., 1930.

————: *Death Valley Men*. N.Y., 1932.

Levy, Benjamin. *Death Valley National Monument: Historical Background Study*. Natl. Park Service, Washington, D.C., 1969.

Long, Dr. Margaret. *Shadow of the Arrow*. Caldwell, ID, 1941; rev. edn. 1950.

Manly, William L. *Death Valley in '49*. San Jose, CA, 1894; and reprint edns. Santa Barbara, 1928, 1929; Los Angeles, 1949; Bishop, CA, 1977; and an abridged edn. Chicago, 1927.

————: "Vermont to California" in *Santa Clara Valley* (San Jose, CA) June 1887 to July 1890.

Mitchell, Roger. *Death Valley Jeep Trails*. Glendale, CA, 1969.

————: *Inyo Mono Jeep Trails*. Glendale, CA, 1969.

Myrick, David. *Railroads of Nevada and Eastern California*. Berkeley, 1962.

Palmer, T. S. *Chronology of the Death Valley Region*. Washington, D.C., 1952.

————: *Place Names of the Death Valley Region in California and Nevada*. n.p., 1948; reprinted Morongo Valley, CA, 1980.

Perkins, Edna. *White Heart of the Mojave*. N.Y., 1922.

Putnam, George P. *Death Valley and Its Country*. N.Y., 1946.

————: *Death Valley Handbook*. N.Y., 1947.

————: *Hickory Shirt*. N.Y., 1949.

Ressler, Theo. C. *Trails Divided*. Williamsburg, IA, 1964.

Roberts, Oliver. *The Great Understander,* by Wm. W. Walter. Aurora, IL, 1931.

Snell, George. *And If Man Triumph*. Caldwell, ID, 1938.

Spears, John R. *Illustrated Sketches of Death Valley*. Chicago, 1892; and reprinted Morongo Valley, 1977.

Stephens, L. Dow. *Life Sketches of a Jayhawker*. San Jose, CA, 1916.

Walker, Ardis Manly. *Manly and Death Valley: Symbols of Destiny*. Palm Desert, CA, 1962.

————: *The Manly Map, and the Manly Story*. Palm Desert, 1954. Death Valley '49ers Pubn. #2.

Weight, Harold O. *Lost Mines of Death Valley*. Twentynine Palms, CA, 1953.

————: *Twenty Mule Team Days in Death Valley*. Twentynine Palms, CA, 1955.

————: *Wm. B. Rood, Death Valley '49er*. Twentynine Palms, CA, 1952.

Wheat, Carl I. "Forty Niners in Death Valley," in *Calif. Hist. Quar.*, 1939.

————: "Pioneer Visitors to Death Valley," in *Calif. Hist. Quar.*, 1939.

————: "Trailing the Forty-niners Through Death Valley," in *Sierra Club Bulletin*, 1939.

Wolff, Dr. John. *Route of the Manly Party of 1849-50 in Leaving Death Valley for the Coast*. (Pasadena ?) circa 1931.

Woodward, Arthur. *Camels and Surveyors in Death Valley*. Death Valley '49ers
Pubn. #7, 1961.
————, ed. *The Jayhawkers Oath and Other Sketches*. Los Angeles, 1949.
Young, Sheldon. "Log from Joliet, Illinois, to Rancho San Francisquito, California, 1849." Typewritten copy in Jayhawker Collection, Huntington Library, San Marino, CA.

In addition there are a number of publications and keepsakes of The Death
Valley '49ers, 1949 to the present, which are well worth reading.

Beyond This Place There Be Dragons
is printed in an edition of 1000 copies
Design by Arthur H. Clark; Linotype set
in Granjon face by Sagebrush Press of
Morongo Valley, California; display type
hand set in Centaur face by Prosperity
Press of Los Angeles. Printed by Publishers
Press, and bound by Mountain States Bindery,
both of Salt Lake City, Utah